A GUIDE TO

The South's

QUIRKIEST ROADSIDE ATTRACTIONS

A GUIDE TO

The South's

QUIRKIEST ROADSIDE ATTRACTIONS

KELLY KAZEK

THE
History
PRESS

Published by The History Press
Charleston, SC
www.historypress.com

First published 2022

Manufactured in the United States

ISBN 9781467153102

Library of Congress Control Number: 2019956028

To all those creative souls who build whimsical new worlds and invite us to experience them—thanks for splashing color alongside the roads without worrying about staying inside the lines.

Contents

Introduction

Every now and then I wonder: Was I born being attracted to weirdness? Or was I an ordinary kid whose mind was somehow warped over the years?

All I know is, if you'd told my ten-year-old self I would one day honeymoon at the World's Largest Catsup Bottle, I would have nodded and said, "Sounds about right." When my big brother, Doofus, and I were kids, we couldn't get enough of the Guinness Book of World Records and Ripley's Believe It or Not! I basically mimicked everything he did, so it was probably Doofus's fault I turned out like I did. Yeah. I'm willing to go with that theory.

However it happened, I never dreamed it would give me a career. I never saw a degree for "weird news reporter" in my college handbook and had no idea I'd ever make a living writing about car-part art, Stonehenge replicas and Bigfoot. Some of my favorite oddities are the things the person who created them didn't even know were weird.

Maybe it's a southern thing. We hate hiding our otherness. We like to put it right out on the front porch where anyone can enjoy it, even when that means an old toilet with petunias planted in it or a dinosaur molded from concrete. We like to put a tiara on it and have it lead the crazy parade. Now much of the rest of the world is catching on to what southerners knew all along: Quirk is cool. Peculiar is popular. Weird is wonderful.

Weird tourism is on the rise, and I, for one, think it makes the world a better place. Wearing our weird on our sleeves is going to be a great unifying movement for this country. Knowing all of us have a little weird in us, that none of us is completely normal, is what makes America a great country.

To help others enjoy the weirdness on our roadsides, I've created a handy guide to such sites as the World's Largest Glass of Bourbon (Kentucky), a dental pick large enough to work on King Kong (Alabama), a house made from beer cans (Texas), a Bigfoot museum (Georgia), spaceship houses (Tennessee, Florida and North Carolina) and pretty much the entirety of Florida.

Unfortunately, there wasn't room to list every quirky site in the South, but there are enough in the following pages to keep you and your family busy with day and weekend trips for years to come. Remember: Always brake for the bizarre. Life is too short to be just like everyone else.

How to Use This Guide

This guide includes unusual and quirky sites from eleven southern states to help you plan road trips of just about any length or theme. Listings in each state are divided into four parts.

ROADSIDE ATTRACTIONS

This section includes objects you can see from the road, making them the perfect stops for family trivia games or selfies. Most have free admission. In some cases, addresses may be estimated.

OUTSIDER ART

Also known as folk art, this unique kind of roadside oddity is the result of creative minds, quick hands, an abundance of time and access to lots and lots of scrap metal, mosaic tile, concrete or whatever is handy. Some collections are indoors; some are outdoors. Some yard art is best gawked at as you pass by. A few charge admission; some request donations. But the work never fails to astound and entertain.

LOCALES

Unlike the roadside attractions section, this listing of unusual locales describes places you will likely want to park your car and get out to explore. Many are quirky museums or historic homes that charge admission. Others are whimsical places to eat or stay overnight. But they are definitely worth the detour.

TOMBSTONE TALES

This section lists just a few of the state's intriguing headstones and the stories behind them. It may include a grave with an interesting backstory or legend, a humorous epitaph or beautiful artwork. Most cemeteries are open during daylight hours only. Many do not have street numbers in their addresses, so you may have to search a little. But when you find them, the funerary art and history lessons are like a visit to a free museum.

LISTINGS BENEATH EACH SECTION are alphabetized by the city in which they are located. When available, phone numbers and addresses are listed to make it easier to find these off-the-beaten path locales. In those cases where no street number was available, I listed the closest address or give directions or, in a few cases, GPS coordinates. You can also check the index in the back of the book for listings by city. The information is up to date as of this writing.

Please keep in mind that locations of objects erected on roadsides have a tendency to change without notice, as do operating hours of small museums and attractions. Call each place before going, or check Google Maps when possible.

Alabama

The wacky side of Alabama takes many forms. You'll find plenty of car-part art and unexpected creations along the roadsides, as well as on display in quirky museums. Looking for world's largest things? Check out the cast-iron statue that moons an entire city or a dental pick large enough to work on King Kong. Visit the Stonehenge replica or stroll along Alabama's own Walk of Fame.

If you're looking for some place a little *different* to eat, try the fare at the Roadkill Café or have dinner inside a cave. You might even decide to spend the night in a silo or the home where F. Scott and Zelda Fitzgerald lived. This list should give you ideas for numerous day and weekend trips off the beaten path.

ALABAMA ROADSIDE ATTRACTIONS

Ready to see Alabama's quirky side? This section includes objects you can see from the road, often free of charge.

Big White Dress Shirt

Andalusia Chamber of Commerce
700 River Falls Street, Andalusia, AL
334-222-2030; Free

To celebrate Andalusia's textile history, a giant white dress shirt—possibly the world's largest—was erected outside the chamber of commerce.

World's Largest Office Chair

Miller Furniture
625 Noble Street, Anniston, AL
256-237-1641

When it was built by Sonny Miller in 1981, the thirty-three-foot-high chair erected in the parking lot of Miller Furniture was billed as the World's Largest Chair. Thanks to the subsequent Chair Wars, it has been unseated. Currently, a sixty-foot-high chair at the entrance of the LA Merchandise Mart in Los Angeles holds the title, so the Miller chair has been relegated to the title World's Largest *Office* Chair. Built of ten tons of steel, it can withstand eighty-five-mile-per-hour winds.

Left: World's Largest Office Chair in Anniston, Alabama. *Photo by Wil Elrick.*

Above: Andalusia, Alabama's tribute to the white business shirt. *Photo by Kelly Kazek.*

Quinlan Castle

2026 Ninth Avenue South, Birmingham, AL
Not open to the public; Visible from the street

Quinlan Castle, an apartment building once owned by the City of Birmingham, was purchased in 2008 by Southern Research Institute for use as lab space. The odd castle rising from a downtown street was designed by architect William Weston and built in 1927. It is listed in the National Register of Historic Places.

The Vulcan is the world's largest cast-iron statue.
Courtesy of Carol M. Highsmith/Library of Congress.

World's Largest Cast-Iron Statue

Vulcan Park and Museum
1701 Valley View Drive, Birmingham, AL
205-933-1409; Admission fee

Vulcan, god of the forge, is the world's largest cast-iron statue at fifty-six feet high, not including his massive pedestal. He was built by artist Giuseppe Moretti for the 1904 World's Fair in St. Louis. In 1938, it was installed atop Birmingham's Red Mountain in honor of the city's iron industry. Vulcan is a local landmark; his bare rear end moons the city of Homewood.

Face in the Courthouse Window

Pickens County Courthouse
20 Phoenix Avenue, Carrollton, AL

The legend of the Face in the Courthouse Window is an oft-told tale that gained traction when it appeared in Kathryn Tucker Windham's beloved book *13 Alabama Ghosts and Jeffrey*. On an upper floor of the Pickens County Courthouse, a face etched into a pane of glass can be seen. What made it?

The legend is printed on a historical marker outside the courthouse, which replaced the previous facility after a fire in 1876: "A freedman, Henry Wells, was accused of burning the second [courthouse] on Nov. 16, 1876. He was arrested in January 1878 and held in the garret of this building. Legend holds that as Wells peered out of the North window at a mob gathering below, lightning struck nearby, indelibly etching his image on the pane."

The Big Peach Water Tower

86 Peach Tower Road, Clanton, AL
Exit 212 off Interstate 65

This massive peach—set atop a 120-foot tall, 500,000-gallon water tower—is a well-known landmark along Interstate 65. It was made by Chicago Bridge and Iron Company and erected in 1992 because Chilton County is Alabama's top peach producer.

World's Smallest City Block

East Troy Street and North College Street, Dothan, AL

A marker within a tiny median triangle in Dothan declares it the "World's Smallest City Block." It includes a yield sign, a stop sign and the granite marker.

Barber Marina's Big Surprises

26986 Fish Trap Road, Elberta, AL
251-987-2628; Free

At the behest of Alabama businessman George Barber, artist Mark Cline created several oversized artworks that are now sprinkled around the small town of Elberta, near Barber Marina. Barber also founded Barber Motorsports Park and Barber Vintage Motorsports Museum in Leeds, which include lots of interesting sculptures.

At the Marina, visitors can see:

Top: The Lady in the Bay in Elberta, Alabama. *Photo by Wil Elrick.*

Bottom: Stonehenge replica in Elberta, Alabama. *Photo by Wil Elrick.*

- LADY IN THE BAY: The oversized head and knees of a woman who appears to be bathing in the bay.
- DINOSAUR HERD: A brontosaurus, T-Rex, stegosaurus and triceratops can be found in the woods around Barber Marina. Look for the "dinosaur crossing" signs.
- ALABAMA'S STONEHENGE REPLICA: Barber also commissioned a fiberglass replica of Stonehenge, which was erected in the woods not far from the dinosaurs.

Spend some time looking around for Barber's other surprises: an ornate fountain, complete with rearing horses; life-size knight statues; a horse-head statue rising from the ground; giant seahorses; cherubs; and creepy ram figures.

World's Largest Boll Weevil

Main Street, in the center of downtown
Enterprise, AL

A pristine white figure of a woman stands in the center of a traffic circle in downtown Enterprise. In her hands, she is holding aloft…a giant black bug. The Boll Weevil Monument, certified as the World's Largest (and probably *only*) Monument to an Insect, is a monument to overcoming adversity. The sculpture was erected in 1919 when the insect was hailed a back-handed hero of sorts: boll weevils destroyed local cotton harvests, forcing farmers to diversify and grow more successful crops.

The monument to the boll weevil in Enterprise, Alabama. *Photo by Wil Elrick.*

Tree That Owns Itself in Eufaula

512 Cotton Avenue, Eufaula, AL

A tree on Cotton Avenue is protected by a fence and marked with a plaque, designating it as the "Tree That Owns Itself." In 1919, a sturdy two-hundred-year-old oak in the yard of Confederate captain John A. Walker endured a tornado and later survived a fire.

To honor the oak's hardiness, local women persuaded the town council to deed the property to the tree. In 1961, the old oak was felled by a tornado. Since then, it has been replaced "several times," according to the Eufaula Chamber of Commerce. But each of the "sons of the Tree That Owns Itself" has also been liberated and stands behind the fence on Cotton Street. A second Tree That Owns Itself is located in Athens, Georgia.

The Hermit Hut

22787 U.S. Highway 98, Fairhope, AL
Free

Henry Stuart, a native of Idaho who was told by doctors he had a year to live, moved to ten acres in Fairhope, hoping the warmer climate would help his condition. He built a simple domed concrete hut, fourteen feet in diameter and hurricane proof. For years, he lived in the hut and slept on a hammock inside. When, decades later, he was still living, he eventually abandoned the hermit hut and moved to Oregon, where he died at age eighty-eight. Alabama author Sonny Brewer decided to live in the hut while writing a novel based on Stuart's story, *The Poet of Tolstoy Park*. The hut, listed in the National Register of Historic Places in 2006, is furnished just as it was when Stuart lived there and is open to the public.

The Hermit Hut of Tolstoy Park. *Photo by Wil Elrick.*

Fairhope Storybook Castles

456 Oak Avenue, Fairhope, AL
Private homes; Drive-by only

In this picturesque town, two castles stand side by side on a residential street, the homes of local sisters. The castles are occupied by Megra and Pagan Sheldon, daughters of artist Craig Sheldon, and their husbands. Sheldon Castle, built by Craig Sheldon after World War II, is Megra's home, while Pagan's husband, Dean, also an artist, built Mosher Castle.

Enter through Shark's Mouth

Souvenir City
217 Gulf Shores Parkway, Gulf Shores, AL
251-948-7280

Since 1956, visitors have entered the mouth of a giant shark to see the wide array of souvenirs and gifts inside the shop.

Giant Purple Octopus

Purple Octopus Souvenirs and Gifts
301 Gulf Shores Parkway, Gulf Shores, AL
251-948-3146

A giant, smiling, polka-dot octopus greets visitors to another massive souvenir store located next door to Souvenir City.

Eggbeater Jesus

First Baptist Church
600 Governors Drive, Huntsville, AL
256-428-9400

While it may seem disrespectful to some to refer to the famous mosaic adorning the outer wall of Huntsville's First Baptist Church as the "Eggbeater Jesus," it is said by local residents with affection. The nickname refers to the artist's rendering of Jesus with seemingly spinning robes, which the church website calls an "obvious centrifugal motion." Huntsville—home to the U.S. Space and Rocket Center and NASA's Marshall Space Flight Center—is called the Rocket City, and the massive artwork was created to represent a scripture referring to a "cosmic Christ."

The mosaic, which has an Age of Aquarius appearance that many find ultracontemporary for a southern church, has been a landmark in Huntsville since 1973 and also has the distinction of being one of the largest mosaics in the United States. About 1.4 million pieces of Italian tile no larger than a thumbnail were needed to create the artwork. The figure of Christ is forty-

This mosaic on Huntsville's First Baptist Church is affectionately known as the Eggbeater Jesus. *Photo by Wil Elrick.*

three feet high with a head more than five feet high. Each of Jesus's eyes is eight inches in diameter. As of 2019, the tiles were falling from the building, and the church deemed the mosaic too costly to repair. Church officials plan to install a replica, tile by tile.

Salem Witch House Replica

133 Walker Avenue, Huntsville, AL
Private home; Drive-by only

In 1995, Dale Rhoades, a historian and collector of antique ironwork, began building a replica of Massachusetts's famous Salem Witch House in downtown Huntsville. The house that inspired it, which has been open as a museum since 1948, is the last surviving structure connected with the infamous Salem Witch Trials of 1692. The home, circa 1640s, was once owned by Jonathan Corwin, a judge in the trials. The replica in Huntsville appears the same on the exterior, with the addition of a one-story wing on each side.

Ruins of Capote's Childhood Home

Lot next to Mel's Dairy Dream
263 South Alabama Avenue, Monroeville, AL

Born Truman Streckfus Persons in New Orleans in 1925, Truman Capote was known as a literary genius and eccentric character. In Monroeville, he was known as the little boy who lived with his mother's cousins. Truman's parents divorced when he was four, so his mother sent him to Monroeville to live with the Faulks. They lived in a home on South Alabama Avenue next door to Nelle Harper Lee, who would also become a legendary author. The misfit Truman was particularly close with Nannie Rumbley Faulk, called "Sook," who inspired characters in his short stories "A Christmas Memory" and "The Thanksgiving Visitor." Today, stones from the home's foundation are preserved as a memorial to Capote.

The Bamboo Forest

Wilderness Park
800 Upper Kingston Road, AL
334-361-3640; Free

A twenty-six-acre preserve in Prattville was the first in the nation to be dedicated as a "wilderness park." In the 1940s, the property owner planted seeds for the bamboo that now covers the area, growing as much as sixty feet high and six inches in circumference. The trees form a canopy overhead, making it a unique spot for hiking and photos.

The Bamboo Forest in Prattville, Alabama. *Photo by Kelly Kazek.*

Fred, the Town Dog

Jackson Street and Alabama Highway 22, Rockford, AL

A headstone in Rockford marks the grave of Fred, a rather ordinary-looking mutt who managed to capture the hearts of the entire town. Fred wandered into Rockford in 1993 and called it home the rest of his life. Fred belonged to no one and everyone, although he spent the majority of his time at Ken's Package Store. Before long, Fred began "writing" a column in the local newspaper about his activities in town. During the dog's life, the town's welcome signs said, "Home of Fred the Town Dog," and Fred was featured on the Animal Planet television network. Fred died on December 23, 2002, and was buried behind the Old Rock Jail, a historic building. He was inducted into the Alabama Animal Hall of Fame in 2004.

Edmund Pettus Bridge

U.S. Highway 80 across the Alabama River, Selma, AL

Selma's Edmund Pettus Bridge is part of Alabama's civil rights history because of its role on Bloody Sunday, the day in 1965 when civil rights activists planning to march to the state capitol were attacked by armed police. The bridge, built in 1940, is listed as a National Historic Landmark.

Singing River Sculptures

Sheffield and Muscle Shoals
Free

Two eighteen-foot aluminum musicians stand in the area known as The Shoals to honor its musical heritage, which is said to have its roots in the Tennessee River. Known as the Singing River Sculptures, the grouping will eventually include as many as fourteen statues in the Quad Cities of Florence, Tuscumbia, Muscle Shoals and Sheffield. So far, one has been erected in downtown Sheffield and another in Muscle Shoals.

Giant Dental Pick

Dr. Barry Booth's office
6525 Spanish Fort Boulevard, Spanish Fort, AL
251-626-3211; Free

Dr. Barry Booth, a dentist in Spanish Fort, commissioned some unusual pieces for his hometown. He designed a giant dental pick and mirror honoring the University of Alabama School of Dentistry. The sixteen-foot-

Sculpture titled *Piknmera* in Spanish Fort, Alabama. *Photo by Kelly Kazek.*

long by eight-foot-high stainless-steel sculpture called *Piknmera* is adjacent to Booth's dental office. Booth also commissioned the fourteen-foot-tall blue paperclip seen nearby. It symbolizes the city "is open for business," he says. The sculpture by artist Casey Downing Jr. commemorates the incorporation of the young town in 1993.

Ruins of Early State Capitol

Capitol Park
2828 Sixth Street, Tuscaloosa, AL
Free

Tuscaloosa was the capital city of Alabama from 1826 to 1846, and a state building was completed in 1829. In 1847, the capital was moved to Montgomery, and the empty capitol became the Alabama Central Female College. It burned in 1923, and the ruins of the building were preserved by the City of Tuscaloosa as Capitol Park, which is open to the public. The site can be rented for events by calling 205-562-3220 or visiting www.tcpara.org.

ALABAMA OUTSIDER ART

This unique kind of roadside oddity comes in many forms. Some collections are indoors; some are outdoors. A few charge admission; others request donations. But the work never fails to astound and entertain.

African Village in America

931 Nassau Avenue SW, Birmingham, AL
Donations

Folk artist Joe Minter's work covers his own yard as well as adjoining lots in his Birmingham neighborhood. Minter set out to make a statement using found objects to create sculptures and biblical symbols. His art, made of everything from dolls to bowling balls to hubcaps, has been shown in galleries, and his story has been featured in numerous publications, including the *New York Times*.

Spirit Trees of Tinglewood Trail

Orr Park
277 Park Drive, Montevallo, AL
205-665-2555; Free

Wood artist Tim Tingle carved numerous animals and mythical beasts into the trees of Orr Park, providing fun surprises for visitors.

A carved tree in Orr Park in Montevallo, Alabama.
Courtesy of Rivers Langley.

Courtyard of Wonders

Kentuck Arts Center
503 Main Avenue, Northport, AL
205-758-1257; Free

For forty-seven years, the Kentuck Arts Center has been supporting local artists with its numerous programs and annual festival. The website says, "Having roots in folk art, Kentuck provides year-round programming with the mission to perpetuate the arts, engage the community, and empower the artist. Feel free to hang out in our Courtyard of Wonders, visit the resident artists' studios, and browse in our Gallery Shop." The centerpiece of the site is Rusty, the Big Red Dog, created in 1983 by artist Larry Godwin. He looks down from the roof of the center.

Museum of Wonder

41 Poorhouse Road, Seale, AL
Donations

Folk artist Butch Anthony created an unusual installation at his property, as well as a drive-through gallery on nearby U.S. Highway 431. Driving through an array of glass-walled shipping containers and viewing everything from a portrait of William Shatner to a taxidermy three-headed chicken is quite the experience, and it's billed as "The World's First Drive-Thru Art Gallery."

Visitors can then return to Anthony's property on Poorhouse Road, where they can walk among his yard art or visit his gallery. He claims to have

more than ten thousand curiosities from "around the world and beyond."

Butch Anthony at his drive-through art installation in Seale, Alabama. *Photo by Kelly Kazek.*

ALABAMA'S LEGENDARY LOCALES

This list describes places you will need to park your car and get out, including quirky museums, unusual historic homes and whimsical places to eat or stay overnight.

The Legend of Huggin' Molly

Huggin' Molly's Restaurant
129 Kirkland Street, Abbeville, AL
334-585-7000

The legend of Huggin' Molly has been told to Abbeville children for decades. She is reportedly a seven-foot-tall, witch-like woman who grabs children who wander alone at night. Molly squeezes them in a rough hug and screams in their ears.

One version of the story claims Molly was the ghost of a woman who dealt with the loss of her infant by hugging local children. Whatever the truth, the legend was used as a cautionary tale by mothers to keep children home safe at night. Today, Abbeville honors the legend with a café named for the witch. Huggin' Molly's is located in a historic pharmacy, complete with a soda fountain, filled with movie memorabilia collected by local businessman Jimmy Rane.

Hitler's Tea Service

Berman Museum of World History
840 Museum Drive, Anniston, AL
256-237-6261; Admission Fee

The Berman Museum of World History catalogues the history of two prolific travelers—Farley and Germaine Berman—who collected art and cultural artifacts from around the world. Among the exhibits are a Tibetan religious icon dating to the fifteenth century, a royal Persian scimitar, a jeweled dagger that belonged to an Egyptian king, one of only two West guns in existence, spy weapons and Adolf Hitler's tea service.

Sloss Furnaces and Fright Furnace

20 Thirty-Second Street N, Birmingham, AL
205-324-1911; Admission fee

Sloss Furnaces operated as a blast furnace for ninety years, producing pig iron from 1881 to 1971. It is one of the nation's first preserved industrial sites and the only blast furnace to be preserved. It is also an event venue and artists' colony. Each fall, it is host to Sloss Fright Furnaces, a Halloween attraction.

Sloss Furnace in Birmingham. *Courtesy of Cullen Steber/Wikimedia Commons.*

Negro Southern League Museum

120 Sixteenth Street South, Birmingham, AL
205-581-3040; Free

This museum commemorating the Negro Southern League contains the largest collection of original Negro League baseball artifacts in the country.

Gee's Bend Quilts

The Gee's Bend Quilters Collective
14570 County Road 29, Boykin, AL
334-573-2323

The town of Boykin was a government settlement developed for black farmers in an area known as Gee's Bend, but it gained worldwide fame thanks to its quilting artisans. Today, about fifty of the town's seven hundred residents are part of a quilters' collective that makes, displays and sells a bold, distinctive style based on African American traditions.

Key Underwood Coon Dog Cemetery

4945 Coondog Cemetery Road, Cherokee, AL

The World's Only Coon Dog Cemetery was established in the woods near Cherokee in 1947 when Key Underwood buried his loyal hunting dog. Only registered coon hounds can be buried in the cemetery. Today, more than three hundred graves are located in the woods. Visitors go to read the unique epitaphs, such as "Hunting Partner and Best Friend," or "If he treed in a mailbox, you'd better open it and look."

Victorian Octagonal House

Petty-Roberts-Beatty House Museum
North Midway Street, Clayton, AL
334-775-9176; Admission fee

Eight-sided homes were a fad in the Victorian era, largely in the New York area, where dozens survive today. Fewer survive in the South. The only one in Alabama is the Petty-Roberts-Beatty House in Clayton, built in 1861, which is now a house museum and event venue. During the Civil War, it was used as headquarters by Union troops that occupied Clayton in 1865.

Ave Maria Grotto

1600 St. Bernard Drive, Cullman, AL
256-734-4110; Admission fee

A hunchbacked monk named Brother Joseph Zoettl tended the grounds of St. Bernard Abbey and eventually began building miniature replicas of biblical sites using stones and found objects. The four-acre park includes the 125 miniature reproductions made by Zoettl over fifty years, until his death in 1961.

Malbis Plantation

29300 Alabama Highway 181, Daphne, AL
251-626-3050

A historic home, scattered structures and an ornate Greek Orthodox church are all that remain of the once-thriving Malbis Plantation, a settlement of Greek immigrants founded in 1906 by Jason Malbis. At its height, the settlement covered ten thousand acres and included a power plant, cannery, hotels, Malbis Bakery, an ice plant, a plant nursery, restaurants, water towers and acres of farmland. The gorgeous church is still in use today. Visitors can also see the French-style manor house where residents lived. Both are listed in the National Register of Historic Places.

Tim Hollis's Pop Culture Museum

Off U.S. Highway 78, Dora, AL
205-648-6110; Tours by appointment

Tim Hollis turned his childhood home into a museum featuring more than one hundred lunchboxes, *Peanuts* collectibles, a Kentucky Fried Chicken lamp and a twenty-year-old box of Batman cereal, among thousands of other relics. Hollis made a two-story addition to his home and built an exact replica of his childhood bedroom in the basement. Hollis gives visitors tours by reservations.

Roadkill Café

25076 State Avenue, Elberta, AL
251-986-5377

This eatery with the fun-and-kinda-gross name doesn't really serve roadkill. The slogan, "You kill it, we grill it," is all in good fun. Guests can choose from traditional southern fare, including fried chicken and cheese grits.

The Roadkill Café doesn't really serve roadkill. *Photo by Kelly Kazek.*

The Rosenbaum House

601 Riverview Drive, Florence, AL
256-718-5050; Admission fee

Alabama's only structure designed by Frank Lloyd Wright, the Rosenbaum home was an example of the famed architect's more modest designs. The home was built for Stanley and Mildred Rosenbaum in 1940 and is considered one of the finest examples of a Usonian home, which Wright designed to be affordable enough for middle-class families. The Rosenbaum home cost between $12,000 and $14,000 to build, including the Wright-designed furniture that remains inside the home. It is now preserved as a museum.

The Original Whistle Stop

Irondale Café
1906 First Avenue North, Irondale, AL
205-956-5258

In 1932, Bess Fortenberry bought a small restaurant and soon became known for her fried green tomatoes. Years later, her niece Fannie Flagg would immortalize the dish in her bestselling novel *Fried Green Tomatoes at the Whistle Stop Café*. The titular café was based on her aunt's restaurant. Although Fortenberry is gone, the restaurant is still serving the famous dish.

World's Largest Collection of Motorcycles

Barber Motorsports Park and Vintage Museum
6030 Barber Motorsports Parkway, Leeds, AL
205-699-7275; Admission fee

George Barber, a racecar driver and former owner of Barber's Dairy, likes large works of art. And he likes them quirky. After selling the family dairy and amassing a mind-boggling assortment of motorcycles and race cars, Barber donated the collection for the creation of a racetrack and museum. The 1,400 motorcycles in Barber Museum were certified by Guinness World Records as the World's Largest Collection of Motorcycles. But visitors to the park will see more than cars and motorcycles. Barber has commissioned and bought numerous works of art that he placed around the grounds to "surprise" guests, including giant metal spiders, oversized ants carrying an oversized cola, a drowning zombie, a Bigfoot and many more. Barber also commissioned strange artworks to place around Barber Marina in Elberta, Alabama.

A display in Barber Motorsports Museum, which houses the World's Largest Collection of Motorcycles. *Photo by Wil Elrick.*

Ricky Bobby Movie Setting
The Talladega Superspeedway

3366 Speedway Boulevard, Lincoln, AL
877-462-3342; Admission fee

Alabama's Talladega Superspeedway is the longest NASCAR oval, with a length of 2.66 miles, and was once one of the sport's largest racing facilities, with a seating capacity of 175,000, although it is now a fraction of that. The speedway was used to film most of the racing scenes for the 2006 movie *Talladega Nights: The Ballad of Ricky Bobby*, starring Will Ferrell.

Ruins of Dicksonia Plantation

427 Alabama Highway 97; Lowndesboro, AL
334-320-5330; Event venue by appointment only

Dicksonia was an antebellum plantation built in 1856, but it burned in 1939. It was replaced by a replica that was thought to be fireproof, but the home burned again in 1964. Today, all that remains is the shell of the once-beautiful home and its stately columns. The ruins were used for scenes in the film *Big Fish*. Today, the owner of the property rents out the ruins for photography and events.

The Rock Pulpit

Sallie Howard Memorial Chapel
Intersection of County Roads 165 and 617, Mentone, AL
256-638-4441; Free

This chapel was built in 1937 by Colonel Milford W. Howard in memory of his first wife. He built it onto a massive boulder so that the rock forms the pulpit inside the church. The church is still used for services and weddings. Milford Howard's ashes are interred in the rock exterior.

Film Set Town of Spectre

Jackson Lake Island
Cypress Lane, Millbrook, AL
334-430-7963; Admission Fee

Fans of the movie *Big Fish* can visit, in person, the fictional town of Spectre featured in the story. The "town" was created as a set by director Tim Burton on a privately owned island near Montgomery. Years later, the current owners have been restoring the structures, which are basically empty shells, to preserve them for future fans. The town is a favorite setting for photographers and now serves as a wedding venue. As for the rest of the island, it is open for fishing, camping and boating.

Buildings constructed as a set for the 2003 film *Big Fish*. *Photo by Wil Elrick.*

Africatown

1959 Bay Bridge Cutoff Road, Mobile, AL
251-300-8941; Free

Africatown is a historic district founded by a group of West African people who were brought illegally to Alabama. In 1860, they arrived aboard the *Clotilda*, the last documented slave ship to reach the United States after international slave trade had been abolished.

The 110 people aboard were sold and enslaved until 1865, when they were freed. Having no money to return to Africa, the people gathered in a community they called Africa Town, now Africatown. It was the first town in the United States that was founded, continuously occupied and run by black people. Today, a welcome center explaining the history of the town is located across from Plateau Cemetery, where many of Africatown's residents are buried.

To Kill a Mockingbird *Setting*

Old Monroe County Courthouse
31 North Alabama Avenue, Monroeville, AL
251-575-7433; Admission fee

Most people know the inspiration for the fictional town of Maycomb in *To Kill a Mockingbird* was the author's hometown of Monroeville. Harper Lee, who won a Pulitzer Prize for the novel, used to watch her father, an attorney, try cases at the 1903 Monroe County Courthouse, just as her character Scout does in the book. The courthouse is now preserved as a museum and restored to its appearance in the 1930s, when Lee was a child. It contains artifacts and memorabilia from the lives of Lee and author Truman Capote and from the book and film versions of *Mockingbird*.

Hank Williams's Death Car

118 Commerce Street, Montgomery, AL
334-262-3600; Admission Fee

Here, visitors can learn about the short life of country superstar Hank Williams, who died at age twenty-nine, but not before writing some of the genre's most influential songs. The array of artifacts includes photos, records, sheet music, clothing, concert posters and even a pair of blue suede shoes (pre-Elvis). The most unusual exhibit on display is Hank Williams's death car. The beautifully restored baby-blue 1952 Cadillac is the car in which Hank Williams died of heart failure in the back seat on New Year's Day, 1953. Oddly, Hank Williams Jr. reportedly drove the car when he was in high school before restoring it.

Lynching Memorial

Memorial for Peace and Justice
417 Caroline Street, Montgomery, AL
334-269-1803; Admission fee

The National Memorial for Peace and Justice opened in 2018 as "the nation's first memorial dedicated to the legacy of enslaved black people, people terrorized by lynching, African Americans humiliated by racial segregation and Jim Crow, and people of color burdened with contemporary presumptions of guilt and police violence," according to its website. The site was developed by the Equal Justice Initiative and includes two museum facilities, as well as outdoor exhibits.

Fort Conde Historic Site

150 South Royal Street, Mobile, AL
251-525-6933; Admission fee

In 1723, when Mobile was a French colony, residents built a fort for protection. To celebrate America's bicentennial in 1976, the City of Mobile opened a 4:5-scale replica of a portion of the fort. It acts as a welcome center and educational site with exhibits from early native and European settlers.

USS Alabama *Battleship Memorial Park*

2703 Battleship Parkway, Mobile, AL
251-433-2703; Admission fee

The USS *Alabama* BB-60 was commissioned in 1942 to serve in World War II in the Atlantic and Pacific theaters. The ship, the subject of numerous ghost legends, is listed as a National Historic Landmark. It was anchored in Mobile Bay following its retirement and opened as a museum in 1965.

The battleship USS *Alabama* is a museum.
Photo by Wil Elrick.

Where the Stones and Aretha Recorded

FAME Studios
603 Avalon Avenue, Muscle Shoals, AL
256-381-0801; Admission fee

FAME (Florence Alabama Music Enterprise) has been an operating recording studio since 1959, although it is now a historic site and open for tours. The studio was owned by Rick Hall, one of the initial founders, until his death in 2018. Numerous famous artists have recorded hits at the studio, including Aretha Franklin, the Rolling Stones, Otis Redding, Tim McGraw, George Strait, Kenny Chesney and Martina McBride. Years of photos and memorabilia are on display.

Natural Bridge Park

County Road 314, Natural Bridge, AL
205-486-5330; Admission fee

Natural formations at the site include a 148-foot-long, 60-foot-high limestone span and a boulder that resembles the profile on an Indian head nickel.

Alabama's "natural bridge" is located in a small town named Natural Bridge. *Photo by Wil Elrick.*

The Civil War Hospital Hotel

The Grand Hotel Marriott Resort, Gulf Club and Spa
One Grand Boulevard, Point Clear, AL
251-928-9201

Guests are surrounded by Alabama Civil War history in a luxury hotel in Point Clear. The oldest part of the hotel was built in 1847 and was used as a hospital during the Civil War. More than three hundred soldiers who died there were buried on the grounds, located near the resort's golf courses, beaches, seven bars and restaurants, an indoor pool, a lagoon-style pool and a spa.

The Alabama Baby

Randolph County Historical Museum
809 Main Street, Roanoke, AL
334-863-5439; Tours by appointment

Ella Louise Guantt became an accidental doll inventor in 1897, when a neighbor girl asked Ella to repair her porcelain bisque doll. She developed a cloth-and-plaster combination to recreate the doll's face, unwittingly starting a doll industry. Guantt had created the first Indestructible Doll, later known as the "Alabama Baby." Dolls were built in a factory behind the house, as many as eight thousand per year at the peak of production. The factory eventually went out of business, and Ella died in 1932.

Eat in a Train

Derailed Diner
27801 County Road 64, Robertsdale, AL
251-960-1152

Visitors can dine in a train car or a repurposed bus in this unique transportation-themed restaurant. Its website says: "The Derailed Diner is a new experience in dining on-the-go, serving up superb breakfast, lunch and dinner, derailed-style. Along with our full-size train dining car, the diner also offers an entirely transportation-themed destination: from the school bus counter, to the tailgate tables, to the space-age drink filling station—the Derailed Diner has something for everyone."

Unclaimed Baggage

509 West Willow Street, Scottsboro, AL
256-259-1525

Ever wonder what happens to all that lost luggage from airlines and cruise ships? The cases and contents are purchased and the items resold at Unclaimed Baggage in Scottsboro. The massive store, more than fifty-five thousand square feet, has been featured on numerous TV shows and in magazines. While much of the merchandise these days comes from overstock sales, people go to see what kinds of abandoned treasures and oddities they might come across. Past finds include a suit of nineteenth-century armor, a 5.7-carat diamond ring, a live rattlesnake, an etched headstone and a set of bagpipes.

Cher's Album-Cover Studio

Muscle Shoals Sound Studio
3614 Jackson Highway, Sheffield, AL
256-978-5151; Admission fee

Muscle Shoals Sound opened in 1969 not far from FAME Studio and became another popular recording spot for artists such as Aretha Franklin, the Rolling Stones, Lynyrd Skynyrd, Rod Stewart, Willie Nelson and George Michael. The studio, listed in the National Register of Historic Places, was restored and is open for tours. The studio's address, 3614 Jackson Highway, appeared as the title of an album Cher recorded there in 1969. A photo of Cher and her band standing in front of the studio is featured on the album cover.

Dine in a Cave

Rattlesnake Saloon
1292 Mount Mills Road, Tuscumbia, AL
256-370-7220

This eatery at Seven Springs Lodge is located in the opening of a cave. Its website says: "Welcome to Rattlesnake Saloon, the watering hole under the rock. This is a place the whole family can come relax and enjoy connecting to local history. Come fill your belly and listen to live local music. After 5 p.m., grab a cold brew... If you are old enough." Rattlesnake Saloon is closed November–January. Seven Springs also offers casual lodging for campers, hikers and horseback riders who frequent the picturesque area. Visitors can camp, sleep in a cabin or rent a room in a grain silo.

Greek Temple Replica

Jasmine Hill Gardens
3001 Jasmine Hill Road, Wetumpka, AL
334-567-6463; Admission fee

Built during the Depression by Benjamin and Mary Fitzpatrick, Jasmine Hill Gardens is a botanical garden filled with replica sculptures. The centerpiece of the gardens is an exact replica of the ruins of the Greek Temple of Hera in Olympia.

The Astrobleme

Wetumpka Impact Crater
Off U.S. Highway 231, Wetumpka, AL
334-567-4811; Free

Wetumpka is the site of a rare astrobleme, or "star-wound," a massive crater caused by a falling meteor as many as eighty-three million years ago. The crater is one of the few above-ground impact sites in the nation and one of only about six in the world, according to the Wetumpka Chamber of Commerce.

ALABAMA TOMBSTONE TALES

This section lists just a few of the state's intriguing headstones and the stories behind them. Most cemeteries are open during daylight hours only. Many do not have street numbers in their addresses, but those listed are as close as possible.

Mary Anderson Grave

Elmwood Cemetery
600 Martin Luther King Drive, Birmingham, AL
205-251-3114

Did you know windshield wipers were invented by an Alabama woman named Mary Anderson (February 19, 1866–June 27, 1953)? In 1903, she was on a trip to New York City when she noticed streetcar drivers were having difficulty seeing through the rain and snow. Anderson developed a device with a rubber blade that the driver could operate with a lever. Anderson reportedly never made any money from the invention.

Paul "Bear" Bryant Grave

Elmwood Cemetery
600 Martin Luther King Drive, Birmingham, AL
205-251-3114

Bear Bryant (September 11, 1913–January 26, 1983), the legendary University of Alabama football coach, died not long after his retirement in 1982. He helmed the University of Alabama's Crimson Tide for twenty-five years, winning six national titles and thirteen SEC championships.

Whiskey Bottle Tombstone

Clayton City Cemetery
North Midway Street, Clayton, AL

The whiskey bottle tombstone in Clayton, Alabama. *Photo by Kelly Kazek.*

The grave of William T. Mullen proves the danger of ignoring a spouse's ultimatum. According to legend, Mullen was an alcoholic, and his wife threatened to mark his grave with a whiskey bottle–shaped headstone to eternally embarrass him. The grave was listed in Ripley's Believe It or Not!

Miss Baker, the Monkeynaut Grave

1 Tranquility Base, Huntsville, AL
800-637-7223; Admission fee to enter space center

The grave of Miss Baker, a squirrel monkey who survived a 1959 trip into space and lived out her life at the U.S. Space and Rocket Center, is located on the museum grounds. She was a beloved figure at the center, where caregivers held public birthday parties and events for the adorable astronaut. She outlived three "husbands," dying in 1984 at the age of twenty-seven. Visitors to her grave leave trinkets and bananas.

Little Nadine's Playhouse Grave

Oakwood Cemetery
1462 First Street, Lanett, AL

The unique grave of a little girl named Nadine Earles is one of the most visited in Alabama. She is buried in a small brick structure known as Little Nadine's Playhouse. Nadine became sick with diphtheria at age four, and her distraught father began building the playhouse as a Christmas gift so she would have it when she was well. When the child died on December 18, the house became her mausoleum. The inscription on the grave inside reads:

> *Our darling little girl*
> *Sweetest in the world*
> *Little Nadine Earles*
> *"Me want it now"*

The house has paned windows, awnings, a lawn and a walkway. A peek through the windows shows toys placed inside. The unusual grave site has appeared in a Ripley's Believe It or Not! book and the book *Weird US: The ODDyssey Continues.*

Little Nadine's Playhouse in Lanett, Alabama. *Photo by Kelly Kazek.*

Hank Williams's Fake Grass

Oakwood Annex Cemetery
1304 Upper Wetumpka Road, Montgomery, AL

Legendary country music artist Hank Williams Sr. died at the age of twenty-nine in 1953. His large headstone is etched with words from his songs as well as images of guitars and boots and a sculpture of his trademark cowboy hat. Even more unusual is the "grass" at the site. Hank Williams Jr. reportedly had the fake turf placed at the graves of his parents, Hank Sr. and Audrey, after fans kept pulling up grass to take with them. An etched stone at the site reads: "Please Do Not Desecrate This Sacred Spot. Many Thanks, Hank Jr."

Grave of Elodie Todd Dawson

Old Live Oak Cemetery
22 Dallas Avenue, Selma, AL

When the beautiful Elodie Todd Dawson died at the young age of thirty-seven, her husband, Confederate officer Nathanial Henry Rhodes Dawson, was devastated. He had a likeness of her carved in Italy to be placed atop her grave. According to legend, he felt the statue's curls were not realistic enough and sent the sculpture back to be recarved. Dawson was the half sister of Mary Todd Lincoln and sister-in-law of Abraham Lincoln.

Last Confederate Veteran?

Hall Cemetery, or Refuge Baptist Church Cemetery
2170 Holly Hills Road, Lincoln, AL

When Pleasant Riggs Crump died at age 104 in 1951, he was believed to be the last surviving Confederate soldier, although the claim is contested. Crump enlisted in the Alabama Infantry at age 16 and reportedly attended the surrender at Appomattox Courthouse. Crump, a deacon at Refuge Baptist Church for 71 years, lived out his life in this small community.

The Faces of Mt. Nebo Cemetery

Mount Nebo Road, Wagarville, AL
Gated cemetery; Call 251-275-2014 for information

A headstone made by Isaac Nettles at Mt. Nebo Baptist Church. *Photo by Kelly Kazek.*

Isaac Nettles Sr., a black inventor born in the 1880s, created cement masks of people in life and later used them to adorn headstones in the cemetery adjoining Mt. Nebo Baptist Church. The unique folk-art stones have been heavily vandalized, although they have been declared historic sites by the National Park Service.

Nettles, who according to lore built a perpetual motion machine that drew the interest of the Ford Motor Company, created four of the odd tombstones, including one that was a bust of his mother and one for his wife, Korea, which was adorned with the faces of the couples' three daughters: Pauline, Marie and Clara. Nettles himself is buried in an unmarked grave, presumably nearby. The cemetery is now gated to deter vandals. Before visiting, contact the Clarke County Historic Museum at 251-275-2014.

Arkansas

From natural wonders—like Hot Springs National Park and the Natural Bridge—to artist-designed quirkiness like the whimsical castle in Wilson Park, Arkansas is filled with fantastical sights. The Popeye statue in Alma and the Beatles-themed town of Walnut Ridge provide fun photo ops. The entire family will enjoy a visit to the boyhood home of Johnny Cash or the post office in Texarkana, the only one located in two different states.

You can stay the night in the haunted Crescent Hotel and eat in a diner where your food is brought to your table by toy train. Get ready for some fun road trips through the Natural State.

ARKANSAS ROADSIDE ATTRACTIONS

This section includes objects you can see from the road, often free of charge.

Popeye Statue

Popeye Park
801 Fayetteville Avenue, Alma, AR
479-632-4127

Alma features a giant bronze statue of Popeye right in the center of its town park. The Allen Canning Company in Alma is responsible for canning much of the nation's spinach, so the town bills itself as the Spinach Capital of the World. The town hosts an annual Spinach Festival each April.

Arkansas's Only Suspension Bridge

Beaver Bridge
Arkansas Highway 187, Beaver, AR

Beaver Bridge is a one-lane suspension bridge built in 1949 across the White River. The 554-foot-long wood-plank span is the only suspension bridge in the state open to motor traffic. Known as the Little Golden Gate Bridge, it is listed in the National Register of Historic Places. It appeared in the 2005 movie *Elizabethtown*.

Left: Popeye statue in Alma, Arkansas. *Courtesy of Brandon Rush/Wikimedia Commons.*

Above: Beaver Bridge in Beaver, Arkansas. *Courtesy of Brandon Rush/Wikimedia Commons.*

Ghost Town of Peppersauce

Walnut Street, Calico Rock, AR
Get directions at Calico Rock Museum & Visitor Center
104 Main Street, Calico Rock

As many as twenty buildings still remain in the abandoned town of Peppersauce, located in Calico Rock, Arkansas. The community was founded in the 1800s as a trading post for French working as trappers along the White River.

The town developed a reputation as a rough outpost and got its moniker from the nickname of the moonshine served in local taverns. It experienced a boom when the railroad was built, but trains began bypassing the town in the 1960s, leading to its demise. Today, visitors can see the abandoned jail, cotton gin, funeral parlor, lumberyard, power plant and more. The buildings are privately owned, so trespassing is forbidden, but they can be seen from the street. The district is listed in the National Register of Historic Places.

Christ of the Ozarks

937 Passion Play Road, Eureka Springs, AR

A sixty-five-foot-high statue of Christ was erected on Magnetic Mountain in 1966. Commissioned by Gerald K. Smith, it was primarily created by Emmet Sullivan, a sculptor who also worked on Mount Rushmore. The nearby amphitheater is where performances of *The Great Passion Play* are performed from May through October.

Christ of the Ozarks. *Courtesy of Bobak Ha'eri/Wikimedia Commons.*

Hogeye the Dancing Razorback Statue

4148 Martin Luther King Jr. Boulevard, Fayetteville, AR

Located on Interstate 49 at exit 62, a twenty-five-foot-tall razorback hog is positioned as if he is dancing. The 3,500-pound sculpture is the work of Eugene Sergeant. It is located in front of Hogeye Inc., a company that makes promotional items.

Planters' Mr. Peanut Sign

4020 Planters Road, Fort Smith, AR

A thirty-foot-tall sign of Mr. Peanut is located on the lawn of the Planters Company. Additional Mr. Peanut statues are located at the visitors' entrance for photo ops.

Giant Arrows Lawn Art

Tenth Street and Garrison Avenue, Fort Smith, AR

D*Face, a renowned urban artist from London, created five giant arrows stuck into the ground on a vacant lot.

The Fouke Monster

Peavy's Monster Mart
104 Highway 71, Fouke, AR
870-653-2497; Free

The Fouke Monster is a Bigfoot reportedly seen in the area of Boggy Creek in the 1970s (although reports of sightings of a hairy, wild man go back as far as 1834). The reports were so widespread that a movie, *The Legend of Boggy Creek*, was made about the creature in 1972.

Because of the legends surrounding Fouke, many people travel to the tiny town each year. Peavy's Monster Mart features a huge, snarling gorilla-like head atop its store, as well as a three-dimensional Bigfoot figure emerging from a wall. Visitors can also take photos at a wooden silhouette of the monster and a mural of the cryptid. Monster Mart sells souvenirs featuring the creature and movie memorabilia. The town of fewer than nine hundred people hosts a Fouke Monster Festival each June.

The Monster Mart in Fouke, Arkansas, pays homage to *The Legend of Boggy Creek*. *Photo by Wil Elrick.*

Gurdon Light Viewing Area

64 Collins Road, Gurdon, AR

This ghost light legend in Gurdon originates with the railroad. Reportedly, visitors often see a green, white or orange orb "bobbing" or floating near the train tracks. Legend says it is the light of a ghostly rail worker who was decapitated by a train and is in search of his lost head.

The Hoo Hoo Monument

207 Main Street, Gurdon, AR

An unusual Egyptian-styled marker with two cats atop it is located on Main Street in downtown Gurdon. Known as the Hoo Hoo Monument, it commemorates the 1892 founding of the International Concatenated Order of the Hoo Hoo, a fraternal society of lumber workers. The bronze marker was made by sculptor George Zolnay and erected in

Hoo Hoo monument in Gurdon, Arkansas. *Courtesy of Viakali/Wikimedia Commons.*

1909. Because it is a rare example of Zolnay's work in Arkansas, the marker is listed in the National Register of Historic Places.

Marker for Babe's (and Baseball's) First 500-Foot Homer

870 Whittington Avenue, Hot Springs, AR

Outside the Arkansas Alligator Farm and Petting Zoo, which was founded in 1902 and is still in business, a marker tells the story of the powerful fly ball that changed Babe Ruth from a pitcher to a hitter. He had been pitching a spring training game but was called to the plate when a batter was needed.

The marker reads, "Ruth trained here nine times and became a very familiar face around Hot Springs. He hiked the mountains, took the baths, played golf, patronized the casinos, and visited the racetrack. On March 17, 1918 (St. Patrick's Day), he launched a mammoth home run from Whittington Park that landed on the fly inside the Arkansas Alligator Farm. It has been measured at 573 feet, baseball's first 500-foot-plus drive." Imagine what baseball might have been like if no one ever figured out Babe Ruth could hit.

Giant Bud Light Can

Belle Point Ranch
20906 Arkansas Highway 22, Lavaca, AR

A silo painted to look like a giant can of Bud Light has stood on the side of the highway since 1976. Arkansas.com says it was created by David McMahon

Sr., a local cattle breeder and beer distributor, in 1975 or 1976. The painted label claims it holds 8,734,902 fluid ounces of brew. In the 1980s, the can could be seen in Bud Light commercials. The silo is on private property but is visible from the road.

Ruins of Monte Ne

14299 Charlton Drive, Rogers, AR

In 1901, William Hope "Coin" Harvey built a health resort and planned community called Mount Ne to take advantage of the nearby springs, thought to be healthful. The resort had one of the first indoor swimming pools in the state. Two hotels in the community, Missouri Row and Oklahoma Row, were the largest log buildings in the world when they were built. Today, the tower from Oklahoma's Row survives, as well as a fireplace from Missouri Row.

Harvey planned to add a massive pyramid. He built an amphitheater and a retaining wall but never completed the pyramid. The community was a failure, and the property was sold after Harvey died in 1936. Beaver Lake was created in 1964, submerging much of the town's remains, although a few can be seen at normal tide levels.

The Only Post Office in Two States

State Line Post Office
500 North State Line Avenue, Suite 101, Texarkana, AR
800-275-8777

The Texarkana Post Office and Federal Courthouse straddles the Arkansas-Texas state line and has two zip codes. It is the only post office located in two states and is one of the most photographed U.S. courthouses. The structure was built in 1932 and still operates as a post office and courthouse, but anyone can take photos of the exterior—while standing in two states.

The combination courthouse and post office building is located in Texarkana, half in Texas and half in Arkansas. *Photo by Kelly Kazek.*

When B.B. King Named His Guitar Lucille

Arkansas Highway 42, Twist, AR

A marker in the tiny town of Twist commemorates the night when legendary blues singer B.B. King named his famous guitar. King would later recall that he was performing at a juke joint in Twist in 1949 (although the marker says the mid-1950s) when fire broke out. The blaze was reportedly caused when a kerosene lantern was overturned by two men brawling over a woman named Lucille. King stepped outside to safety before realizing his guitar was inside. He risked his life to run back into the fire to rescue his guitar and then christened it Lucille. King had numerous guitars through his career, all named Lucille.

Beatles-Themed Town

Walnut Ridge, AR

Inside the surviving walls of an old brick building in the downtown area of Walnut Grove is a sculpture of silhouettes of the four Beatles replicating the cover of the *Abbey Road* album. Visitors to the town can also see wooden cutouts of the Beatles, a brightly painted "Imagine" piano, window paintings and plaques explaining why this little burg of five thousand residents is a destination for Beatles fans.

It began on Friday, September 18, 1964, when the Beatles were flying from a performance in Dallas for some R&R. They planned to spend the weekend at Pigman Ranch in nearby Alton, Missouri, which was owned

Sculpture commemorating a visit from the Beatles in Walnut Ridge, Arkansas. *Photo by Kelly Kazek.*

by Reed Pigman Sr., the man who operated the charter airline the Beatles used for travel. The closest airport that could accommodate the plane was at Walnut Ridge, and the group hoped to secretly land and head to the ranch for a break from a heavy tour schedule. But word soon leaked, and local teens were in a frenzy. When the group arrived back at the airport Sunday to fly to New York, hundreds of Walnut Ridge residents crowded the airport, getting autographs and handshakes.

Walnut Ridge also erected a Guitar Walk, which honors the fact that Highway 67 through Arkansas was named the Rock 'n' Roll Highway in 2009 because of the singers who traveled it in the 1950s. The Guitar Walk is a 115-foot-long, 40-foot-wide concrete walk shaped like an Epiphone guitar.

Rush Ghost Town

Arkansas Highway 14, Buffalo National River, Yellville, AR
870-741-5443; Free

In the 1880s, a mining community grew up along the Buffalo National River. The 1,300-acre property is now a historic district overseen by the National Park Service.

"The heyday of the mining district came during World War I. All of the mines were in full operation, producing zinc for the war effort," the Park Service says. "As the war wound down, so did the market for zinc. Soon the valley seemed a ghost town in comparison to the busy years of several thousand inhabitants. A mining revival in the 1920s was short-lived, but 'free-oreing' supported local miners until World War II. During the 1940s several of the processing mills were dismantled for salvage. Until the closing of the post office in the 1950s, Rush maintained a community identity. Gradually, the remaining inhabitants left, until Rush became known as a ghost town."

Remaining signs of the town include old log cabins, rock foundations, a blacksmith shop, two stores, roadbeds, old equipment and the mines. Note: The mines are abandoned and very dangerous. Entry is barred. Rush is listed in the National Register of Historic Places.

ARKANSAS OUTSIDER ART

This unique kind of roadside oddity comes in many forms. Some collections are indoors; some are outdoors. A few charge admission; others request donations. But the work never fails to astound and entertain.

Quigley's Castle

274 Quigley Castle Road, Eureka Springs, AR
479-253-8311; Admission fee

Billed as Ozark's Strangest Dwelling, this unique home was designed by Elise Quigley and built beginning in 1943 by her husband, Albert, and a neighbor. The home was made using lumber cut from the property. The exterior is covered in stones collected by Elise since her childhood. Inside, the home has a two-story space to house the tropical plants Elise loved. She also cultivated sprawling outdoor gardens. By 1950, the home and gardens had become a tourist attraction, and the family began charging admission for tours. Elise and Albert have passed away, but the family still owns the house and offers tours. The home is listed in the National Register of Historic Places.

Quigley's Castle, Eureka Springs, Arkansas. *Courtesy of Brandon Rush/Wikimedia Commons.*

Castle at Wilson Park

Wilson Park
675 North Park Avenue, Fayetteville, AR
479-444-3471

Fayetteville's historic Wilson Park is known for an unusual feature: a whimsical castle structure that was built to hide a formerly bland concrete springhouse that feeds the park's swimming pool.

According to the city's website, a contest was held in the late 1970s for design ideas. Sculptor Frank Williams's castle was the winner: "The Castle has become increasingly popular over the years, receiving thousands of visitors annually. Over time, the structural integrity began to weaken, requiring renovations to the original project. These improvements were completed in 1999 and 2004. Rock walls on the planting spaces were constructed, aggregate walkways were added, entry areas were enlarged, the bridge rails were re-built, and the dam below the bridge was reinforced." In recent years, artist Eugene Sargent created "benches that resemble flowers and leaves, a flower fountain was fashioned for the pond, and in 2009 a 'worm' retaining wall was added."

The Castle in Wilson Park in Fayetteville, Arkansas. *Courtesy of Brandon Rush/Wikimedia Commons.*

Wizard's Cave and Labyrinth

Terra Studios Art Gallery and Park
12103 Hazel Valley Road, Fayetteville, AR
479-643-3185; Free

What happens when a group of artists is let loose on six acres of gardens? An incredible art park filled with fantasy creatures, murals and fountains, as well as a Wizard's Cave and a labyrinth. It's free to enter and play. The park is outside Terra Studios, the art gallery known for creating those small blown-glass figures called Bluebirds of Happiness. The website says, "Six beautiful acres studded with sculpture gardens, murals, sparkling glass, fantasy creatures and peaceful fountains. The fountains may contain fish or fabled dragons or simply the sparkling sound of moving water. Hundreds of artists have contributed to this one-of-a-kind art park....While you're here, be sure to visit the Wizard's Cave....The cave, with dripping water, glass stalactites and sparkling crystals, hosts a variety of inhabitants." The park is open daily.

Concrete Dinosaurs

Mountainburg City Park
201 U.S. Highway 71, Mountainburg, AR

A local man named Douglas W. Birchfield put his artistic side to work in 1980 and created concrete dinosaurs for children to play on. The folksy critters, including a T-rex, brontosaurus and triceratops, are located in the city park. Birchfield added ladders inside the brontosaurus and triceratops so children could climb inside.

Dinosaur Park in Mountainburg, Arkansas. *Courtesy of Carol M. Highsmith/Library of Congress.*

Lacey Michelle's Castle

11113 Cricket Cutoff Road, Omaha, AR
870-426-4330

Shelby Ravallette fulfilled a promise to his daughter after the little girl died at age seven in 1987. The stonemason began building a castle in the Ozark Mountains to honor her memory, and it became a lifelong labor of love. He continues to work on the structure. The walls are two feet thick, and the castle features a turret, fireplaces and stone staircases.

Ravellette keeps a pet cow on the grounds, which also includes flower and vegetable gardens on seventy acres. Ravallette collects rainwater for the gardens and opened an apartment in the castle to rent to visitors. Guests can eat on a patio outside on furniture made from massive stones. Learn more about Lacey Michelle's Castle in the movie *God's Architects*.

ARKANSAS'S LEGENDARY LOCALES

This list describes places where you will need to park your car and get out, including quirky museums, unusual historic homes and whimsical places to eat or stay overnight.

Birthplace of Walmart

Walmart Museum
105 North Main Street, Bentonville, AR
479-273-1329; Free

Sam Walton, founder of Walmart, opened his first dime store in Bentonville in 1950. He soon expanded on his idea, and Walmart was born. The little five-and-dime now houses the Walmart Museum.

Art Deco Greyhound Bus Station

Retro Greyhound bus station in Blytheville, Arkansas. *Courtesy of nyttend/ Wikimedia Commons.*

Welcome Center and Transportation Museum
109 North Fifth Street, Blytheville, AR
870-763-2525; Free

An incredible example of an art deco–style Greyhound bus station now serves as a welcome center with exhibits from the city's transportation history. The bright blue station, listed in the National Register of Historic Places, closed in 2001. It was restored and reopened in 2010.

Arkansas's Natural Bridge

1120 Natural Bridge Road, Clinton, AR
501-745-2357; Admission fee

This one-hundred-foot sandstone arch was formed over millions of years in the Ozark Mountains. In pioneer days, it was used as a transportation bridge. Also on the site are a log cabin museum and gift shop that are open mid-March through mid-November.

While you're in the area, stop and enjoy another natural attraction, Pivot Rock, at 1708 Pivot Rock Road, Eureka Springs, 479-253-8860.

Natural Bridge in Clinton, Arkansas. *Courtesy of the Clinton Chamber of Commerce.*

Boyhood Home of Johnny Cash

Dyess Colony
110 Center Drive, Dyess, AR
870-764-CASH (2274); Admission fee

Johnny Cash was three years old when his family moved to Dyess Colony, a town created in 1934 as an agricultural settlement as part of the New Deal. His parents, Ray and Carrie Cash, were among the nearly five hundred families recruited to move to the experimental colony, and they came with their five children—including Johnny, whose given name was "J.R." Two more children were born while the family lived in Dyess. Johnny lived in the settlement until he finished high school. The Cash home, one of the few that survived from the colony, was restored by the Arkansas State University and opened as a museum.

Johnny Cash's boyhood home in Dyess, Arkansas. *Courtesy of Thomas R. Machnitzki/ Wikimedia Commons.*

America's Most Haunted Hotel

Crescent Hotel and Spa
75 Prospect Avenue, Eureka Springs, AR
855-725-5720

The historic Crescent Hotel & Spa opened in 1886 and is billed as the "most haunted hotel" in the country. A historical archive is located on the fourth floor and is open to guests. Ghost tours are also offered at various times. The massive resort closed and was used as a women's college from 1908 to 1924 and a junior college from 1930 to 1934.

Historic Crescent Hotel in Eureka Springs. *Courtesy of TXphotolady/Wikimedia Commons.*

It was a controversial hospital from 1937 to 1940 when it was operated by Norman G. Baker, a millionaire inventor who claimed in radio programs to be a doctor. He told patients he had cures for cancer and other diseases. In 1940, he was finally exposed and sent to prison, abandoning the hotel.

In 1946, the hotel was purchased by a group of businessmen who owned it until 1967, when it was heavily damaged by fire. It was purchased in 1997 and restored as a modern luxury hotel. Numerous ghost stories are attached to the Crescent, including many from the hospital years when patients died. Listed in the National Register of Historic Places, the hotel has been featured on the TV shows *Ghost Hunters* and *Paranormal Witness*.

Great Passion Play

Holy Land
935 Passion Play Road, Eureka Springs, AR
800-882-7529; Admission fee

The Great Passion Play at Holy Land is performed at an amphitheater in the Ozark Mountains. The drama of Jesus's life is performed by more than 170 human actors, as well as animals. The set is three stories high. Guests can tour the staging area, as well as the wardrobe rooms, set design, special effects, lighting and sound, according to the pageant's website.

Visitors can also walk through a life-sized replica of the Eastern Gate in Jerusalem into an authentic marketplace filled with biblical characters.

Texaco Bungalow

77 Mountain Street, Eureka Springs, AR
479-253-9999

A 1930s art deco–style service station was turned into a tiny inn with two spaces for rent, located in the city's historic residential district downtown.

Magical Treehouse Castle

Oak Crest Cottages and Treehouses
526 West Van Buren, Eureka Springs, AR
479-253-9493

This treehouse castle lodge sleeps two people twelve feet in the air. Rates start at $140 per night. This company also offers other quirky accommodations, like more traditional treehouses and "hobbit caves."

Sleep Near Lions and Tigers

Turpentine Creek Wildlife Refuge
239 Turpentine Creek Lane, Eureka Springs, AR
479-253-5841; Admission fee

A rescue center for large wild cats offers lodging not far from the animal habitats. Guests can choose from rooms in the lodge, a treehouse, safari tents or RVs. The shelter is also open for day tours.

Thorncrown Chapel

12968 Highway 62 West, Eureka Springs, AR
479-253-7401; Donations

Thorncrown Chapel is a gorgeous wood-and-glass structure that rises forty-eight feet above a woodland area of the Ozarks. Its website says it "contains 425 windows and over 6,000 square feet of glass. It sits atop over 100 tons of native stone and colored flagstone, making it blend perfectly with its setting. The chapel's simple design and majestic beauty combine to make it what critics have called 'one of the finest religious spaces of modern times.'" Designed by architect E. Fay Jones, the chapel opened in 1980 and quickly became a popular tourist destination. It has won numerous design awards and honors.

Chaffee Barbershop Museum

7313 Terry Street, Building 803, Fort Smith, AR
479-434-6774; Free

A barbershop in Fort Smith was known as the place where army enlistees had their hair shaved into flattops, including its most famous customer, Elvis Presley, who had his hair cut in 1958. When Elvis's famous sideburns and pompadour were cut, fans everywhere cried but were heartened by the rock star's patriotic attitude. The museum preserves the chair where Elvis sat and other memorabilia.

Old-Timey Amusement Park

The Park at West End
Garrison Avenue and North Second Street, Fort Smith, AR
479-784-2368; $1 for Ferris wheel rides, free park entry

Those who miss the kitschiness of old-timey amusement parks will love the Park at West End. The small park, located in downtown Fort Smith, features a Ferris wheel that was made for the 1935 World's Fair in San Diego. Open from April through October, the park also has a vintage Italian carousel with hand-painted horses, a diner in a refurbished Pullman railcar, an English double-decker bus snack bar and quirky art and figures everywhere.

Legendary Gallows Replica

Fort Smith National Historic Site
301 Parker Avenue, Fort Smith, AR
479-783-3961; Admission fee

Replica of historic gallows at Fort Smith, Arkansas. *Courtesy of the National Park Service.*

The National Park Service operates this historic site that includes replicas of gallows and a courtroom that are the source of legend. From 1873 to 1896, justice was administered by famed hanging judge Isaac Parker, who was responsible for sending eighty-six men to their deaths for the crimes of rape and murder.

Replicas of the courtroom and gallows were built in another location in the 1950s, but in 1981, a new replica was built on the site of the original gallows following written descriptions found in newspaper accounts. Nooses are hung from the gallows to commemorate significant dates in the gallows' history. The macabre site is one of the most visited in the park.

Clinton's Birthplace Museum

117 South Hervey Street, Hope, AR
870-777-4455; Free, small fee for guided tours

William Jefferson Clinton III was born in Hope in August 1946, three months after the death of his father in a car wreck. His widowed mother, Virginia, and her parents lived in a small frame home in Hope for four years. The home was built in 1917. It is now operated by the National Park Service.

Bathe in the Hot Springs

Bathhouse Row
Central Avenue, Hot Springs, AR
501-620-6715; Free museum, fee for baths

Just as in the Victorian era, visitors to Hot Springs can bathe in the healing waters that gave the city its name. The hot mineral water flows from dozens of fountains around the downtown area, allowing visitors to fill bottles to take home. Bottles and jugs are available for sale at several downtown stores.

The eight surviving bathhouses, built between 1892 and 1923, are gorgeous architectural wonders. Two survive as actual bathhouses: Buckstaff, which offers the complete Victorian experience in its vintage baths, and Quapaw, a more modern spa that allows visitors to come sit in the waters for a twenty-dollar fee.

This museum on historic Bathhouse Row in Hot Springs exhibits the original baths and health equipment. *Photo by Wil Elrick.*

The houses are owned by Hot Springs National Park. Its visitors' center, located in the old Fordyce Bathhouse, is now a free museum where guests see what types of equipment people used to try to restore their health. Other bathhouses are now shops, and one is a brewery where you can purchase beer made from the hot spring waters.

Maxwell Blade's Odditorium and Curiosities Museum

119 Central Avenue, Hot Springs, AR
501-623-6200; Admission fee

It would be difficult to find a stranger and more perfect venue for an Odditorium than a former drive-through mortuary. This museum, opened by magician Maxwell Blade, displays dozens of macabre and strange objects, including ventriloquist dummies, magic artifacts and antique medical equipment.

Gangster Museum of America

510 Central Avenue, Hot Springs, AR
501-318-1717; Admission fee

From the 1920s to the 1940s, Hot Springs was a gangster hotspot. The museum website says it was a time when "mineral water, gambling, bootlegging, and other extreme pleasures brought visitors from all over the world to Hot Springs, Arkansas. The Gangster Museum of America is an historic and entertaining account of how some of the most notorious criminals in America co-existed with the quaint population of this little valley town in the mountains of central Arkansas." It includes a casino display and exhibits on Al Capone, Lucky Luciano, Owney Madden and more.

Al Capone's Hotel

Arlington Resort Hotel & Spa
239 Central Avenue, Hot Springs National Park, AR
501-623-7771

This massive hotel featuring twin towers is the third version of the Arlington. The first was built in 1875, and another was constructed in 1893. When the second hotel burned in 1923, it was rebuilt a third time at Central Avenue and Fountain Street. In the 1930s, it was a favorite stop for gangster Al Capone, who reportedly preferred room 443. The hotel was also visited by Franklin D. Roosevelt, Harry Truman, George H.W. Bush, Bill Clinton, Babe Ruth, Tony Bennett, Barbra Streisand and Yoko Ono.

Historic Arlington Hotel in Hot Springs. *Photo by Wil Elrick.*

All Aboard Restaurant and Grill

6813 Cantrell Road, Little Rock, AR
501-975-7401
20320 I-30 North, No. 170, Benton, AR
501-794-2272

This fun restaurant, which has two locations, has a unique way of getting your order to your table: It is delivered by a train that runs around the ceiling and then drops a box filled with food on a platform above the appropriate table. The platform is then lowered to

All Aboard Diner in Little Rock, Arkansas, where food is delivered by model train. *Photo by Wil Elrick.*

the table by an elevator-type conveyance. The eatery's website says it uses locally grown organic foods whenever possible.

ESSE Purse Museum & Store

1510 Main Street, Little Rock, AR
501-916-9022; Admission fee

This unique museum is one of only three in the world dedicated to purses. Displays show a variety of women's handbags and the items they carried in them to illustrate the daily lives of females through the twentieth century. The website says visitors will find "that a purse is not just a utilitarian bag in which a woman carries her necessities, but an extension of her personal space, her essence, and of the things that make her 'her.'" There is also a gift shop.

Mammoth Springs Frisco Depot

Frisco Lane, Mammoth Spring, AR
870-625-7364; Free

This depot, the oldest railway station in Arkansas, was built in 1886. It has been preserved as a museum, complete with life-size figures portraying attendants, train crew and passengers. The depot was restored to its Victorian appearance, complete with diamond-shaped panes in dormer windows and a slate roof. Visitors can hear audio presentations accompanying displays of railroad and local artifacts.

Jones Bar-B-Q Diner

219 West Louisiana Street, Marianna, AR
870-295-3807

You won't find any menus at Jones Bar-B-Q Diner. Only one item is offered: barbecued pork on Wonder Bread. The iconic café is a two-booth establishment with the owners, James and Betty Jones, residing upstairs. The café was awarded a prestigious James Beard Award in 2012 in the America's Classics category.

Uncle Sam, World's Largest Diamond

Crater of Diamonds State Park
209 State Park Road, Murfreesboro, AR
870-285-3113; Admission Fee

This state park is "one of the only places in the world where the public can search for real diamonds in their original volcanic source," according to the park's website. Crater of Diamonds, a state park since 1972, is a thirty-seven-acre plowed field on the eroded surface of a volcanic crater. Visitors

Crater of Diamonds
State Park in Arkansas.
*Courtesy of Doug Wertman/
Wikimedia Commons.*

can keep any gemstones they find. A marker shows the location of the spot where the World's Largest Diamond was discovered in 1924. Nicknamed Uncle Sam, it was 40.23 carats before cutting.

Sleep in a Teepee

Diamond John's Riverside Retreat
81 Roy Road, Murfreesboro, AR
870-285-4027

Located just a mile and a half from the popular Crater of Diamonds State Park, Diamond John's Riverside Retreat is known for its teepee lodging. The site has four cabins and four teepees overlooking the Little Missouri River, where guests can swim and fish. Three smaller teepees hold four adults, while the largest accommodates eight.

Lum and Abner Jot 'Em Down Store and Museum

4562 Arkansas Highway 88 West, Pine Ridge, AR
870-326-4442

The *Lum and Abner* radio programs from the 1930s through the early 1950s were based on the real community of Pine Ridge. The show mentioned real stores, which were built in 1904 and 1909. The stores are now open as a museum and store, where visitors can hear old *Lum and Abner* radio programs while browsing exhibits, an operational historic post office and the souvenir store.

The Old Mill

T.R. Pugh Memorial Park
3800 Lakeshore Drive, North Little Rock, AR
501-791-8537; Free

You've probably seen the picturesque mill in Pugh Park and didn't even know it. The replica of an 1880s mill was built in 1933 and appeared in the opening scenes of *Gone with the Wind*, which premiered in 1939. These days, the mill is a popular spot with photographers and picnickers. The park is also decorated with a unique bridge that looks as if it is made of entwined trees and branches, but it was really made of concrete by sculptor Dionicio Rodriquez, who added other touches of whimsy around the grounds. The mill is listed in the National Register of Historic Places.

Orange-Shaped Diner

The Mammoth Orange
103 North Highway 365, Redfield, AR
501-397-2347

This iconic diner with a bright orange, round-shaped top serves up breakfasts, burgers, hot dogs and milkshakes. Diners can even pull up a stool and eat outside the big orange. It opened in 1963.

Daisy Airgun Museum

202 West Walnut Street, Rogers, AR
479-986-6873; Admission fee

This museum exhibiting all kinds of Daisy airguns is a nonprofit organization formed to preserve vintage Daisy products. The website says, "Since 1960, Daisy's corporate offices in Rogers, Arkansas, have housed an impressive airgun collection. In 1999, the company decided to utilize that collection to create a first class and entertaining museum which would serve as a tourism attraction for our city." The museum, housed in an 1896 building, opened in March 2000.

Daisy Airgun Museum in Rogers, Arkansas. *Courtesy of Doug Wertman/Wikimedia Commons.*

ARKANSAS TOMBSTONE TALES

This section lists just a few of the state's intriguing headstones and the stories behind them. Most cemeteries are open during daylight hours only. Many do not have street numbers in their addresses, but those listed are as close as possible.

Morris, the General Manager Cat

Crescent Hotel and Spa
75 Prospect Avenue, Eureka Springs, AR
855-725-5720

Morris the cat, who lived to the ripe ol' age of twenty-one, had an important position and an office at the historic Crescent Hotel. Morris was known as the "general manager" and official greeter at the hotel. When Morris died in 1994, he was buried in a place of honor on the grounds. A memorial plaque in the lobby of the hotel also offers a tribute:

> *In Memory of Morris, the Resident Cat at the Crescent Hotel,*
> *He filled his position exceedingly well,*
> *The General Manager title he wore, was printed right there on his own office door,*
> *He acted as greeter and sometimes as guide,*
> *Whatever his duties, he did them with pride,*
> *He chose his own hours and set his own pace,*
> *The guests were impressed with his manners and grace,*
> *Upstairs and down he kept everything nice,*
> *They might have had ghosts, but they never had mice,*
> *Due to the fact he was growing quite old, he'd doze by the fire when the weather got cold,*
> *His years were a dignified twenty and one, when at last he retired his nine lives were done,*
> *He filled his position exceedingly well,*
> *the Resident Cat at The Crescent Hotel.*

Henry Humphrey: Victim of Bonnie and Clyde

804 Fayetteville Avenue, Alma, AR

Henry Humphrey, the city marshal of Alma, first encountered the gang of Clyde Barrow and Bonnie Parker the night of June 22, 1933. Humphrey was making rounds through the town when gang members forced him into a local bank, tied him up and robbed the bank. Unfortunately for Henry, he ran into the gang again the next day, and this time, he and the gang exchanged gunfire. Henry Humphrey died. In 1986, the town honored Humphrey with a memorial in front of the Alma Police Department. He is the only city officer killed in the line of duty.

Sam Walton Grave

Bentonville Cemetery
400 Southwest F Street, Bentonville, AR
479-271-5945

Sam Walton (1918–1992), the founder of Walmart, is buried beneath an unassuming marker in Bentonville, where the company was established.

The Goat Woman of Smackover

Liberty Methodist Church Cemetery
2 Ouachita, Louann, AR

Rhena Salome Miller Meyer (1905–1988) was known as the Goat Woman of Smackover, Arkansas. Before settling in the town, she was a one-woman band with a circus. She and her husband, Charles, lived in a 1915 Model-T

Downtown Smackover, Arkansas. *Courtesy of Valis55/ Wikimedia Commons.*

circus truck. After her husband died in 1963, Rhena accumulated many pet goats and began giving shows in which she played music and the goats "sang" along. The circus truck, the only known one of its kind, is displayed at the Arkansas Museum of Natural Resources in Smackover.

Caddo Indian Memorial

Arkansas Highway 8 near Village Avenue, Norman, AR

A Caddo Native American burial ground was discovered not long ago on the southern end of town, and town officials erected a fence to protect the area. Recently, descendants of the Caddo Indians added benches and plaques with historical information. The graves are not individually marked.

Mystery Grave of Arkansas

Fairview Cemetery
Arkansas Highway 59, Van Buren, AR

Who is buried in a primitive-looking tomb in Fairview Cemetery in Van Buren? The grave is thought to predate the founding of the cemetery in 1816, but no one knows who is buried there. A plaque attached to the foot of the tomb tells the local legend that perhaps one of Hernando de Soto's men was buried there during one of his 1541 expeditions. Most historians, however, doubt de Soto reached Van Buren.

Another theory says the stones mark the grave of a Viking, one of a group who allegedly lived in Oklahoma more than one thousand years ago. The mystery remains unsolved.

Florida

lorida, bless its heart, is the quirkiest of states. Some claim it isn't even truly southern, yet it is filled with inherently southern roadside wonders.

Enjoy castles? There are plenty to see in the Sunshine State. You'll find the ruins of Braden Castle and the Coral Castle, a mysterious tribute to unrequited love. Then there's the shiny silver Solomon's Castle, which features a moat and a restaurant in a pirate ship.

If you like shiny things, you might also visit the Futuro house, which looks like a UFO. You can also walk into the mouth of the World's Largest Alligator or pose with a giant conch shell. Whichever direction you head in Florida, you'll find something unusual. Trust me on this.

FLORIDA ROADSIDE ATTRACTIONS

This section includes objects you can see from the road, often free of charge.

Ninety-Three-Foot Spiral Slide

Aventura Mall
19501 Biscayne Boulevard, Aventura, FL
305-935-1110; Free

A ninety-three-foot-high spiral slide, a curious structure designed by Belgian artist Carsten Höller, is located at a new wing in Aventura Mall, a high-end retail center anchored by Nordstrom and Bloomingdale's. "The Aventura Slide Tower leads a double life: towering landmark and exhilarating slide," the mall's website says.

Tootsie in a Patriotic Bikini

6111 Fifteenth Street East, Bradenton, FL

A former Uniroyal Gal named Tootsie painted wearing a red, white and blue bikini makes for a patriotic photo op.

The World's Smallest Police Station. *Courtesy of ebyabe/Wikimedia Commons.*

World's Smallest Police Station

Across from Carrabelle Chamber of Commerce
102 Avenue A North, Carrabelle, FL
850-697-3691

Although many towns claim to have the world's smallest police station, this one-person call center truly earns the title. The "station" looks like a phone booth and was actually the emergency call box in the 1960s. Thanks to vandalism, the current booth is a replica. It has been featured on TV shows such as *Ripley's Believe It or Not*, *The Tonight Show with Johnny Carson* and the *Today* show.

Swampy, World's Largest Alligator

Jungle Adventures
26205 East Highway 50, Christmas, FL
407-568-2885; Admission fee

This two-hundred-foot-long alligator is actually a building that houses Jungle Adventures. There's an admission fee for the adventure part, which includes exhibits with live animals, but it's free to take a look at Swampy from the outside.

Memorial to Brownie the Town Dog

Riverfront Park
60 East Orange Park, Daytona Beach, FL
386-671-3400

At the corner of Orange Avenue and Beach Street near the Halifax River stands a memorial to one of Daytona's most beloved residents: a stray dog named Brownie. The dog wandered into town in 1939

and was treated like a prince, with a custom doghouse, expensive foods and even his own bank account, according to BrownietheTownDog.org. By the time Brownie died in 1954, he had been featured in numerous publications. He is honored with a bronze statue in his likeness.

The memorial to Brownie the Town Dog.
Courtesy of Eddie Jams/Wikimedia Commons.

Boot of Circus Giant

9815 U.S. Highway 41, Gibsonton, FL

A replica of an oversized boot honors the late Al Tomaini, who worked as a circus giant and was a well-respected leader in Gibsonton, a circus-wintering town. The thirty-five-inch-high boot is set atop a pillar etched "Al and Jeanie Tomaini: Gibsonton Civic Leaders." Al was seven feet, eleven inches, or eight feet, four inches, depending on the source, while his two-foot-five-inch wife with missing limbs was billed as the Half Girl. The memorial is located on the site where the couple ran the Giant's Fish Camp & Restaurant.

Betsy the Giant Lobster

86700 Overseas Highway, Islamorada, FL

A thirty-foot-high and forty-foot-long spiny lobster named Betsy, created by sculptor Richard Blaze, is on display at the Rain Barrel Artisan Village.

Goofy Gator Statue

Next to the Jacksonville Fire Museum at 1408 Gator Bowl Boulevard, Jacksonville, FL

A twenty-two-foot-tall grinning alligator that once stood outside Casper's Gatorland in St. Augustine was given a new home near Metropolitan Park.

Baby Bridges

Cancer Survivors Park
101 West State Street, Jacksonville, FL

Small-scale replicas, also called the "Baby Bridges," make up the Five Bridges Cancer Survivors monument, representing the Dames Point, Matthews, Acosta, Hart and Main Street bridges. They were created by students from Florida Community College.

Christ of the Deep

Twenty-five feet beneath the ocean, Key Largo, FL

A massive statue, submerged about twenty-five feet in the sea in John Pennekamp Coral Reef State Park, is a dive destination. The four-thousand-pound statue, *Christ of the Deep*, was sculpted by Italian artist Guido Galletti. Two other copies were made from the artist's original cast, one in Italy and one in Grenada.

Christ of the Deep, or the Abyss. *Courtesy of Sebastian Carlosena/Wikimedia Commons.*

Giant Mermaid on a Building

The Mermaid Gift Shop
7511 West Irlo Bronson Memorial Highway, Kissimmee, FL
407-396-1407

Come for the incredible selfie opportunity, stay to browse through gifts and souvenirs.

Monument of States

Lakefront Park
300 East Monument Avenue, Kissimmee, FL

In 1943, Kissimmee residents wanted to do something to honor those killed in the 1941 attacks on Pearl Harbor. The Monument of States was

created by Dr. Charles Bressler-Pettis. The National Park Service says, "In its design, each state would donate a rock particular to their location for placement on the monument….Over time, cities and even other countries would send objects to affix to the towering monument at the request of Pettis, thereby creating an evolving and visually prominent tourist attraction."

Monument of States.
Courtesy of Visitor7/Wikimedia Commons.

Ruins of St. Anne's Shrine

St. Anne's Shrine Road, Lake Wales, FL
Free

A shrine was built in 1920 to commemorate a local miracle. A Canadian man believed the waters of Lake St. Anne had cured his son, so he built a monument. After the lovely stone shrine became something of a tourist attraction, it was partially demolished in 1950, but the altar, steps and arch remain.

Memorial to Lost Seamen

John's Pass Village & Boardwalk
12901 Village Boulevard, Madeira Beach, FL
727-238-3671

A nine-foot-high statue of a massive hand holding a fragile boat, known as the *Hand of Fate*, was erected in 2012 beside the channel in John's Pass Village, where many sailors headed out to sea, never to return. It was carved by Robert Bruce Epstein.

World's Largest Chicken Wing

Hooter's
192 Johns Pass Boardwalk West, Madeira Beach, FL
727-797-4668

This half-ton replica of a chicken wing hangs from a sign declaring it the World's Largest.

Lichtenstein Mermaid

Jackie Gleason Theatre
1700 Washington Avenue, Miami Beach, FL
305-673-7300

Outside the Jackie Gleason Theatre, a Roy Lichtenstein sculpture called *Mermaid* is showcased on the lawn. The 1979 artwork is made of concrete and steel, among other things, and features a live palm tree.

The Roy Lichtenstein statue *Mermaid* in Miami Beach. *Courtesy of Carol Highsmith/Library of Congress.*

Half-Buried Giant Woman

Lake Eola Park
512 East Washington Street, Orlando, FL

A forty-foot-long woman sculpted by artist Meg White, a statue called *Discovery of Muse*, looks as if she is lying in the park, covered with a blanket of shrubbery.

Giant Conch Shell

10100 U.S. Highway 1, Port St. Lucie, FL
772-355-5616

A five-thousand-pound replica of a conch is located in front of the Shell Bazaar, where it has remained since the store opened in 1953. Another Giant Conch Shell, this one fifteen feet high and made of metal, is located in a high school parking lot at 2100 Flagler Avenue, Key West, Florida.

A mosaic-covered, two-headed alligator. *Courtesy of GWilson12/Wikimedia Commons.*

Two-Headed Alligator Statue

4500 North Nebraska Avenue, Tampa, FL

He's colorful. He's tiled. He's an alligator. He has two heads. That's all you really need to know about this work of art/photo op in Tampa's Seminole Heights neighborhood. Reportedly, a two-headed 'gator has been the neighborhood's mascot since the homes were built in 1911, based on a local legend. The six-foot-tall statue is the creation of resident Justin Arnold, who claimed to have found a two-headed alligator carcass nearby in 2014.

Giant Kissing Sailor & Nurse

McKee Botanical Garden
350 U.S. Highway 1, Vero Beach, FL
772-794-0601; Visible from the road

A twenty-five-foot-tall statue of a World War II sailor kissing a dental nurse on V-J Day can be seen outside McKee Botanical Garden. It is located at the corner of North Gulfstream Avenue and Bayfront Drive. It was created by artist Seaward Johnson.

Monument to the Possum

At Second Avenue and Washington Street, Wausau, FL

Known as the "Possum Capital of the World," the small town of Wausau takes its responsibility to honor the marsupials seriously. A twelve-foot granite monument to the opossum was erected downtown in 1982. It is etched with the likeness of an opossum and the inscription: "Erected in grateful recognition of the role the North American possum, a magnificent survivor of the marsupial family pre-dating the ages of the mastodon and the dinosaur has played in furnishing both food and fur for the early settlers and their successors. Their presence here has provided a source of nutritious and flavorful food in normal times and has been an important aid to human survival in times of distress and critical need."

Monument to the possum in Wausau, Florida. *Courtesy of Carol Highsmith/Library of Congress.*

Twenty-Four-Foot-Tall Potty Chair

3317 Old Thornhill Road, Winter Haven, FL
Private Property; Visible from road

This monumental potty chair—the old-fashioned kind with a hole to place over a toilet for elderly or disabled folks—is the work of artist Steven Chayt, who said he had been pondering the idea for more than twenty years before building it in 2015.

FLORIDA OUTSIDER ART

This unique kind of roadside oddity comes in many forms. Some collections are indoors; some are outdoors. A few charge admission; others request donations. But the work never fails to astound and entertain.

Carrabelle Bottle House

604 Southeast Avenue F, Carrabelle, FL
850-653-7197; Private residence

Begun in 2012 by Leon Wiesner, the Carrabelle Bottle House and the small-scale lighthouse beside it are made using bottles for walls. Wiesner lives in and continues to work on the home. On his website, he says, "We live here year around and are willing to show you the house and surroundings at any time, just call. Visitors are always welcome."

Mosaic House of Dunedin

1524 Alamo Lane, Dunedin, FL
Private residence; Drive-by only

Carol Sackman and her husband, Blake White, are working artists who turned their Dunedin home into a mosaic masterpiece. A mosaic-tiled arch stands in front of the home, greeting guests with the message "Changes Make Waves." The home is painted in bright, beachy colors, and mosaic art can be found on its walls, porch floors and in the garden.

The Coral Castle

28655 South Dixie Highway, Homestead, FL
305-248-6345; Admission fee

How did one diminutive man move massive boulders of coral rock to create fairy-tale surroundings for the woman he loved? No one knows.

But the proof is located in Homestead, Florida. Edward Leedskalnin, a native of Latvia, worked from 1923 to 1951 to build this odd coral structure in hopes of recapturing the heart of his beloved Agnes Scuffs, who had broken off their engagement.

It didn't work, but Ed managed to create an everlasting roadside attraction. The mysterious part? The website says, "With no outside assistance or large machinery Ed single-handedly built the Coral Castle, carving and sculpting over 1,100 tons of coral rock, as a testimony to his lost love, Agnes. What makes Ed's work remarkable is the fact that he was just over 5 feet tall and weighed only 100 pounds. In this part of Florida, the coral in some areas can be up to 4,000 feet thick. Incredibly, he cut and moved huge coral blocks using only hand tools. He had acquired some skills working in lumber camps and came from a family

The Coral Castle in Homestead, Florida. *Courtesy of Ebyabe/Wikimedia Commons.*

of stonemasons in Latvia. He drew on this knowledge and strength to cut and move these blocks."

Because Ed worked at night, no one ever witnessed his labors. "When questioned about how he moved the blocks of coral, Ed would only reply that he understood the laws of weight and leverage well," the online history explains. "This man with only a fourth-grade education even built an AC current generator, the remains of which are on display today. Because there are no records from witnesses his methods continue to baffle engineers and scientists, and Ed's secrets of construction have often been compared to Stonehenge and the great pyramids."

Whimzeyland

1206 Third Street, Safety Harbor, FL
Private residence; Drive-by only

A home in Safety Harbor was once known as the Bowling Ball House, after its owners, artists Todd Ramquist and Kiaralinda, filled their yard with art made from painted balls.

Over the course of two decades, the couple has added a variety of artworks in myriad shapes and sizes, using colored bottles, mosaic tiles, found objects and, of course, painted bowling balls. Brightly colored paths swirl through the gardens, leading to the colorful home and a gazebo. Not even the chimney escaped decoration—it is covered in purple paint and topped with a bright sunshine face and the word *whimzey* is spelled down its length.

Mr. Imagination's Wall

211 East First Street, Sanford, FL
407-323-2774; Free

Gallery owner Jeanie Taylor specializes in folk art. After she met Gregory Warmack, a local man known as "Mr. Imagination," she invited him to decorate a wall outside her Sanford gallery in the historic Hotchkiss Building. The works on the building were created using bits and pieces of artifacts from the lives of locals. Warmack's work can also be seen in the Smithsonian Anacostia Museum of Art, the American Visionary Museum in Baltimore, the National Botanical Gardens in Washington, D.C., the American Folk Art Museum in New York City and more.

Tiny Town

2520 Emerson Avenue S, St. Petersburg, FL
561-866-4422; Private residence
Free

Located past St. Petersburg's old warehouse district is a brightly colored scale-replica town created by artist Dan Painter. Vintage-looking buildings and signs line his yard, including a small drive-in movie screen with an old Ford parked out front, an auto shop called Dan's Rattle and Crank, the Flamingo Motel, complete with swimming pool, a gas station and more. Although the "town" was built on Painter's land, he welcomes visitors, according to the *Tampa Bay Times*. You just have to find him at home.

Hong Kong Willie's Creations

East Fletcher Avenue, Tampa, FL
Take Exit 266 from Interstate 75
813-770-4794; Visible from the road

Hong Kong Willie is actually a bait shop and fishing business, but it's the art out front that draws many visitors. Art made of found objects such as life preservers, fishing nets, painted buoys—even a helicopter—are located in front of the business.

FLORIDA'S LEGENDARY LOCALES

This list describes places you will need to park your car and get out, including quirky museums, unusual historic homes and whimsical places to eat or stay overnight.

Ruins of Braden Castle

Braden Castle Park
Braden Castle Drive, Brandenton, FL
941-746-7700

In the 1840s, brothers Joseph and Hector Braden came to the area and bought 1,100 acres to raise sugar cane. They built their home—a two-story structure—from tabby, a mixture of shells and sand often used in coastal construction. The tabby castle was eventually abandoned and became a favorite site for treasure hunters. It burned in 1903, and the remains were left on the property, becoming a tourist attraction. The ruins are located in Braden Castle mobile home park.

The ruins of Braden Castle. *Courtesy of Paul R. Burley/Wikimedia Commons.*

Boyett's Grove

4355 Spring Lake Highway, Brooksville, FL
352-796-2289

Sure, this is a place for visitors to Florida to pick fresh citrus fruit, but it's also where you can find all the other Sunshine State kitsch you've been seeking. Alligators? Check. Souvenirs? Check. Ice cream cones? Tropical birds? Check and check. And then there's the aquarium and dinosaur cave and—you have to see it to believe it.

The Bubble Room

15001 Captiva Drive, Captiva, FL
239-472-5558

This family-style restaurant has been an icon on Captiva Island since 1979. Its name is derived from the strings of vintage "bubbling" Christmas lights that grace the interior of the shack-like eatery year-round. It is also known for the antique animatronic Santas and toys that can be found around the restaurant. The music you hear while dining was all recorded in the 1920s–1940s.

The Bubble Room in Captiva, Florida, in 1992.
Photo by Kelly Kazek.

Spiritualist Town of Cassadaga

1112 Stevens Street, Cassadaga, FL
386-228-2880

A house in Cassadaga, Florida. *Courtesy of Ebyabe/Wikimedia Commons.*

Cassadaga, a small unincorporated community, is known as the Psychic Capital of the World because of the large number of professed mediums and psychics living and working there.

The community started in 1875 with a spiritualist camp meeting held by George P. Colby. Since then, the community became a mecca for like-minded people. Today, it is a preserved historic district where visitors can see a welcome center, the Cassadaga Hotel, Colby Memorial Temple, a library, the Caesar Forman Healing Center, a bookstore, a park and more. Guests are welcomed and will always find someone to help them portend the future. The town's mission statement is "Spiritualism has no dogma or creed, just a simple set of nine principles to help guide our lives."

Kapok Tree Inn

923 North McMullen Booth Road, Clearwater, FL
727-725-8733

Once an iconic restaurant in Clearwater, the Kapok Tree Inn was preserved and reopened as an event venue.

Named for a tree from India planted on the site in the 1870s, the Kapok Tree Inn was an eclectic eatery built in 1958 by a bandleader named Richard B. Baumgardner. The two-hundred-seat establishment offered fairly typical country meals but in lavish surroundings "with hundreds of imported, or locally manufactured, columns and statues and paintings and chandeliers, tied delightfully in with the grounds' tropical foliage. Over the years, word-of-mouth alone propelled this utterly unique restaurant and its grounds to the status of local and international sensation," according to kapokspecialevents.com. "It was truly a sprawling complex, with souvenirs and gift shops bearing its name. Throughout its life, The Kapok Tree Inn was named again and again as one of the nation's best restaurants for business dining." The restaurant closed in 1991, and the site eventually became an event venue, with much of the interior design intact.

Drive-In Church

3140 South Atlantic Avenue, Daytona Beach, FL
386-767-8761

This church in Daytona Beach offers a drive-in movie–type experience. Congregants can worship in the sanctuary, outside on picnic blankets or in their cars. The website explains: "You will be greeted by a member of the congregation who will give you a bulletin as well as a pre-packaged communion set. They will also help you locate 88.5FM on your radio dial….From there, you simply select where you'd like to park and participate in worship."

Giant Wooden Indian Heads

Peter Wolf Toth Museum
102 Arthur Avenue, Edgewater, FL
386-795-0291; Free

Sculptor Peter Wolf Toth is known for his massive wooden carvings of Native American heads scattered across the United States. To date, he has created more than seventy-four of the statues, which range from fifteen to forty feet high, on what is known as the "Trail of the Whispering Giants." He donates his works to various cities in honor of Native Americans; he sells smaller versions at his gallery to help fund his work.

Cruise-Ship Hotel

B Ocean Resort
1140 Seabreeze Boulevard, Fort Lauderdale, FL
954-564-1000

This hotel was built in 1956 to resemble a cruise ship. Initially called the Yankee Clipper Hotel, it was renamed in 2015. Guests can stay in one of more than four hundred rooms or experience a live "mermaid" show at the Wreck Bar. The hotel can be seen in the 1999 movie *Analyze This*.

Oldest Surviving Goofy Golf

401 Elgin Parkway NE, Fort Walton Beach, FL
850-862-4922; Fee to play

In 1958, James W. Hayes had an amazing idea to draw families to his business: create a miniature golf course and fill it with wacky homemade dinosaurs and other creations. The result, Goofy Golf, went on to become a chain established by Lee Koplin in Panama City Beach. Hayes's original Goofy Golf animals can still be seen at the Fort Walton Beach location, where guests are greeted by the twenty-three-foot-tall T-rex named "Hammy."

Jules' Undersea Lodge

51 Shoreland Drive, Key Largo, FL
305-451-2353

Those looking to stay in unusual lodging will find perhaps the strangest room in the world in Key West—it's underwater. Divers who want to experience deep-sea living can rent the lodge for lunch or stay from as little as three hours to overnight. Visitors must dive twenty-one feet to reach the lodge.

Boat from The African Queen

99701 Overseas Highway, Key Largo, FL
305-451-8080; Fee for rides

The *African Queen* was built in England in 1912 to shuttle cargo for a railway company, but it became famous when it costarred with Hollywood elite. AfricanQueenflkeys.com says, "Made famous in the 1951 movie of the same name starring Humphrey Bogart and Katherine [*sic*] Hepburn she

The steamboat *African Queen* offers tours in Key Largo. *Courtesy of Ebyabe/Wikimedia Commons*

still remains a timeless classic. This famous steamboat is available for daily canal cruises and dinner cruises in the Port Largo Canal area and also for private events."

Hemingway's Six-Toed Cats

Hemingway Home and Museum
907 Whitehead Street, Key West, FL
305-294-1136; Admission fee

Sure, people go to the onetime home of legendary author Ernest Hemingway to learn more about his life in Key West, but many go mainly to see descendants of his polydactyl cats. Hemingway had a soft spot for the six-toed cats, and the curators of the museum have carried on his legacy by providing homes to numerous stray cats, who live the high life on the property.

Orange-Shaped Building

Eli's Orange World, Kissimmee, FL
407-239-6031

This building with a bright-orange, domed top has been a Florida landmark since 1981. It is billed as the World's Largest Orange. Inside, visitors can buy fresh citrus fruit, souvenirs, gifts and apparel.

Tupperware Museum

14901 South Orange Blossom Trail, Kissimmee, FL
407-826-5050; Free

What southerner wouldn't want to learn more about Tupperware in order to store even more of Meemaw's leftovers? Visitors can check out exhibits on the history of food containers at the Tupperware Headquarters.

Dupree Gardens Ruins

Ehren Cutoff, Land O' Lakes, FL
Free

Like many once popular Florida attractions, Dupree Gardens went the way of the Dodo bird. The roadside gardens, created by Tampa attorney J. William Dupree, covered nine hundred acres and included a lodge, a tearoom and even rides on the lake in a glass-bottomed boat.

The historical marker says, "Even though gasoline rationing had caused the facility to be 'Closed For The Duration' in 1943, a New York City auction of Dupree Gardens' camellia blooms netted $250,000.00 for the War Bond effort in 1944. Dupree Gardens, still a beautiful garden spot, briefly

Ruins of Dupree Gardens. *Courtesy of candleabracadabra/ Wikimedia Commons.*

reopened in 1946 for some civic events. The tearoom burned in 1995. The lodge (converted to a home by the Hendrix family), the gatehouse (now in ruins) and some scattered plantings are all that remains of this early Florida theme park." Driving north on U.S. Highway 41, turn right at Ehren Cutoff and drive three-quarters of a mile to a pull-off area.

Parking Garage as Art

Block of Forty-First Street NE, Miami, FL
Fee to Park

Leave it to Miamians to find a way to make parking garages more beautiful. The folks with Design District in downtown Miami are behind Museum Garage. The seven-story building is a work of art, with each of the five sides showcasing a variety of colors and styles.

"Starry Night" House

306 West Sixth Avenue, Mount Dora, FL
Private residence, drive-by only

Most people recognize Vincent van Gogh's famed painting *Starry Night*, even if they didn't know its name. The famous work was recently the subject of controversy in Mount Dora when a couple decided to paint a mural on the back of their home. Homeowners Nancy Nemhauser and Lubomir Jastrzebski commissioned artist Richard Barrenecheat to paint the home because the work of van Gogh brings comfort to their autistic son. City leaders objected to the mural, which faces Old U.S. Highway 441, but eventually agreed to let it stay.

Sugar Mill Ruins

600 Mission Drive, New Smyrna Beach, FL
386-736-5953; Free

Cruger-dePeyster Plantation, which included its own mill made of coquina-shell construction, was founded on six hundred acres circa 1830 to grow sugar cane. In 1835, the plantation was attacked during the war between Seminole Indians and the federal government. Today, the ruins of the mill are part of a seventeen-acre historic park.

The Shell Factory

16554 North Cleveland Avenue, North Fort Myers, FL
239-995-2141; Admission fee

When in Florida, one must do iconic Florida things, such as visit the Shell Factory and Fun Park. The grounds include an impressive array of roadside attractions, even for Florida, such as a shell museum, Christmas house, petting farm, dinosaur land, zip lines, paddleboats, cafés, music venues, mini golf and more.

The legendary Shell Factory. *Courtesy of Freesharer4/ Wikimedia Commons.*

Skunk Ape Research Center

40904 Tamiami Trail East, Ochopee, FL
239-695-2275; Admission fee

Do you believe in the Skunk Ape? The smelly cousin of Sasquatch who lives in the Florida swamps? That's not the important thing, because Dave Shealy believes enough for all of us. He has collected materials about and evidence of the Skunk Ape at his research facility, which also acts as a souvenir shop and roadside attraction featuring live alligators and snakes.

Solomon's Castle

4533 Solomon Road, Ona, FL
863-494-6077; Admission fee

This shiny silver castle was built by sculptor Howard Solomon. The three-story high, twelve-thousand-square-foot castle comes complete with turrets. What makes it so shiny? The façade is covered in aluminum printing plates.

Not satisfied with just owning a castle, Solomon built a sixty-foot replica of a pirate's ship to house a restaurant. The ship eatery is known locally as the "Boat in the Moat." More recently, Solomon added a lighthouse to the property.

Goofy Golf in Panama City Beach

12206 Front Beach Road, Panama City Beach, FL
850-234-6403; Fee to play

Since 1959, children have come to Goofy Golf to play a round of mini golf, gawk at the assortment of colorful critters, crawl into the mouth of the dragon and sit in the hand of the giant monkey.

Futuro House in Pensacola Beach

1304 Panferio Drive, Pensacola Beach, FL
Private residence; Drive-by only

The Futuro House, located directly on Pensacola Beach, was painted white rather than the standard silver and appeared to be unused in July 2019. It was erected atop a small home in the 1960s when the Futuros were first manufactured, according to the FuturoHouse.com.

A neighbor erected a mannequin in an alien mask to provide a touch of whimsy. The prefabricated homes were designed in the 1960s to

withstand hurricanes, and the one on Pensacola Beach has outlasted several. Only about sixty Futuro homes survive in the world.

A second Futuro home located in Tampa is set atop the 2001 Odyssey, a strip club at 2309 North Dale Mabry Highway. The Futuro house serves as the club's VIP room. Visible from the road.

A Futuro house on Pensacola Beach, Florida. *Photo by Wil Elrick.*

Ruins of Bongoland

950 Old Sugar Mill Road, Port Orange, FL
386-767-1735; Admission fee

Florida is one of those places where visitors aren't surprised to come across a dinosaur in the woods. But in the Dunlawton Sugar Mill Gardens in Port Orange, many other critters lurk in the foliage. Guests might happen upon a prehistoric giant sloth or a T-rex, survivors of Bongoland, a 1940s tourist attraction. The roadside stop was built by Dr. Jerry Sperber, a dermatologist fascinated by dinosaurs. He dotted the landscape with life-sized models of long-extinct animals he made from chicken wire and concrete and opened it to the public. The property also included a miniature train, live animals and a replica of a Seminole village. Unfortunately, the attraction didn't make much money and closed in 1952, leaving the animals to roam the woods for eternity.

The Truman Show *Movie Town*

Community of Seaside
31 Natchez Street, Santa Rosa Beach, FL
Private residences; Drive-by only

Visit this planned community where *The Truman Show* was filmed, including 36 Natchez Street, which served as the house where Jim Carrey's character lives. Note: The house number may say "36 Natchez," as in the film, but the street address is 31 Natchez on Google Maps.

A house seen in the movie *The Truman Show. Courtesy of Jakesilb14/Wikimedia Commons.*

FLORIDA TOMBSTONE TALES

This section lists just a few of the state's intriguing headstones and the stories behind them. Most cemeteries are open during daylight hours only. Many do not have street numbers in their addresses, but those listed are as close as possible.

The Flying Wallendas Grave

Manasota Memorial Park
1221 Fifty-Third Avenue E, Brandenton, FL
941-755-2688

The world-famous aerialist Karl Wallenda, a member of the legendary Flying Wallendas, is buried alongside his second wife beneath a headstone etched with the words: "Aerialists Supreme." Karl (1904–1978), perhaps the most famous Wallenda, died while walking a tightrope between two buildings in Puerto Rico. His wife, Helen Kreis Wallenda, also was a performer. They were married from 1936 until Karl's death. She died in 1996.

Jackie Gleason Grave

Our Lady of Mercy Catholic Cemetery
11411 Twenty-Fifth Street NW, Doral, FL
305-592-0521

The famous actor and comedian best known for the TV series *The Honeymooners* and the movie *Smokey and the Bandit* was born in New York but is buried near Miami. Gleason (1916–1987) is buried beneath a beautiful marble mausoleum. One side is etched with his famous tagline, "And away we go."

The grave of Jackie Gleason. *Courtesy of Liber8tor/Wikimedia Commons.*

Boat-Shaped Grave

Lemon Bay Cemetery
500 South Indiana Avenue, Englewood, FL

The memorial on the grave of a prominent man in the local fishing industry, Herbert Harvey "Bill" Anger (1915–1990), is shaped like a concrete boat, complete with steering pedestal and wheel. Two cables hold the boat to posts, as if it had just docked.

She Really Was Sick

Key West Cemetery
701 Pauline Street, Key West, FL

The grave of B.P. Roberts (1929–1979) is one of the most visited in historic Key West Cemetery—and there are lots of quirky ones to visit. Her grave is marked with a stone that says, "I Told You I Was Sick."

Another humorous epitaph in the cemetery is on the grave of Alan Dale Willcox (1947–2009), which says, "If You Are Reading This, You Desperately Need a Hobby." The marker for Gloria M. Russell (1926–2000) says, "I'm Just Resting My Eyes."

Dolphin from TV's Flipper

Dolphin Research Institute and Center
58901 Overseas Highway, Grassy Key, Marathon, FL
305-289-1121

Mitzi the dolphin (1958–1972) became famous in the mid-1960s when she was trained to be the star of the TV show *Flipper*. The show ran on NBC from 1964 to 1967. Mitzi's grave is marked by the life-sized statue of a dolphin that appears to be leaping from the grave, along with the epitaph: "Dedicated to the memory of Mitzi. The original Flipper." She was one of several dolphins who portrayed Flipper on the show.

Mitzi the Dolphin is memorialized at the Dolphin Research Center. *Courtesy of Panoramio/Wikimedia Commons.*

Grave in the Middle of the Road

Canova Drive near the intersection of Columbus Avenue, New Smyrna Beach, FL

Charles Dummet (1844–1860) was killed in a hunting accident at the age of fifteen. Reportedly, his distraught father buried him on his beachfront property. Although there wasn't much activity in the area in 1860, the location of the grave was problematic one hundred years later when the city was growing. Rather than moving the remains, developers built the road around it, creating a tiny island with palms and grass and flowers. That's the way it remains today. The headstone is etched: "Sacred to the Memory of Charles Dummett, Born Aug. 18, 1844–Died April 23, 1860."

Georgia

*T*he Peach State is home to the Georgia Guidestones, mysterious giant slabs etched with guidelines for humanity. Who had them made? What do they mean? Visitors have to make up their own minds. If you like your roadside oddities less mysterious but just as unique, Georgia is filled with folk artists creating such works as the World's Largest Grit, or a village of fairy houses.

If you're a fan of movies, you can visit numerous real sites used in classic films, including the Whistle Stop Café from *Fried Green Tomatoes* and the bench from *Forrest Gump*. No matter what your interests, you will find a plethora of ideas for day and weekend trips through Georgia.

GEORGIA ROADSIDE ATTRACTIONS

This section includes objects you can see from the road, often free of charge.

Cagle Castle

12570 Arnold Mill Road, Alpharetta, GA

A tiny castle built in 1950 by Rudy McLaughlin for his wife, Ruth, is a private home that can be seen from the road. The 1,900-square-foot, two-bedroom home is surrounded by a pool "moat" and colorful gnome statues.

R.E.M. Murmur *Trestle*

220-270 South Poplar Street, Athens, GA

Known as the R.E.M. Murmur Trestle, this railroad trestle is featured on the back of the group's 1983 album *Murmur*. It was preserved as a tourist attraction, where thousands of R.E.M. fans pilgrimage each year.

The railroad trestle in Athens, Georgia, featured on the cover of R.E.M.'s *Murmur* album. *Photo by Wil Elrick.*

Tree That Owns Itself in Athens

277 South Finley Street, Athens, GA

An oak tree whose roots jut into the pavement at the corner of South Finley and Searing Streets in Athens is known as the Tree That Owns Itself. Sometime in the 1820s, Colonel William Henry Jackson deeded the land where it grew to the tree so that no one could cut it down. The original tree fell in 1942, and the current tree grew from its acorn. It is sometimes referred to as the Son of the Tree That Owns Itself.

The Son of the Tree That Owns Itself in Athens, Georgia. *Photo by Kelly Kazek.*

World's Only Double-Barreled Cannon

301 College Avenue, Athens, GA

The double-barreled cannon on the lawn of Athens City Hall is the only one in existence. It was built in 1863 by a local inventor when residents feared attack by Union forces during the Civil War. The cannon was loaded with two balls connected by a chain in hopes that the balls and chain would shoot out and cut down enemy soldiers. However, the projectiles went askew when test-fired, and the invention was abandoned.

The world's only double-barreled cannon, in Athens, Georgia. *Photo by Wil Elrick.*

The Autoeater Sculpture

100 Tenth Street NE, Atlanta

This sixteen-ton marble sculpture with a car emerging from it was created by artists Julia Venske and Gregor Spänle.

The Great Fish

265 Pharr Road NE, Atlanta

The Atlanta Fish Market restaurant is home to a sixty-five-foot-long statue of a fish leaping into the air. It was installed in 1995.

White House Replica

3687 Briarcliff Road Northeast, Atlanta
Private residence; Drive-by only

This three-quarter-scale replica of 1600 Pennsylvania Avenue was built in 2002 by Fred Milani. Most of the interior of the 16,500-square-foot-home was not replicated from the original White House, although it does have an oval office and Lincoln Bedroom.

"First" Brunswick Stew Pot

Bay Street/U.S. Highway 341, Brunswick, GA

Located in Mary Ross Park on Bay Street/U.S. Highway 341 at the end of Gloucester Street is a monument to the making of the first pot of Brunswick stew. An old cooking pot is set on a base that is etched with the claim: "In this pot the first Brunswick Strew was made on St Simon Isle July 2, 1898." Other cities also lay claim to being the birthplace of Brunswick stew.

Airplane Stuck in Wacky House

Sam's Tree House
360 Piedmont Street, Calhoun, GA

This wacky treehouse was built in 1992 by Sam Edwards, an author and former aide to President Jimmy Carter. The "house" is made of wood but adorned with found objects such as a small airplane that serves as the bedroom, a submarine prop used in an Elvis Presley movie in the 1960s, a boat, helicopter and more.

Fruitcake Capital of the World

Claxton, GA

Although you can no longer tour the fruitcake bakeries in Claxton, billed as the Fruitcake Capital of the World, you can take photos of the water tower bearing the claim, as well as at two bakeries:
- Claxton Fruit Cake Company at 203 West Main Street.
- Georgia Fruit Cake Company at 5 South Duval Street.

During business hours, you can also stop and buy a few cakes to take home.

Gaggle of Roadside Giants

500 Nathan Dean Boulevard, Dallas, GA
1212 Industrial Boulevard, Dallas, GA

Local plumber Mike Whitman collects giant roadside figures and displays them across the city of Dallas.

A new twenty-foot-tall plumber figure, created by Bell Plastics in California, stands in a parking lot on Nathan Dean Boulevard not far from an eighteen-foot-tall Uniroyal Gal painted as Wonder Woman.

A twenty-foot-tall Mr. Bendo is located on Industrial Boulevard. Whitman reportedly bought three new giants in 2019 that have not been erected yet: a Paul Bunyan, a clown and a Mortimer Snerd figure from International Fiberglass.

A giant plumber promotes Mike Whitman's plumbing business in Dallas, Georgia. *Photo by Kelly Kazek.*

Native Rock Eagle Effigy

350 Rock Eagle Road, Eatonton, GA
706-484-2899; Free

The Rock Eagle Effigy in Putnam County is a ceremonial site constructed as many as three thousand years ago by Native Americans. The 102-foot-long and 120-foot-wide bird shape was created from thousands of pieces of quartzite. A stone fort was built at the site of the Rock Eagle Effigy as a viewing tower.

The eagle effigy created by Native Americans in Eatonton, Georgia. *Photo by Wil Elrick.*

Georgia Guidestones

1031 Guide Stones Road, Elberton, GA

The Georgia Guidestones, known as the American Stonehenge, were erected in 1980 in Elberton. Their origins are a mystery. A man calling himself R.C. Christian ordered the tablets to be etched with a message for humanity in eight languages. It was created by Elberton Granite Finishing Company, but no one knows the true identity of Christian. The monument is nineteen feet, three inches tall with a capstone atop five astronomically aligned slabs. It weighs 237,746 pounds.

The ten guides are written in English, Spanish, Swahili, Hindi, Hebrew, Arabic, Chinese and Russian. The Guidestones have been featured on TV shows such as *Mysteries at the Museum* and *Brad Meltzer's Decoded*.

The Guidelines:
1. Maintain humanity under 500,000,000 in perpetual balance with nature.
2. Guide reproduction wisely—improving fitness and diversity.
3. Unite humanity with a living new language.
4. Rule passion—faith—tradition—and all things with tempered reason.
5. Protect people and nations with fair laws and just courts.
6. Let all nations rule internally resolving external disputes in a world court.
7. Avoid petty laws and useless officials.
8. Balance personal rights with social duties.
9. Prize truth—beauty—love—seeking harmony with the infinite.
10. Be not a cancer on the earth—Leave room for nature—Leave room for nature.

The Georgia Guidestones in Elberton, Georgia. *Photo by Kelly Kazek.*

World's Largest Tiger Statue

Green Street, downtown Gainesville, GA

This statue of Brenau University's Golden Tiger mascot is eight feet tall and fourteen feet long. It was commissioned by Ike Belk, former head of the department store chain, and sculpted by Greg Johnson in 2013.

Jimmy Carter Peanut

Highway 45 North/Buena Vista Road, Plains, GA

This thirteen-foot-tall peanut statue sports a wide grin in tribute to former president Jimmy Carter. Erected in 1976, it is located outside a convenience store.

Cracked Earth: A World Apart

102 West River Street, Savannah, GA

A unique memorial to those who died in World War II, this twenty-foot-high bronze sphere is split in two parts to represent a war that divided the world. Visitors can walk between the halves to read names.

Monument to Bob, the Town Turkey

8690 Main Street, Woodstock, GA

Artist Bruce Weintzetl created this metal monument to Bob, a turkey who liked to wander around Woodstock, after the turkey was killed by a hit-and-run driver in 2012.

GEORGIA OUTSIDER ART

This unique kind of roadside oddity comes in many forms. Some collections are indoors; some are outdoors. A few charge admission; others request donations. But the work never fails to astound and entertain.

Sleepy Hollow Fairy Garden

Sleepy Hollow in Blairsville, Georgia. *Courtesy of Carol M. Highsmith/Library of Congress.*

5279 Highway 515 East, Blairsville, GA
706-379-9622; Free

Tucked out of the way in the Blue Ridge Mountains of Blairsville is a wondrous fairyland created by former Disney artist Art Millican Jr. Art builds and sells fairy, gnome and bird houses of all shapes and sizes, as well as hand-cranked automaton toys. Millican, who also provided consulting and design services for Dollywood and Michael Jackson's Neverland Ranch, built a workshop and created an entire village that visitors can walk through.

Pasaquan

238 Eddie Martin Road, Buena Vista, GA
706-507-8306; Donations

Pasaquan is a preserved, seven-acre "internationally recognized visionary art environment" created by Eddie Owens Martin in Bueno Vista, according to its website. Martin changed his name to St. EOM and worked for thirty years on the site.

Pasaquan in Buena Vista, Georgia. *Courtesy of Rivers Langley/Wikimedia Commons.*

He died in 1986, and the site began to deteriorate. In 2014, the Pasaquan Preservation Society and Columbus State University partnered to restore and open the site to the public.

SamG Land

1390 Tom Born Road, Clarkesville, GA
706-949-3504; Free

Sam Granger started building SamG Land in November 2016 when he completed his centerpiece, the World's Largest Grit. Since then, he has been at work adding new features, using mostly recycled items. Full of humor and sarcasm, SamG takes a different approach and often pushes the limits of correctness and appropriateness, while still trying to spread his message of love. SamG Land is a world he has made for himself, but the artist loves to share it with others as well.

Paradise Garden

200 North Lewis Street, Summerville, GA
706-808-0800; Admission fee

Paradise Garden, a site in the National Register of Historic Places in Summerville, contains the works of Howard Finster, a renowned folk artist. Finster died in 2001, and the site is now open to the public for tours and maintained by the Paradise Garden Foundation. In 1976, when Finster was fifty-nine years old, he said he received a message from God telling him to create five thousand sacred works of art. He completed that number by 1985 and would eventually make nearly forty-seven thousand works before he died in 2001.

The Paradise Gardens website explains Finster's inspiration in his own words: "One day I dipped my finger in some white paint and picked it up, and when I picked it up, it formed a face before I ever seen a face, and I turned it around to look and see if I had too much paint and there was two eyes, a mouth, a nose, and everything. A whole face. My finger looked like a face. And there was a feeling just came over me and said, 'paint sacred art.' I said 'Lord, I can't paint. I don't have no education in that.' So I took

Howard Finster's Paradise Gardens in Summerville, Georgia. *Photo by Kelly Kazek.*

a dollar bill out of my wallet and started posing on the picture of George Washington. Some kids were around watching me work and that was the first time I felt I was an artist."

Paradise Gardens features all kinds of quirky art, statues made from found objects, a covered bridge filled with works of art and even a concrete coffin that contains the two-hundred-year-old remains of an unidentified teenage girl.

Pope's Store Museum

192 Pope Store Road in Ochlocknee, GA
Free

There is no parking lot, no sign, or even a place to pull off the road to see some of the most important art surviving in Georgia. Set along a residential road in Ochlocknee off Georgia Highway 111, an unusual concrete entryway leads to a home whose façade was embellished by one of the first female roadside artists in the country. The property of Laura Pope Forester (1873–1953) was once home to more than two hundred statues and bas-reliefs, but the majority were tragically destroyed, leaving the entry gate, the decorated home and a few other pieces of art inside and around the house.

Pope's Store in Grady County, Georgia. *Photo by Kelly Kazek.*

In addition to being one of the only folk-art gardens created by a woman, it is also the nation's oldest. The farm became a tourist attraction during Pope's lifetime—it was featured on postcards and referred to as "Pope's Museum." Forester made the impressive archway leading to her home, which bears a series of sculpted faces, in the 1940s. The fifteen-foot-high, one-hundred-foot-long entry gate is decorated with "lacework" made from cast-iron sewing machine legs, wagon wheels and other items.

The majority of the statues and busts were of women, but sometimes men were featured, including Douglas MacArthur and Dwight Eisenhower. She added marble slabs engraved with the names of all local people who died in World War II on one side and the authors of the 1945 Georgia Constitution on the other. Gate and home visible from the road. Tours can be booked by visiting www.popesmuseum.com or calling Michelle Dean at 229-307-0037.

GEORGIA'S LEGENDARY LOCALES

This list describes places you will need to park your car and get out, including quirky museums, unusual historic homes and whimsical places to eat or stay overnight.

Ruins of Barnsley Mansion

Barnsley Resort
597 Barnsley Gardens Road, Adairsville, GA
770-773-7480; Admission fee

A picturesque resort in north Georgia is known as a place for people who like to ride, shoot or golf. It wouldn't be so different from other resorts of its kind—except that its property is home to the ruins of an Italianate mansion, the Barnsley family cemetery and gardens. Each Christmas season, the ruins are beautifully decorated, with lights and garland draped from the old mantels and stairways.

The brick ruins are what's left of the 1848 manor house, called Woodlands, which featured indoor plumbing and French and Italian marble. It was built by Godfrey Barnsley for his wife, Julia, who died before its completion. The home was damaged by the occupation of Union troops during the Civil War and again in a 1906 tornado. It became a resort in 1999.

Prisoner-of-War Camp and Museum

Andersonville National Historic Site
496 Cemetery Road, Andersonville, GA
229-924-0343; Free

Visit the site of the largest and most infamous prisoner-of-war camp of the Civil War. At Camp Sumter, or Andersonville Prison, thirteen thousand prisoners died while incarcerated. The site includes a National Cemetery, the National Prisoner of War Museum, which features exhibits on all American wars, and a memorial to POWs. The small village of Andersonville has more points of interest, including the Drummer Boy Civil War Museum, a pioneer farm with a gristmill and more.

World's Longest Freestanding Escalator

CNN Center
190 Marietta Street NW, Atlanta
1-877-4CNNTOUR; Admission fee

A ride on this marvel billed as the World's Longest Escalator is available only when you take the CNN Studio Tour. The escalator is 196 feet long and eight stories high.

Hunger Games *Mansion of President Snow*

Swan House
130 West Paces Ferry Road NW, Atlanta
404-814-4000; Admission fee

An Atlanta mansion built in 1928 served as the mansion of President Snow in the *Hunger Games* movies. The gorgeous home is now open for movie tours, where visitors can see props used in the movies and take photos in President Snow's office. Open for pre-booked tours.

World's Largest Drive-In Restaurant

The Varsity
61 North Avenue NW, Atlanta
404-881-1706

In 1928, Frank Gordy opened the Varsity in a tiny brick building and later took over a neighboring shop. In 1940, the two small original buildings were combined and renovated to give the eatery a streamlined art deco look. The restaurant now covers five acres and has parking for six hundred cars that are served by "carhops." Each day, the restaurant serves about 2 miles of hot dogs (if laid end-to-end), 300 gallons of chili, 1 ton of onion rings and 2,500 pounds of potatoes.

Waffle House Museum

2719 East College Avenue, Avondale Estates, GA
770-326-7086; Tours by appointment

This museum is housed in the first Waffle House restaurant, opened in 1955 by Joe Rogers Sr. and Tom Forkner. The building was restored to its original appearance and filled with Waffle House memorabilia from the past sixty years.

Burger Bus

288 Gilmer Ferry Road, Ball Ground, GA
678-454-2422

Guests can eat specialty hamburgers in a bus.

Expedition: Bigfoot!

1934 Highway 515, Cherry Log, GA
706-946-2601; Admission fee

This fun museum features displays about Bigfoot. See a variety of footprint casts, figures of differing types of cryptids and models of Sasquatch heads. The museum features stations where visitors can listen to Sasquatch grunts or watch videos of eyewitness interviews.

Inside Expedition: Bigfoot! *Photo by Wil Elrick.*

Babyland General Hospital

300 NOK Drive, Cleveland, GA
706-865-2171; Admission fee

Babyland General Hospital is known as the "birthplace" of the Cabbage Patch Kids. Xavier Roberts, the creator of Cabbage Patch Kids, bought an old clinic and created a "hospital," where he sells dolls. Visitors can visit the birthing rooms, nursery and adoption center, where they can purchase collectible Cabbage Patch Kids.

Barbecue in a Bus

Country's Barbecue on Broadway
1329 Broadway, Columbus, GA
706-596-8910

Visitors to downtown Columbus can eat barbecue in a converted 1930s Greyhound bus station, complete with an old refurbished bus equipped with booths.

World's Largest Lunchbox Museum

Located inside the River Market Antiques
318 Tenth Avenue, Columbus, GA
706-653-6240; Admission fee

Visit Allen Woodall Jr.'s collection of 3,500 metal lunchboxes from the 1950s to the 1980s.

Haunted Jekyll Island Millionaires Club

Jekyll Island Club Resort
371 Riverview Drive, Jekyll Island, GA
855-535-9547

A large, beautiful clubhouse built in 1886 for millionaires is now a resort for those who vacation on Georgia's Jekyll Island. In the late 1800s and early 1900s, Jekyll was the vacation spot for America's wealthiest families, including the Vanderbilts, Morgans and Pulitzers. In 1886, the men who headed these families incorporated an exclusive hunting and recreational group and called it the Jekyll Island Club. Not happy with having only a clubhouse, the men purchased the entire island for $125,000. It was nicknamed the "Millionaire's Club." For their summer trips to the island, the families built eighteen homes they called "cottages"—mansions to regular folk.

When the men built their clubhouse, they spared no expense. The massive and beautiful club was built in the Queen Anne style, including a turret, and featured numerous suites and game rooms. The club closed at the end of the 1942 season, and the owners paid for a staff to keep up the buildings and property until 1947, when the island was sold to the State of Georgia. For a while, the state operated the site, but it closed in 1971.

The club was restored and opened as a luxury resort in 1985 so guests can experience the same splendor as the men who helped shape our nation. Visitors who aren't staying overnight can eat at the resort or walk around the exterior. In addition, visitors can see the millionaire's cottages on tours of the island's 240-acre historic district. Interiors of some homes are open to the public. Tours begin at 101 Old Plantation Road. Call 912-635-4036 for information.

Uncle Remus Museum

214 South Oak Street, Eatonton, GA
706-485-6856; Admission fee

This museum pays homage to Joel Chandler Harris, author of the books about Uncle Remus and critters such as Br'er Rabbit. A portion of the museum is housed in the original home of Joseph Sidney Turner, who was the inspiration for the "little boy" in the tales. The museum is a log cabin made from two slave cabins, similar to the one occupied by the Uncle Remus character.

Site of World's First Stuckey's

100 Candy Court, Eastman, GA
Free

The building that housed the first Stuckey's roadside stand and candy plant is currently home to Southside Market, an antique mall. In 1937, W.S. Stuckey opened a stand in Eastman to sell pecans. In 1948, he built a candy plant on the site so he could produce candy, including the famous Stuckey's Pecan Log. Although it no longer sells Stuckey's merchandise, the building is open to visitors who are curious about the roadside chain's beginnings. While there, take a photo with the Stuckey's historical marker in front of the store.

This eatery is located near Hartwell Dam. *Photo by Kelly Kazek.*

Best Biskits by a Dam Site

4413 Elberton Highway, Hartwell, GA
706-377-3503

This quirkily named business, Best Biskits by a Dam Site, is located near Hartwell Dam.

Film Set Whistle-Stop Café

443 McCracken Street, Juliette, GA
478-992-8886

The movie *Fried Green Tomatoes* is set in Alabama, but it was filmed in Juliette and other small Georgia towns. A 1927 general store in the tiny town of Juliette, which is little more than a street lined with a dozen or so homes and buildings, was tapped to serve as the titular eatery. After filming, the painting on the

The set where 1991's *Fried Green Tomatoes* was filmed was made into a real café in Juliette, Georgia. *Photo by Kelly Kazek.*

windows and some items built for the set, such as booths, were left behind. The building was turned into a real Whistle Stop Café serving traditional meat-and-three meals. It stays busy, so go early. Several nearby buildings were also altered, including one that served as a bank and was covered in faux brick, which is still there. Other houses and buildings are now quaint shops.

Drive a Tank, Crush a Car

Tank Town USA
10408 Appalachian Highway, Morganton, GA
706-633-6072; Admission fee

This outdoor park allows visitors to drive tanks, excavators and bulldozers, with an option to crush a car.

Tank Town USA in Morganton, Georgia. *Photo by Wil Elrick.*

Abandoned Milledgeville State Lunatic Asylum

Central State Hospital
620 Broad Street, Milledgeville, GA
478-445-4128; Free; By appointment only

This massive campus was once the largest psychiatric facility in the country and possibly the world. At its peak in the 1960s, it housed more than twelve thousand patients. Construction began in 1837, and the facility opened in 1842 as Milledgeville State Lunatic, Idiot and Epileptic Asylum. It would eventually grow to include two hundred buildings.

Patients were moved to regional centers, and the historic buildings were closed by 2012, with the exception of the administration building.

Abandoned buildings at Central State Hospital in Milledgeville, Georgia. *Photo by Wil Elrick.*

Hospital buildings from the 1800s and early 1900s were left abandoned and are in ruins. Signs are posted warning visitors of the dangers of entering the buildings, most of which have collapsed roofs. However, photos can be taken from the sidewalks. The hospital now has a museum and offers tours of the two-thousand-acre property, including the cemetery.

Town of Santa Claus

Santa Claus City Hall, 25 December Drive
912-526-6949

This tiny town in Toombs County, Georgia, has only about 165 permanent residents, but it welcomes visitors year-round to celebrate Christmas. A Santa statue stands beside the town's welcome sign, and street signs bear names like Candy Cane Road, December Drive and Rudolph Way, perfect for photo ops.

Forrest Gump's Bench

Savannah History Museum inside the Visitor's Center
303 Martin Luther King Jr. Boulevard, Savannah, GA
912-651-6825; Admission fee

As many as four fiberglass benches were used in filming the 1994 classic
Forrest Gump. Scenes of Tom Hanks portraying Gump were filmed on the
north side of Chippewa Square, facing Bull Street. One bench was donated
to the city and can be seen in the Savannah History Museum.

Stone Mountain Park

1000 Robert E. Lee Boulevard, Stone Mountain, GA
800-401-2407; Admission fee for park

Stone Mountain refers to a natural attraction, a famous man-made carving,
a city and a theme park. It is the name of a granite dome—its base has
a circumference of five miles—located northwest of Atlanta. The dome is
best known for the relief carved into its face of three Confederate figures:
Jefferson Davis, Robert E. Lee and Stonewall Jackson.

The carving, set 400 feet above the ground, is 90 feet long by 190 feet
high. It was begun in 1923 and completed in 1964 by three sculptors in
succession: Gutzon Borglum, Augustus Lukeman and Walker Kirkland. It
was privately owned until 1958, when it was sold to the State of Georgia. A
massive park is now located on the site where visitors can eat and shop, as
well as take the Skyride to the summit of the mountain, interact with farm
animals or play in a variety of "adventure lands" such as the Dinotorium,
Geyser Towers, Megabugs and SkyHike.

The city of Stone Mountain is a quaint southern village of about six
thousand residents.

Home with Fifty Exits

Lapham-Patterson House
625 North Dawson Street, Thomasville, GA
229-226-7664; Free

This home was built between 1884 and 1885 as a winter cottage for C.W. Lapham, a wealthy shoe merchant from Chicago. The Victorian home, whose walls and angles were built slightly askew, had gas lighting, hot and cold running water, indoor plumbing and modern closets. Because Lapham had survived the Great Chicago Fire, he built at least fifty exits to the home (twenty-four doors as well as specialty windows) so he could find a way out in the event of a blaze.

Vidalia Onion Museum

100 Vidalia Sweet Onion Drive, Vidalia, GA
912-538-8687; Free

Learn about the history and impact of the sweet onions grown in the region. Children can meet the mascot, Yumion, and try their hand at grading onions. Then be sure to take a selfie at the Vidalia Onion fountain located downtown.

GEORGIA TOMBSTONE TALES

This section lists just a few of the state's intriguing headstones and the stories behind them. Most cemeteries are open during daylight hours only. Many do not have street numbers in their addresses, but those listed are as close as possible.

Lion of Atlanta

Oakland Cemetery
248 Oakland Avenue SE, Atlanta
404-688-2107

Also known as the Lion of the Confederacy, this intricate sculpture of a dying lion atop a Confederate flag marks the site of the graves of unknown dead. It was commissioned by the Atlanta Ladies Memorial Association and carved from Georgia marble in 1894 by T.M. Brady. The historic cemetery, established in 1850, is also the resting place of *Gone with the Wind* author Margaret Mitchell.

Sideways the Dog Grave

Near Tech Tower at 225 North Avenue NW, Atlanta

A little terrier named Sideways stole the hearts of Georgia Tech University students in the mid-1940s. The dog was injured when she was thrown from the window of a moving car in 1945, when she was a puppy. She had surgeries for her injuries but walked at an angle the rest of her life. She was a common sight on campus, often wandering into classrooms or onto athletic fields.

The beloved little dog died in 1947, possibly from accidentally ingesting rat poison in a dorm. She was buried to the west of Tech Tower beneath a marker that reads: "Ever faithful and true, companion of the student body and G.A. Tech." The marker is set at an angle on the grave to honor the little dog. Students traditionally place pennies on the grave for luck.

Circus Train Wreck Memorial

Riverdale Cemetery
1000 Victory Drive, Columbus, GA
706-653-4579

On November 22, 1915, a train carrying the members and acts of the Con T. Kennedy Carnival Show were passing through Columbus on the way from Atlanta to Phoenix, Arizona. At 1:26 p.m., the train collided with a passenger train; both were traveling at about thirty miles per hour. No deaths occurred on the passenger train, which was made of steel, but numerous performers and two carloads of animals were killed when fire broke out on the wooden carnival train. The exact number of fatalities is unknown, although media estimates at the time ranged from fifteen to twenty-four. Owner Con Kennedy erected a marker in the shape of a circus tent at the site of the mass grave in Riverdale Cemetery.

Inventor of Coca-Cola Grave

Linwood Cemetery
721 Linwood Boulevard, Columbus, GA
706-321-8285

John Stith Pemberton (1831–1888), the pharmacist credited with creating Coca-Cola, is buried in historic Linwood Cemetery. Pemberton served as an officer in the Confederate army and was wounded in his chest in the Battle of Columbus, leading to an addiction to morphine. Coca-Cola, initially called Pemberton's French Wine Coca, was developed while Pemberton experimented with alternatives to morphine and cures for addiction. Oddly, he used cocaine as an ingredient in his elixir, thinking it would help overcome addiction. At the time, little was known about the effects of cocaine, and it was eventually removed from the drink. Most historians now agree it was formulated in Columbus, but it was first mass-produced in Atlanta, which claims to be the home of Coca-Cola. Visitors regularly leave Coke bottles on the grave.

The grave of Dr. John S. Pemberton in Linwood Cemetery in Columbus, Georgia. *Photo by Wil Elrick.*

Calculator the Dog Grave

Sacrifice Field, Baltzell Avenue, Fort Benning Military Base

Calculator was a mongrel who showed up at Fort Benning and charmed everyone on the base. He learned that if he held one paw as if injured, he would get more treats and earned the name "Calculator" because he "put down three and carries one," the soldiers said. Of course, it could also refer to his adorable manipulations. He liked to ride in military vehicles going into town or sleeping in the barracks. He was buried on the base beneath a large boulder with a plaque that reads: "Calculator. Born ? – Died Aug. 29, 1923. He made better dogs of us all." The boulder has since been moved to Sacrifice Field.

Allman Brothers Plot

Rose Hill Cemetery
1071 Riverside Drive, Macon, GA
478-742-5084

Duane Allman, famed guitarist of the Allman Brothers Band, was buried in Rose Hill Cemetery upon his death in October 1971 in a motorcycle crash in Macon. The band's bass player, Berry Oakley, is buried next to Duane. Eerily, Oakley died in a motorcycle crash a year later just a few blocks from the site of Duane's crash. For many years, fans would come to the grave site to drink or leave trinkets, and eventually, a fence was erected.

Gregg Allman, who died of cancer in 2017 at the age of sixty-nine, was buried across from them. His marker is etched with words from the group's song "Melissa": "Again the morning's come/Again he's on the run/ Sunbeams shining through his hair/Appearing not to have a care/We'll pick up your gear and/Gypsy roll on, roll on." The site was refurbished in 2019 to create a family plot.

Statue of Life-Size Circus Elephant

Pleasant Grove Primitive Baptist Church Cemetery
2354 Georgia Highway 37, Moultrie, GA

A five-and-a-half-foot-tall marble statue of a baby elephant marks the grave of circus owner William "Billy" Duggan (1899–1950) in Pleasant Grove Primitive Baptist Church Cemetery. The statue is based on Nancy, a baby in a group of elephants trained by Duggan for his circus. He had just bought an animal exhibit and was set to open the Hagen-Wallace Circus when he died while wintering in Florida.

A statue of a baby elephant marks the grave of circus owner William F. Duggan Sr. in Moultrie, Georgia. *Photo by Kelly Kazek.*

Headstone of "Human Bunny"

Myrtle Hill Cemetery
20 Myrtle Street SW, Rome, GA

This gorgeous cemetery rises up a hill that offers sweeping views of the city. Many graves are marked with beautiful funerary art; others have interesting epitaphs. One of the most unusual is on the grave of Nelle Allison Wyatt (1925–2009), whose headstone lists her name, as well as "Human Bunny," her life-sized stuffed animal reportedly buried with her. She apparently received Bunny on her eighth birthday in 1933; the stone gives Bunny's "birth" and "death" dates as 1933–2009.

Little Gracie Watson Grave

Bonaventure Cemetery
330 Bonaventure Road, Savannah, GA

The grave of Gracie Watson (1883–1889) is one of the most frequently visited sites in Georgia. Gracie, the daughter of W.J. and Frances Watson,

128

was, by all accounts, a charming and precocious little girl. Her father was manager of the Pulaski House Hotel, where Gracie was often found entertaining guests. She developed pneumonia in 1889 and died at Easter. Her father commissioned a statue in the likeness of his beloved little girl from sculptor John Walz. The sculpture drew so many tourists that the grave was damaged numerous times. It is now behind an iron fence where people can look but not touch.

Millionaire's Bird Dog Cemetery

Di-Lane Wildlife Management Area
4121 Herndon Road, Waynesboro, GA

This cemetery is exclusively for the field trial bird dogs owned by Henry Berol, heir to the Eagle Pencil Company fortune. Berol, who lived in New York, hunted at Di-Lane Plantation and even had a cook for his beloved dogs. As many as one hundred dogs are interred in the cemetery. Open to the public during daylight hours.

Kentucky

Kentucky is known, of course, for gorgeous horse farms and the famous Derby. Did you know it also has a Stonehenge replica made from real boulders, all kinds of unique cave systems and fun tourist traps in the mountains, such as Mike's Mystery House?

Just one visit to Louisville will check off numerous "world's largest" on your bucket list, including baseball bat, highball bourbon glass, golden statue of David and even a vampire bat. It is also a great state to learn about the making of whiskey—check out distillery tours in numerous towns. Between stops, enjoy the blue grass and rolling hills.

KENTUCKY ROADSIDE ATTRACTIONS

This section includes objects you can see from the road, often free of charge.

Giant Bourbon Barrel

Barton 1792 Distillery
300 Barton Road, Bardstown, KY
866-239-4690

The oversized barrel is in a picnic area at the end of the free distillery tour.

Hatfield and McCoy Feud Monument

Orrville Morris Park
Kentucky Highway 1056, Blackberry, KY

Numerous sites in Kentucky commemorate the legendary feud between two mountain families, the Hatfields (who were based mainly on the Kentucky side of the Tug River) and McCoys (who lived on the West Virginia side). You can see graves of victims and statues of key figures, buy souvenirs and take driving tours.

But you may as well start in Blackberry, Kentucky, with the Hatfield and McCoy Monument, which gives a timeline of the feud. Located not far from the site of the first killing in the feud, the monument is made up of a low snake-shaped wall that represents the Tug River lined with plaques that give a timeline of events from 1863 to 1924, when the feud ended.

An eight-foot-high wooden statue of Randolph McCoy was unveiled in 2018 in nearby Hardy, Kentucky. It can be seen at the McCoy Well and Homeplace on Highway 319. (The home was burned in the feud.) A likeness of William Anderson "Devil Anse" Hatfield stands on his grave site in Omar, West Virginia.

Bronze Big Red Mascot

Augenstein Alumni Center
292 Alumni Avenue, Bowling Green, KY
270-745-2586

The mascot for Western Kentucky University is Big Red, a character that looks a lot like a Muppet. The bronze version, located in front of the Alumni Center, is about the size of an average person and welcomes visitors with open arms, making hugging photo ops easy.

Forest Giants in a Giant Forest

Bernheim Arboretum and Research Forest
2075 Clermont Road, Clermont, KY
502-955-8512; Donations

Woodland troll at Bernheim Arboretum and Research Forest in Clermont, Kentucky.
Courtesy of Kentucky Tourism.

To celebrate the ninetieth anniversary of Bernheim Forest, Danish artist Thomas Dambo created three huge wooden trolls. The whimsical, carved giants make up a family, including a pregnant Mama Loumari and her children, Little Nis and Little Elina. They are located on a two-mile trail loop. Note: The giants are expected to remain until 2022, so be sure to check after that.

Bernheim Arboretum and Research Forest is a 15,625-acre preserve that was founded in 1929 by Isaac Wolfe Bernheim and donated to the people of Kentucky.

Notre Dame Cathedral Replica

St. Mary's Cathedral Basilica of the Assumption
1140 Madison Avenue, Covington, KY
859-431-2060

St. Mary's Basilica, a small-scale replica of the Notre Dame Cathedral, was built by Most Reverend Camillus Paul Maes, the bishop of the Diocese of Covington. Construction began in 1894 and stopped in 1915. It was never completed. The statuary seen on the front of Notre Dame was never added to St. Mary's. Inside St. Mary's, which was ranked as a "minor basilica"

A replica of Notre Dame Cathedral in Covington, Kentucky. *Courtesy of Poghia/Wikimedia Commons.*

in 1953 by Pope Pius XII, is a twenty-four-foot-by-sixty-seven-foot stained glass window featuring 117 figures. It is one of more than 80 stained-glass windows in the church.

9/11 Memorial

136 South Main Street, Greenville, KY
270-338-1895

A memorial to those who died in the September 11, 2001 terror attacks stands in downtown Greenville. The monument stands eighteen feet tall and is made from a seventeen-foot box beam that was part of the North Tower of the World Trade Center. Atop the beam is a bronze sculpture of an eagle clutching an American flag. Beneath them, two granite columns represent the Twin Towers.

Memorial Sundial

Kentucky Vietnam Veterans Memorial
365 Vernon Cooper Drive, Frankfort, KY

A memorial to Vietnam veterans was designed in the 1980s by architect Helm Roberts. It includes a giant sundial with a unique feature: Each of the 1,103 soldiers gets his own moment in the sun because each name is placed where the shadow of the dial's point touches it on the date of that person's death.

Giant Floral Clock

Kentucky State Capitol
700 Capital Avenue, Frankfort, KY
502-564-3449

A clock thirty-four feet in diameter and covered in growing flowers was dedicated in May 1961 by Governor Bert T. Combs. The clock, located behind the state capitol, was created as a joint project of the Garden Club of Kentucky and the state.

Giant floral clock in Frankfort, Kentucky. *Courtesy of ACdixon/Wikimedia Commons.*

Florence Y'all Water Tower

500 Mall Circle Road, Florence, KY
859-371-5491

The iconic water tower in Florence, Kentucky. *Courtesy of the City of Florence.*

A red- and white-striped water tower that can be seen from Interstate 75 is a much-photographed landmark. The original slogan, Florence Mall, was meant to promote a planned mall, but the Kentucky Bureau of Highways deemed it improper because it advertised a business that didn't exist yet. Seeking an inexpensive solution, city leaders decided to paint over parts of the M to form a Y and add an apostrophe.

Mother Goose Building

2800 North Main Street, Hazard, KY
888-857-5263

This oval building with a giant nesting goose atop it was originally built as a home. The eyes are working car headlights, and the windows are egg-shaped. It was built by George Stacy from 1935 to 1940. He lived there until his death in 1954. It has been used for a variety of businesses since then and remains a local landmark.

Mother Goose building in Hazard, Kentucky. *Courtesy of Robtk /Wikimedia Commons.*

King Arthur's Round Table

Round Table Literary Park
720 North Drive, Hopkinsville, KY

Visitors to this local park will find a replica of King Arthur's Round Table with stumps for seats and a sword stuck in a stone.

Trains Share Street with Cars

Trains on Main, Downtown LaGrange, KY
800-813-9953

In this small town, trains actually run along Main Street. A history on TourOldham.com says, "'On-street running' or 'street running' is the routing of a railroad track or tramway track running directly along public streets, without any separation. The rails are embedded in the roadway pavement, and the train shares the street directly with pedestrians and automobile traffic....While there are other street runners in the U.S., La Grange, Ky. has the only street runner left in America that actually runs on Main Street."

A train runs through downtown LaGrange, Kentucky, alongside cars. *Courtesy of SimRacin40/Wikimedia Commons.*

Tourists can see and hear the trains as they eat or shop downtown. The city also has an observation tower for visitors to watch trains.

World's Largest Dixie Cup

451 Harbison Road, Lexington, KY

A water tower shaped like a cup stands on the property of a plant that once manufactured Dixie cups. The company later became part of Georgia-Pacific Corporation, which has offices at the site, but the cup remains.

Patriotic House Façade

Heigold House
332 Frankfort Avenue, Louisville, KY

Christian Heigold, a stonemason and German immigrant, built a mansion in 1853 with an ornate façade decorated in patriotic carvings as well as likenesses of his family. Heigold etched his belief in the American dream into his mansion's brick-and-stone exterior, many say to prove his allegiance during a time when immigrants were often attacked in Louisville. His works included busts of presidents James Buchanan and George Washington, the motto "Hail to the City of Louisville" and more. Heigold died in 1865 and

LOUISVILLE'S REALLY BIG THINGS

The city of Louisville doesn't take itself too seriously, which makes it a fun tourist stop. The downtown district is filled with museums, restaurants, distilleries, historic buildings and sculptures, but it is also home to several "world's largest" objects.

Here are a few you shouldn't miss:

World's Largest Baseball Bat

800 West Main Street, 877-775-8443

Before touring the factory where Louisville Sluggers are made, be sure to get a photo with the 120-foot-tall baseball bat leaning against the building. Nearby, at 822 West Main Street, Kentucky Mirror and Plate Glass displays a sculpture of a baseball breaking a giant window to capitalize on the photo opportunities.

Photo by Wil Elrick.

World's Largest Vampire Bat

1006 West Main Street, 502-583-0636

Another business having fun with its proximity to the world's largest baseball bat is Caulfield's Novelty, a costume shop. Displayed on the side of its building is a giant vampire bat whose red eyes light up.

Photo by Kelly Kazek.

World's Largest Bourbon Glass

528 West Main Street, 502-272-2623

Photo by Wil Elrick.

Standing across from the Evan Williams Bourbon Experience, visitors can see the outline of a massive bottle of bourbon in the windows of the five-story building. For the uppermost floors, the bottle is an outline on the panes but at the second floor, it becomes a real giant bottle neck with a real stream of "bourbon" that continuously pours into a giant highball glass on the first floor. The glass and bottleneck are visible upon entering the lobby.

World's Largest Golden Replica of David

A thirty-foot-tall golden version of *David* in downtown Louisville. *Photo by Wil Elrick.*

700 West Main Street

If you're going to copy Michelangelo's David, *why not double its size and make it golden? Situated on a sidewalk outside 21c Museum Hotel on Main Street, the massive fiberglass replica stands thirty feet high and is painted gold. It was created in 2012 by New York City artist Serkan Ozkaya for the 21c Museum Hotel.*

Giant Eyeglasses, Troll and Clasped Hands

A few objects that aren't the world's largest but are pretty darn big (and lots of fun) are giant eyeglasses at Falls City Eyecare, 1562 Bardstown Road; friendly troll at 150 West Washington Street; and huge clasped hands outside the Nia Center at 2900 South Twenty-Ninth Street.

The ornate façade of the Heigold house is preserved in downtown Louisville. *Courtesy of Kesavaraj/ Wikimedia Commons.*

left the home to his son. It was originally located on Marion Street and was one of the few homes in the area to withstand the flood of 1937. In 1953, city officials demolished all but the front of the home, which was moved to Thurston Park to be displayed and later to a traffic median on Frankfort Avenue. It is listed in the National Register of Historic Places.

World's Largest Burgoo Pot

Moonlite Bar-B-Q
2840 West Parrish Avenue, Owensboro, KY
270-684-8143

The owners of Moonlite Bar-B-Q have proclaimed a cooking pot in front of the building as the World's Largest Burgoo Pot, and so far, no one has challenged that. Burgoo is a stew of meat and veggies popular in Kentucky. The restaurant has been in business more than seventy years, and the pot was created in the 1970s or '80s. Owensboro is also home to the International Barbecue Festival, held each May.

KENTUCKY OUTSIDER ART

This unique kind of roadside oddity comes in many forms. Some collections are indoors; some are outdoors. A few charge admission; others request donations. But the work never fails to astound and entertain.

Apple Valley Hillbilly Garden and Toyland

Apple Valley Hillbilly Garden and Toyland in Calvert City, Kentucky. *Courtesy of Apple Valley Hillbilly Garden and Toyland.*

9351 U.S. Highway 68, Calvert City, KY
270-366-2301; Donations

This amazing complex is part folk-art garden and part toy museum. The Facebook page says, "We are a sprawling eclectic art tribute to old by-gone tacky roadside attractions." Visitors can see a 1928 Gulf service station and store. The Toyland museum houses more than three thousand toys and six running trains.

Finn's Flock

Waterfront Park
401 River Road, Louisville, KY
502-574-3768

In 2001, a set of twenty-eight painted metal birds created by folk artist Marvin Finn were installed in Riverfront Park for local residents to enjoy. The whimsical birds are known as Finn's Flock. The artist died in 2007.

Jerry's Junk

1737 East Frankfort Avenue, Louisville, KY
Private property; Visible from the street

For decades, Jerry Lotz has decorated the corner lot of his home with an eye-popping collection of artifacts he calls "junk." Although Jerry has now retired from giving tours, visitors can stand at the fence and see a chimp wearing a saddle, a twelve-foot-around tire, King Kong holding a huge ice cream cone, a biplane from a Disney kiddie ride skewered on a pole, a yellow brick road and an eighty-ton New York Central Railroad caboose.

Kentucky Stonehenge

201 Lynn Avenue, Munfordville, KY
270-524-4752

Munfordville resident Chester Fryer built his own version of Stonehenge in his yard. Rather than making an exact replica, Fryer searched for the largest boulders he could find and created a rock garden designed to reflect the points on a compass rose. Additional rocks mark the cardinal directions. Fryer created numerous other rock gardens on his property, including some with religious themes and some reflecting "Earth's mysteries," according to KyStonehenge.com.

Stonehenge replica in Munfordville, Kentucky. *Photo by Wil Elrick.*

KENTUCKY'S LEGENDARY LOCALES

This list describes places you will need to park your car and get out, including quirky museums, unusual historic homes and whimsical places to eat or stay overnight.

Sleep in a Jail Cell

Jailer's Inn Bed and Breakfast
111 West Stephen Foster Avenue, Bardstown, KY
502-348-5551

The oldest part of Nelson County Jail was built in 1819. It housed prisoners until 1987. The online history says, "Records indicated that John Rogers, architect of St. Joseph Cathedral, performed certain carpentry on this structure. The upper floor of this native limestone building, with 30-inch-thick walls, contained two cells and an 'upstairs dungeon' to house prisoners." The back jail was built in 1874, when the front part of the building became the jailer's home. The structure, listed in the National Register of Historic Places, is now a bed-and-breakfast where guests can sleep in the Jail Cell Room or in a variety of other themed rooms.

Ride a Boat Through a Cave

Lost River Cave
2818 Nashville Road, Bowling Green, KY
270-393-0077; Admission fee

Visitors can take an underground boat ride in Lost River Cave, a seven-mile cave system beneath Bowling Green. The history on the cave website says, "In 1986 the Cave entrance and the 25-acre wooded valley was donated to Western Kentucky University by its owners: WKU professor Dr. Raymond Cravens, WKU Physical Plant Administrator Owen Lawson and Mr. and Mrs. Leroy Highbaugh. The donation served as the springboard for the restoration and preservation of Lost River Cave and the surrounding natural environment." Visitors can also go ziplining and participate in nature activities in the seventy-two-acre park.

Eat in the Jail Where Hank Williams Slept

Jailhouse Pizza
125 Main Street, Brandenburg, KY
270-422-4660

Guests can dine on pizza, sandwiches and salads—complete with a helping of Outlaw Bread or Sheriff's Fries—in the 1906 building that served as the Meade County Jail until the mid-1970s. Hank Williams Sr. reportedly was arrested while in town and spent the night at the jail.

Duncan Hines's Kitchen

Western Kentucky University Museum
1444 Kentucky Street, Bowling Green, KY
270-745-2592; Admission fee

Western Kentucky Museum is filled with fascinating memorabilia and artifacts of Kentucky natives, including a pair of the World's Largest Underpants that were a gag used by the real Patch Adams. One of the most interesting is the Duncan Hines exhibit, which features a replica kitchen that includes his real stove and kitchen accessories and a vignette of a vintage supermarket.

Duncan Hines is not just a brand name—he was a real man. Born in Bowling Green in 1880, Hines became a traveling salesman and began making lists of places to eat while on his travels. At the time, there was not a central way for people to find places to eat. His self-published list was a hit, so he created one for lodging. In the 1950s, Hines sold rights to his name and the lists to a company that made cake mixes, and a brand was born.

Four-Legged Mayors of Rabbit Hash

Rabbit Hash General Store
10021 Lower River Road, Burlington, KY
859-586-7744

Rabbit Hash is an unincorporated community, but many of its buildings are listed in the National Register of Historic Places. The name is known for

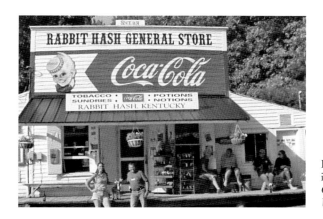

Rabbit Hash General Store
in Burlington, Kentucky.
*Courtesy of Stuart Ferguson/
Wikimedia Commons.*

two reasons: 1) Community members like to elect four-legged candidates as mayor, and 2) The old Rabbit Hash General Store.

The current mayor is a pit bull named Brynneth Pawltro, who won in 2016 by raising $3,367 during her campaign. She is the fourth canine mayor.

The picturesque general store, built about 1831, was a popular tourist stop before it was heavily damaged by fire in 2016. The funds raised in the mayoral election helped fund rebuilding efforts, and the store re-opened in 2017, still advertising the sale of "sundries, potions and notions."

Big Mike's Mystery House

Big Mike's Rock & Gift Shop
566 Old Mammoth Cave Road, Cave City, Ky
270-773-5144; Admission fee

Big Mike's would be a typical mountain town souvenir shop with the exception of three things: a real giant dinosaur skull inside, a fake giant dinosaur in front of the building and the Mystery House. The indoor

Big Mo outside Big Mike's Souvenirs.
Photo by Kelly Kazek.

dinosaur attraction is "Big Mo," the World's Largest Fossilized Mosasaur Skull, which came from a prehistoric sea creature estimated to be forty feet long and sixty-five million years old. In its glass case, the massive skull was impressive, but Big Mike couldn't leave it at that—he built a replica mosasaur of concrete in front of the shop, complete with sharp teeth. The Mystery House, which basically relies on fooling the eye with angles and optical tricks, offers lots of fun photo ops.

Wigwam Village No. 2

601 North Dixie Highway, Cave City, KY
270-773-3381

Wigwam Village in Cave City is one of three that survive from the original seven, built in the 1930s and 1940s. Businessman Frank A. Redford built the first Wigwam Village Motor Court in nearby Horse Cave, Kentucky, about 1935. It consisted of a teepee-shaped restaurant surrounded by fifteen teepee-shaped guest rooms.

Eventually, there would be seven Wigwam Villages in six states. Those still in operation are No. 2 in Cave City; Wigwam No. 6 in Holbrook, Arizona, built in 1949; and Wigwam No. 7 in San Bernardino/Rialto, California, built in 1947. Guests can spend the night on original 1930s furnishings at Wigwam Village No. 2. Accommodations are rustic but reasonable.

Wigwam Village in Cave City, Kentucky. *Photo by Kelly Kazek.*

Punkyville

1546 U.S. Highway 27, Falmouth, KY
859-654-3046; Free

In 2003, Charles "Punky" Beckett, a retired construction worker, began building a small-scale town right next to his home. He constructed replicas of a jail, dentist's office, hotel, gas station and more to house his huge collection of antiques, novelties, vintage signs and even old cars. It's like a museum, but Beckett doesn't charge folks who stop to check out his town.

The Car Where Patton Died

The General George Patton Museum
4554 Fayette Avenue, Fort Knox, KY
502-624-3391; Admission fee

One of the more macabre items at the Patton Museum is the 1938 Army Cadillac in which he was a passenger when it wrecked in December 1945. Patton hit the glass partition between him and the driver and broke his neck and injured his spine. He died twelve days later. He was buried in Luxembourg because, according to the museum, "he wanted to spend eternity near his fellow dead warriors."

The museum is filled with artifacts collected and catalogued by Patton himself, including, the museum says, "Patton's ivory-handled revolvers; a footlocker that Patton converted into a mobile bar; a World War I machine gun, the only weapon that ever wounded Patton, which he later had removed from its bunker, labeled, and shipped home; and the saddle of Julio Cardenas, Pancho Villa's second-in-command, which Patton confiscated after shooting Cardenas off of it." The museum is located next to the Gold Depository at Fort Knox.

Collection of Ventriloquist Dummies

Vent Haven Museum
33 West Maple Avenue, Fort Mitchell, KY
859-341-0461

The Vent Haven Museum displays an array of ventriloquist dummies collected by Cincinnati businessman William Shakespeare Berger (1878–1972). Berger was the former president of the International Brotherhood of Ventriloquists. He spent sixty years collecting more than nine hundred unusual and rare ventriloquist puppets. Each July, the museum hosts a ventriloquist "ConVENTion."

The Stegowagenvolkssaurus

W. Frank Steely Library
100 Nunn Drive, Highland Heights, KY
859-572-5457; Free

Visitors to the library at Northern Kentucky University will see a one-of-a-kind creature: an artwork built from a full-sized Volkswagen Beetle called the Stegowagenvolkssaurus. Cincinnati art professor Patricia A. Renick had the idea to build the sculpture in 1973 as a commentary on use of fossil fuels in automobiles. She took a yearlong leave of absence from her job to work on the sculpture, starting with a donated 1964 Beetle from a junkyard. She built the twenty-foot-long creature in her garage after extending the space with a tent. The artwork was exhibited for a while before being disassembled and stored in a Chicago building. Although the parts were damaged and in disarray, the sculpture was reassembled following Renick's death in 2007 and donated to the library, which is across the river from Cincinnati. During her lifetime, Renick also created the Triceracopter, a dinosaur built from a Vietnam-era helicopter. It is on display at the University of Cincinnati's Langsam Library, 2911 Woodside Drive, Cincinnati, Ohio.

Stegowagenvolkssaurus on display at the Steel Library at Northern Kentucky University. *Courtesy of the University of Cincinnati.*

The Haunted Hospital

Waverly Hills Sanitorium
4400 Paralee Drive, Louisville, KY
502-933-2142; Admission fee

Waverly Hills Sanatorium, an eerily beautiful Tudor Gothic Revival structure, has been abandoned since its closure in 1961. The original two-story structure was expanded in the early 1900s when a severe outbreak of tuberculosis hit the area.

The building is listed in the National Register, and the Waverly Hills Historical Society was formed to prevent it from being demolished. The group capitalizes on the ghost tales surrounding the building to raise funds, hosting haunted house tours and light shows at Christmas. The sanitorium has been featured on TV shows such as *Ghost Hunters*, *Scariest Places on Earth*, *Ghost Adventures*, *Ghost Asylum* and more.

Ride in a Steam Locomotive

Kentucky Railway Museum
136 South Main Street, New Haven, KY
800-272-0152; Admission fee

The Kentucky Railway Museum was chartered in 1954 with the donation of a steam locomotive from the Louisville and Nashville Railroad, which still runs on the museum's own railway. Today, the museum covers a five-thousand-square-foot replica depot filled with memorabilia and more than seventy pieces of restored rail cars and equipment. Visitors can enjoy rides on Locomotive No. 152, as well as take special dinner, theater and holiday excursions.

World's Longest Cave

Mammoth Cave National Park
1 Mammoth Cave Parkway, Mammoth Cave National Park, KY
270-758-2180; Admission fee

The centerpiece of Mammoth Cave National Park is the cave itself, which is the longest known cave system in the world. More than 400 miles of the cave have been explored. Visitors can choose from a variety of tours and activities. The 52,830-square-foot park is listed as a National Heritage Site and an international Biosphere Reserve. The staff advises using directions on the website rather than satellite navigation.

Natural Bridge and Skylift

2135 Natural Bridge Road, Slade, KY
606-663-2214; Free

The centerpiece of this park, established in 1895, is a seventy-eight-foot sandstone arch that is sixty-five feet high. Natural Bridge State Park covers 2,400 acres of protected land in the Daniel Boone National Forest. It was originally opened as a public attraction by the Lexington & Eastern Railroad before becoming a Kentucky State Park in 1926. A sky lift takes visitors to the Natural Bridge area, which also regularly plays host to traditional Appalachian square dances.

Mantle Rock

Mantle Rock Road, Smithland, KY
859-259-9655; Free

Another natural bridge is Mantle Rock, located in Mantle Rock Nature Preserve. The centerpiece is the 30-foot-high sandstone bridge that spans 188 feet. Visitors can see bluffs, shelters, honeycomb formations, fluorite deposits and a rock-lined stream. The preserve is a site on the Trail of Tears National Historic Trail, which follows the Cherokee Nation after being forced to Oklahoma. The park offers a variety of hiking trails.

Kentucky Castle

230 Pisgah Pike, Versailles, KY
859-256-0322

This intriguing castle was built in 1969 by Rex and Caroline Bogaert Martin, who were inspired by German castles and planned to have seven bedrooms, fifteen bathrooms and a tennis court, but the couple divorced before finishing the structure.

Ownership was passed around for years before being reconstructed in 2003, giving the castle a total of sixteen bedrooms (four in the turrets), twelve luxury suites, a library, game room, music room, dining hall, ballroom, swimming pool, formal garden, basketball court, bar and tennis court. It was then open as a restaurant and hotel. The castle's website says, "Kentucky Castle is committed to becoming the world's greatest farm to table restaurant, boutique hotel, and event space." Guests can also book tours of the castle.

Noah's Ark Encounter

1 Ark Encounter Drive, Williamstown, KY
855-284-3275; Admission fee

Visitors can climb aboard a full-scale replica of Noah's Ark, built by dimensions outlined in the Bible. The ark is 510 feet long, 85 feet wide and 51 feet high. Activities include a zoo of exotic animals, ziplining and more.

KENTUCKY TOMBSTONE TALES

This section lists just a few of the state's intriguing headstones and the stories behind them. Most cemeteries are open during daylight hours only. Many do not have street numbers in their addresses, but those listed are as close as possible.

Daniel Boone Grave

Frankfort Cemetery
215 East Main Street, Frankfort, KY
502-227-2403

Although Daniel Boone died in 1820 and was buried in Missouri, his body was brought to a new burial site in Frankfort Cemetery in 1845. The renowned explorer and his wife, Rebecca, were the first to be interred in the newly established cemetery overlooking the Kentucky River.

Woman Who Danced Herself to Death

Youngs Park
530 Linden Avenue, Harrodsburg, KY

In Harrodsburg, Kentucky, one pioneer, Dr. Christopher Columbus Graham (1784–1885), capitalized on the area's natural resources. In the 1820s, he purchased two natural springs—Greenville and Harrodsburg Springs—and created a spa known as Graham Springs, which became one of the era's greatest attractions.

In 1842, he used proceeds from the attraction to build Graham Springs Hotel, one of the most magnificent in the state. Not long after the hotel opened, a beautiful woman in her twenties came to the hotel with a man, according to legend. She registered as Virginia Stafford, daughter of a Louisville judge.

One night, at a party, the young woman danced with her partner and then with many of the other men present. Suddenly, the woman's partner

The grave of the "woman who danced herself to death" in Harrodsburg, Kentucky. *Courtesy of the City of Harrodsburg.*

realized she had died in his arms. Shocked, the staff tried to reach the judge, only to learn he had no daughter named Virginia.

Not knowing what else to do, hotel staff and guests held a funeral for the woman, and she was buried in front of the hotel. Townspeople began referring to it as the grave of the Lady Who Danced Herself to Death.

In about 1920, the hotel burned, and the land where the mysterious woman was buried became a city park. Her grave was left undisturbed. After the fire, people claimed to see the figure of a woman dancing around the grave site on moonlit nights. The figure in white would twirl to music no one else could hear.

The mystery of her identity remains, although historians now believe she was likely Mollie Black Sewell of Tennessee. The Lady Who Danced Herself to Death still lies beneath a grave surrounded by a white picket fence that bears a sign that reads:

> *Unknown*
> *Hallowed and*
> *Hushed be the*
> *place of the dead.*
> *Step Softly.*
> *Bow Head.*

Man o' War Memorial

4089 Iron Works Parkway, Lexington, KY
859-233-4303

Even those who know little of horses or thoroughbreds have heard of the legendary Man o' War. The champion was born on March 29, 1917, and became a popular attraction on the racing scene in the 1920s. He lived thirty years, dying just a month after his groom, Will Harbut, died in October 1947. Man o' War's owner had the horse embalmed and buried in a fancy casket. His grave was topped with a life-sized bronze likeness. In 1977, the horse was disinterred and, along with his statue, moved to Kentucky Horse Park, where he holds a place of honor.

Speedy, the Mortuary Mummy

Maplelawn Park Cemetery
1335 North Thirteenth Street, Paducah, KY
270-442-2538

Before he found a final resting place, Charles Henry "Speedy" Atkins was mummified and displayed in a funeral home. Atkins, who had no family, drowned in 1928 when he was about fifty-three years old. He was friends with the attendant at the local African American funeral home, so Atkins's body was taken there. Instead of burying him, the attendant preserved Speedy into a wooden-like figure and displayed him. After Atkins's body was featured on the TV shows *Ripley's Believe It or Not* and *That's Incredible*, he was finally laid to rest in 1994.

Frito-Lay Magician

Cave Hill Cemetery
701 Baxter Avenue, Louisville, KY
502-451-5630

Harry Leon Collins was born in 1920 in Glasgow, Kentucky, and loved magic. During World War II, he was assigned to the entertainment branch of the Marines and performed magic for the troops. After the war, he moved to Louisville and became a Frito-Lay salesman. He worked for twenty years

The grave of Harry Collins, the corporate magician for Frito-Lay in Cave Hill Cemetery. *Photo by Kelly Kazek.*

as the Frito-Lay man by day and magician at night and became well known around the city.

Collins was named the company's "corporate magician" in 1970, likely the first of his kind. He would promote the brand by traveling and performing magic shows, always exclaiming "Frito-Lay!" before the big reveal. His grave is marked with a life-sized statue of him wearing his tux and performing a magic trick, his cape draped nearby.

Colonel Harland Sanders Grave

Cave Hill Cemetery
701 Baxter Avenue, Louisville, KY
502-451-5630

Harland Sanders (1890–1980), the founder of Kentucky Fried Chicken, is buried in a place of honor in historic Cave Hill Cemetery in Louisville. Sanders operated a roadside fried chicken stand during the Great Depression and opened his first franchise in 1952. The chain would grow until there were restaurants in every state in the nation. Sanders, an honorary colonel, became the company mascot, dressed in his iconic white suit and black tie. KFC is the fourth-largest chain in the world.

Sanders's grave is marked with four columns surrounding a bronze bust that was sculpted by his daughter, Margaret. His wife, Claudia Ellen Sanders, who died in 1996, is also buried at the site. The slab over their graves says Sanders was the "Founder of the Kentucky Fried Chicken Empire." Visitors have left objects on his grave, including KFC buckets, ketchup packets and pennies.

The grave of Colonel Sanders in Cave Hill Cemetery in Louisville, Kentucky. *Photo by Kelly Kazek.*

Wooldridge Statues

Maplewood Cemetery
408 North Sixth Street, Mayfield, KY
270-251-6210

Colonel Henry Wooldridge (1822–1899) was an eccentric Civil War veteran who is known for erecting statues of himself on his burial plot years before he died. Wooldridge, who moved to the Mayfield area after the war, bought a large plot in Maplewood Cemetery in 1892 when the last of his siblings died. The plot features eighteen figures, including one of himself on horseback and another of himself carved from marble, as well as statues of his mother, sisters, brothers, two nieces and even likenesses of his hunting dogs.

The main statue of Wooldridge was sculpted of marble in Italy, while the other figures were made locally of limestone. Wooldridge is buried at the site in an above-ground tomb. No other family members are interred in the plot. The site is listed in the National Register of Historic Places and was featured on the TV show *Ripley's Believe It or Not*. The site can be seen in the 1989 Bruce Willis film *In Country*.

The Wooldridge monuments in Mayfield, Kentucky. *Courtesy of C. Bedford Crenshaw/ Wikimedia Commons.*

McCoy Family Feud Cemetery

Dils Cemetery
104 Chloe Road, Pikeville, KY
800-844-7453

Dils Cemetery is part of the Hatfield-McCoy Feud Historic District and is listed in the National Register of Historic Places. Members of the McCoy family—from the infamous Hatfields and McCoys feud—are buried in the cemetery, including patriarch Randolph McCoy and his wife, Sarah; their daughter Roseanna (the one who famously ran away with Johnse Hatfield); and their son, Sam, and his wife, Martha.

Louisiana

Everyone knows New Orleans has its share of weirdness—the Voodoo Museum, Museum of Death, Museum of the American Cocktail, not to mention all those incredible statues, haunted hotels and cemeteries. But the rest of Louisiana is no slouch when it comes to strange. You might find a house in a swamp filled with driftwood artworks, giant frog statues guarding a bridge or a huge Dalmatian with light-up spots.

Visitors have been seeking adventure at the Abita Mystery House for decades but they can also visit ruined forts, a monument to a pilot who vanished while chasing a UFO and a giant red crawfish on the side of the road, waiting for you to stop and take a selfie with it. When you've checked off all the "usual weirdness," this list should give you plenty of other road trip ideas.

LOUISIANA ROADSIDE ATTRACTIONS

This section includes objects you can see from the road, often free of charge.

Giant Cans of Syrup

C.S. Steen Syrup Mill Inc.
119 North Main Street, Abbeville, LA
337-893-1654

Five generations of the Steen family have been making pure cane syrup at a mill in Abbeville. Outside, three tanks are painted to look like bright yellow cans of Steen's 100% Pure Cane Syrup.

Muffler Man Cowboy

Topps Western World
3003 Topps Trail, Bossier City, LA
318-746-1836

A classic Muffler Man with a cowboy hat and lasso advertises Topps Western World and the business next door, Topps Trailer Sales.

A cowboy Muffler Man at Topps Western World.
Courtesy of John Margolies/Library of Congress.

World's Largest Ronald Reagan Statue

North New Hampshire Street at East Lockwood Street, Covington, LA

A ten-foot-high, saluting Ronald Reagan stands atop a six-foot pedestal in downtown Covington, Louisiana. The town had no ties to the former president, but a friend of his, Patrick F. Taylor, noticed the town had a road dedicated to Reagan. Taylor had planned to create a monument to Reagan and made an agreement with the city council to donate it to Covington. It was donated in 2008, by Taylor's estate, after his death and Reagan's.

Giant Rubber Shrimp Boots

Houma Area Visitors Center
114 Tourist Drive, Gray, LA

A nearly eight-foot-tall pair of shrimp boots are outside the visitors' center in Gray, looking as if they were just kicked off.

Monument to the First Prize Fight

303 Williams Boulevard, Kenner, LA

A statue of two men boxing commemorates the first World Championship Heavyweight Prize Fight held in the United States. The fight between Jem Mace of England and Tom Allen, who was also from England but competed in America, occurred May 10, 1870. The bare-knuckle fight was held in Kenner's Old Sugar House near the Mississippi River. Mace won.

9/11 Memorial in Lafayette

Parc San Souci
201 East Vermilion Street, Lafayette, LA
337-291-5566

On the East Congress Street side of the park stands a 9/11 memorial erected in 2002. It was made from two beams from the World Trade Center, limestone from the Pentagon and dirt from the Flight 93 crash site in Shanksville, Pennsylvania.

International Boundary Marker, Republic of Texas

Louisiana Highway 765 Louisiana Highway 765, Logansport, LA

This marker created in 1840 and placed in 1841 shows the international border between the United States and the Republic of Texas, which was then its own country. Before then, boundary disputes left after the Louisiana Purchase created a neutral area open to outlaws because it was not under any government jurisdiction. With the marker placed, authorities were able to make arrests and weed out bandits.

It is sometimes said to be the only international boundary marker left in the United States, but a stone erected by explorer Andrew Ellicott in 1799 is located in Mobile, Alabama. It marked the boundary line between the Mississippi Territory, then held by the United States, and West Florida, which was under Spanish rule. It is located on U.S. Highway 43 in Ellicott Stone Historical Park. Both markers are listed in the National Register of Historic Places.

Giant Safety Pin

Sydney and Walda Besthoff Sculpture Gardens
1 Collins Diboll Circle, New Orleans
504-658-4100

An oversized safety pin can be seen on Victor Avenue, in the New Orleans Museum of Art Sculpture Gardens. It was created in 1999 by sculptors Claes Oldenburg and Coosje van Bruggen. Numerous other fascinating works are scattered around the public garden.

The Doullut Steamboat Houses

Holy Cross neighborhood
400 and 503 Egania Street, New Orleans
Private residences; Drive-by only

Two of New Orleans' most beautiful homes are located in the Lower Ninth Ward. The ornate homes were built in an unusual mix of styles by a family of riverboat pilots. The first was built in 1905 by a husband-and-wife team of pilots, Milton P. Doullut and Mary Doullut, who, as one of the first

One of the Doullut Houses in New Orleans. *Courtesy of Carol M. Highsmith/ Library of Congress.*

licensed female pilots in Louisiana, took the helm in a skirt. Milton, also a shipbuilder, and his son, Paul Doullut, built another as a home for Paul, also a riverboat captain, about 1913.

They are built in the Steamboat Gothic style, with elements that look like riverboats, such as the railings, oval windows and swag-style trim. The Doulluts also added pagoda-style roofs and cupolas, reportedly influenced by the Japanese exhibit at the 1904 World's Fair in St. Louis.

Scrap-House Katrina Memorial

900 Convention Center Boulevard, New Orleans

Artist Sally Heller created a memorial to those lost in Hurricane Katrina, and it was erected in 2009 across from the Convention Center. The sculpture, made from scrap metal, depicts a house thrown into a tree and knocked askew by the storm.

Frog Guardians

Louisiana Highway 1, just north of Highway 168, Rodessa, LA

In a community that was once named Frog Level, two large concrete frogs sit atop pillars etched with the words *Alabama* and *Georgia*. The monument was installed in the 1800s to recognize the people from those states who settled the town. The name reportedly comes from the noisy frogs in the area. The City of Rodessa was incorporated in 1896, absorbing the communities of Spoonful and Frog Level.

Giant Light-Up Dalmatian

801 Crockett Street, Shreveport, LA
318-673-6500

An unusual artwork was erected on the lawn of Central ARTSTATION in Shreveport. A nineteen-foot Dalmatian statue has 254 spots that light up at night. It was designed by William Joyce and Brandon Oldenberg.

LOUISIANA OUTSIDER ART

This unique kind of roadside oddity comes in many forms. Some collections are indoors; some are outdoors. A few charge admission; others request donations. But the work never fails to astound and entertain.

Kenny Hill's Sculpture Garden

5337 Bayouside Drive, Chauvin, LA
985-594-2546; Free

Folk artist Kenny Hill spent ten years, from 1990 to 2000, building more than one hundred concrete sculptures on his property before moving away.

Many of the sculptures are religious in nature, with the largest artwork being a forty-five-foot-tall lighthouse made of seven thousand bricks. Scaling the exterior of the lighthouse are numerous figures, such as soldiers, angels, cowboys and a self-sculpture of Hill.

Since the property was abandoned by Hill, it was restored by art enthusiasts from Nicholls State University. It is now home to the NSU Art Studio, which offers tours of Hill's garden.

Kenny Hill Sculpture Garden in Chauvin, Louisiana. *Courtesy of the National Park Service.*

Charles Smith's African–American Heritage Museum

901-907 South Walnut Street, Hammond, LA
504-931-5744; Free

Folk artist Charles Smith's "museum" is a yard filled with his sculptures. The themes range from patriotic to religious to social commentary; the figures depict famous people and ordinary folks, animals and alien-looking creatures and lots and lots of busts. Smith, a U.S. Marines veteran of the Vietnam War, says God led him to create his artworks. He welcomes visitors.

BMike's Studio BE

2941 Royal Street, New Orleans
Free

In the wake of Hurricane Katrina's devastation, street artist Brandan "BMike" Odums transformed many abandoned spaces with his art, creating colorful murals to represent hope. In 2016, he opened Studio BE in an abandoned warehouse and covered the thirty-five thousand square feet with his works. BMike's bright, oversized art touches on many themes, including life in New Orleans and important figures in black history. The artist invites school groups to visit.

LOUISIANA'S LEGENDARY LOCALES

This list describes places you will need to park your car and get out, including quirky museums, unusual historic homes and whimsical places to eat or stay overnight.

Abita Mystery House

22275 Louisiana 36, Abita Springs, LA
985-892-2624; Admission fee

This unusual little roadside attraction has been drawing people to the area for decades, originally under the name UCM (you-see-'em) Museum. Guests enter through a vintage service station to view a jumble of objects made by artist John Preble, from folk-art miniatures, to pottery, to sculptures based on local legends, such as Darrel the Dogigator (half alligator and half dog) and Edmond the Allisapien (half alligator, half human).

Abita Mystery House in Abita Springs, Louisiana. *Courtesy of Infrogmation/ Wikimedia Commons.*

Louisiana State Penitentiary Museum

17544 Tunica Trace, Angola, LA
225-655-2592; Donations

The prison originated in 1880 when criminals were held in the slave quarters of a local plantation known as Angola and forced to work the farmland. It was known as one of the nation's bloodiest prisons until reforms were made. Since 1965, it has been known as the site of a popular prison rodeo.

Angola was the filming site for *Dead Man Walking*, *Monster's Ball* and *The Farm*. Today, it houses a museum covering more than 130 years of prison history.

The old state capitol in Baton Rouge, Louisiana. *Courtesy of Avazia/ Wikimedia Commons.*

Old State Capitol Castle

100 North Boulevard, Baton Rouge, LA
225-342-0500; Admission fee

A gorgeous historic castle in Baton Rouge was once the state's seat of government. The Old Louisiana State Capitol housed the state legislature from the mid-nineteenth century until a new building was completed in 1932. The original capitol was built in 1852 to look like and function like a castle and is now a museum and wedding venue.

Bonnie and Clyde Ambush Museum

2419 Main Street, Gibsland, LA
318-843-1934; Admission fee

The building that housed the café where Bonnie and Clyde ate their last meal is now a museum filled with artifacts from the lives of the infamous, young lovers-slash-gangsters. Bonnie Parker and Clyde Barrow were ambushed by law officers and killed nearby while still in their car. There is

The Bonnie and Clyde Ambush Museum in Gibsland, Louisiana. *Courtesy of Billy Hathorn/ Wikimedia Commons.*

a granite marker at the ambush site about two and a half miles out of town on Louisiana Highway 154.

Mardi Gras Museum

Central School Arts & Humanities Center
809 Kirby Street, Lake Charles, LA
337-430-0043; Admission fee

Visitors to the Mardi Gras Museum get a look at one of the largest collections of festival costumes in the South. The museum also gives a history of festivities, tells the story of King Cake and offers a look at the pageantry of parades.

Steel Magnolias *House*

320 Jefferson Street, Natchitoches, LA
318-238-2585

This home was the centerpiece of the 1989 movie *Steel Magnolias*, serving as the home of the fictional Eatonton family. The 5,900-square-foot home was built about 1841 and is now a bed-and-breakfast inn with rooms named for the movie's characters. The home is furnished with crystal chandeliers, marble mantels above

The house used in the film *Steel Magnolias* is a bed-and-breakfast inn in Natchitoches, Louisiana. *Photo by Wil Elrick.*

eight gas-lit fireplaces and many of the original antiques. The screenplay was adapted from a play written by a Natchitoches native, Robert Harling, based on the death of his sister, Susan.

The Carousel Bar in Hotel Monteleone in New Orleans. *Courtesy of Hotel Monteleone.*

Carousel Bar

214 Royal Street, New Orleans, LA
504-523-3341

This unique spot was the first, and remains the only, rotating bar in New Orleans. It opened in 1949 inside the historic Hotel Monteleone. The bar is designed like a real carousel and completes a rotation every fifteen minutes.

New Orleans Historic Train Garden

5 Victory Avenue, New Orleans, LA
504-483-9386; Admission fee

The Historic New Orleans Train Garden, built by artist Paul Busse, is part of the Botanical Garden. The miniature village "features typical New Orleans home and building architecture made with botanical materials, and replicas of streetcars and trains that wind around the track," according to the city's parks department. "Visitors walk along a pathway representing the water surrounding the city and 'stops' along the track give brief histories of the neighborhoods and the train and streetcar lines that served them. As visitors walk, they overlook 1,300 feet of track carrying streetcars and trains like those that traveled the city in the late 1800s to the early 1900s, at 1/22 of their actual size."

Fisherman's Castle at Irish Bayou

3337 U.S. Highway 11, New Orleans, LA
Private residence; Drive-by only

Simon Hubert Villemarrette started the castle in 1981 to be a small tourist attraction for the upcoming 1984 World's Fair in New Orleans but never completed it. The castle, a local landmark, was one of the few things standing in the wake of Hurricane Katrina. It was refurbished in 2016 as a private residence. It can be seen from Interstate 10.

Irish Bayou Castle in New Orleans.
Courtesy of Infrogmation/Wikimedia Commons.

House of Broel Miniatures Museum

2220 St. Charles Avenue, New Orleans
504-494-2220

This antebellum mansion is not only a museum unto itself, but it also houses the collection of intricate dollhouses made by owner Bonnie Broel.

Madi Gras World in New Orleans. *Courtesy of Carol M. Highsmith/Library of Congress.*

Mardi Gras World

1380 Port of New Orleans Place, New Orleans
504-361-7821; Admission fee

Get a behind-the-scenes look at the making of lavish floats used in the city's legendary Mardi Gras parades. The works of Kern Studios date to 1932, "when the first mule-drawn float was built on the back of a garbage wagon," its website says.

Museum of Death

227 Dauphine Street, New Orleans
504-593-3968; Admission fee

This tour, not for the faint of heart, is for history buffs interested in the pageantry and business of death. The museum includes artifacts related to funerary customs, burial traditions and more, including body bags, coffins, skulls, antique mortician equipment, Manson family photos, crime-scene photos, memorabilia of serial murderers and more.

Museum of the American Cocktail

1504 Oretha Castle Haley Boulevard, New Orleans
504-569-0405; Admission fee

This museum is a fun stop for fans of happy hour. It includes exhibits about New Orleans and southern food, drink and culture and hosts events throughout the year.

Voodoo Museum

724 Dumaine Street, New Orleans
504-680-0128; Admission fee

This small, two-room museum is one of the few in the world entirely dedicated to the practice of voodoo. Visitors can learn about the ancient art and get readings from a voodoo priest.

Nottaway Plantation

31025 Louisiana 1, White Castle, LA
225-545-2730

Nottaway Plantation & Resort was built in the 1850s as a sugar cane estate and is the largest existing antebellum mansion in the South. Today, it is a high-end hotel and a member of Historic Hotels of America, renowned for its stunning architecture.

LOUISIANA TOMBSTONE TALES

This section lists just a few of the state's intriguing headstones and the stories behind them. Most cemeteries are open during daylight hours only. Many do not have street numbers in their addresses, but those listed are as close as possible.

Married Dogs Grave

Houmas House
40136 Highway 942, Darrow, LA
225-473-9380; Fee for mansion tours

The graves of two Labrador retrievers named King Sam and Princess Grace, who were "married" in a 2003 ceremony, are marked with a cast-iron dog statue. The canine couple was buried on the grounds of the historic Houmas House, which was also the filming location for the 1964 movie *Hush…Hush, Sweet Charlotte*, starring Bette Davis and Olivia de Havilland. At least eighteen other movies and TV shows were filmed at the home, including 1975's *Mandingo*, 1988's *Fletch II*, *The Bachelor*'s season 21 and 2018's *Green Book*.

Grave of a Truly Married Man

Monroe Old City Cemetery
Elysian Fields Road, Monroe, LA
(In the triangle formed with Manassas and Desiard Streets)

Gossips whispered that Annie Livingston never married her husband, Sidney Saunders. When he died, she erected a marble statue of him holding a carving of their marriage certificate.

Pilot Who Vanished Chasing UFO

Sacred Heart Catholic Church Cemetery
9986 Bayou Des Glaises Street, Moreauville, LA
318-985-2774

Felix Moncla was twenty-seven years old when he and his copilot disappeared without a trace, along with their U.S. Air Force jet. The jet was sent to respond to a mysterious radar blip. The plaque on his memorial reads, "Disappeared Nov. 23, 1953, Intercepting a UFO over Canadian Border."

Body Parts Chapel

St. Roch Cemetery
1725 St. Roch Avenue, New Orleans
Limited tours

In 1867, Reverend Peter Thevis began praying to Saint Roch, the patron saint of good health, to protect his parishioners from yellow fever. When none of his congregants died, they erected a Gothic Revival chapel to honor Saint Roch. It has become a site where people pray for healing, often leaving items to designate what needs healing, from polio braces to glass eyes to molded feet.

Saint Roch Chapel
in New Orleans.
Courtesy of Infrogmation/
Wikimedia Commons.

Nicolas Cage's Pyramid

St. Louis Cemetery No. 1
425 Basin Street, New Orleans
504-596-3050; Admission fee

Amid crumbling tombs in New Orleans's oldest cemetery is a nine-foot-high cement pyramid that will one day entomb the earthly remains of eccentric actor Nicolas Cage. Cage, who made several films in New Orleans, briefly owned the LaLaurie Mansion, home to one of the city's most horrific tales of torture and murder. In 2010, he had the tomb built so he could be buried near voodoo priestess Marie Laveau.

The tomb built by Nicolas Cage in New Orleans. *Courtesy of GeraldShields11/Wikimedia Commons.*

Tomb of the Voodoo Priestess

St. Louis Cemetery No. 1
425 Basin Street, New Orleans
504-596-3050; Admission fee

The tomb of Marie Laveau is one of the most visited in St. Louis Cemetery No. 1, which was established in 1789. She was known as one of the most powerful practitioners of voodoo in New Orleans in the nineteenth century. She died in 1881 and is reportedly buried in the tomb of her husband's family, the Glapions. Visitors to the grave would write Xs on the outside of the tomb in hopes Marie would bring them luck. The marks, however, damaged the tomb. It was fully restored in 2014, and anyone who marks on the tomb will receive a heavy fine. In addition, all tours are now guided, and visitors cannot wander the grounds freely.

The grave of Marie Laveau in New Orleans. *Courtesy of Dan Soto/Wikimedia Commons.*

Tomb of Unknown Slave

St. Augustine Catholic Church
1210 Governor Nicholls Street, New Orleans
504-525-5934

On the grounds of St. Augustine Catholic Church, founded in 1841—the country's oldest African American parish—is a memorial dedicated to the enslaved. The church was founded by free people of color, who were the only congregants known to have purchased additional pews for use by enslaved people. Civil rights activists Homer Plessy and A.P. Tureaud attended the church, among other notable New Orleans residents.

In 2004, the church dedicated a memorial sculpture of a cross made from rusted chain and hung with shackles. A nearby plaque is marked "The Tomb of the Unknown Slave."

It says, "This St. Augustine/Treme shrine honors all slaves buried throughout the United States and those slaves in particular who lie beneath the ground of Treme in unmarked, unknown graves. There is no doubt that the campus of St. Augustine Church sits astride the blood, sweat, tears and some of the mortal remains of unknown slaves from Africa and local American Indian slaves who either met with fatal treachery, and were therefore buried quickly and secretly, or were buried hastily and at random because of yellow fever and other plagues." The shrine was meant as a reminder that people are always "walking on holy ground."

Arm of St. Valerie

St. Joseph Co-Cathedral
721 Canal Boulevard, Thibodeaux, LA

St. Valerie of Limoges was a martyr who was beheaded in the Roman period. Her arm bone became a religious relic and was gifted to St. Joseph's pastor, Charles M. Menard, by Cardinal Costantino Naro when Menard made a pilgrimage to Rome in 1867. The bone was sealed inside a waxen replica of Valerie, which was dressed in velvet finery and placed in a reliquary inside St. Joseph. When the church burned in 1916, the relic was one of the few items saved. The cathedral was rebuilt in 1920, and the figure with the arm bone was placed in a glass sarcophagus and displayed in the new building, where it remains today.

Mississippi

Some things you expect to find in Mississippi—gorgeous historical homes and juke joints still rocking after fifty years—but others may surprise you. Did you know Mississippi was the birthplace of the teddy bear? Yep. They even have a festival to celebrate. It also has a petrified forest, a museum dedicated to aprons, a café inside a giant woman's skirt and an abandoned two-hundred-acre model of the Mississippi River Basin.

If those aren't odd enough, you can visit the grave of Douglas, a Confederate camel, or tour an octagonal mansion that has been left in its unfinished state since 1861. While you're in Mississippi, you should plan to make some of the typical Elvis stops and maybe try a slugburger, the regional delicacy.

MISSISSIPPI ROADSIDE ATTRACTIONS

This section includes objects you can see from the road, often free of charge.

Angel Tree

North Beach Boulevard, Bay St. Louis
South of the Demontluzin Avenue intersection

Three people—Doug Niolet, Kevin Guillory and Nikki Moon—clung to an oak tree to survive the forty-foot-high storm surge of Hurricane Katrina in 2005. The tree died and was cut down, but the survivors asked chainsaw artist Dayle Lewis to carve its limbs into angels and then re-erected it in a concrete base. It is now displayed only a few hundred feet from where the tree stood when they clung to it.

Coffee Pot on a Building

904 South First Street, Brookhaven, MS

In 1931, James J. Carruth opened Brookhaven's first drive-in restaurant, the Coffee Pot Inn. As a tourist draw, an oversized metal coffee pot was erected on the roof. At the time, the building had two stories and served as the Carruth home and the Greyhound bus stop. A historical marker was erected at the site in 2016, saying that in 1936, Eddie Hinnant played a piano on the roof in an attempt to break his previous piano-playing record of 110 continuous hours. The building is now empty.

The Coffee Pot Inn building in Brookhaven, Mississippi. *Courtesy of the City of Brookhaven.*

Statue of Scissors the Twice-Champion Pig

6628 Mississippi Highway 32, Charleston, MS

Scissors the pig was successful enough that he had his own house on Pine Crest Farm near Charleston. The Duroc-Jersey hog was twice named champion at the National Swine Show, in 1917 and 1918. The pig, which weighed as much as 1,800

Home of Scissors the pig in Charleston, Mississippi. *Courtesy of Thomas R. Machnitzki/Wikimedia Commons.*

pounds, was owned by Colonel Thomas Griffin James. A statue of Scissors is located in the yard of his former home.

Devil's Crossroads in Clarksdale, Mississippi. *Courtesy of Carol M. Highsmith/Library of Congress.*

Devil's Crossroads

North State Street, Clarksdale, MS
(Intersection of Old Highway 61 and Highway 49)

The mythical site where legendary blues musician Robert Johnson reportedly sold his soul to the devil in exchange for his talents is marked by a sign and three blue guitars. It is located near the Delta Blues Museum.

Marshall Jesus Sculpture

438 Silver Ridge, Gulfport, MS

A tree that had been standing in the yard of a private residence since 1940 was damaged by Hurricane Katrina in 2005. In 2012, the homeowners commissioned artist Dave Perez to sculpt a six-foot-high Jesus head from the tree's trunk. The owners, the Marshall family, reportedly welcome visitors to take photos, according to Gulfcoast.org.

9/11 Memorial in Hattiesburg

801 Main Street, Hattiesburg, MS

In downtown Hattiesburg, a memorial of two stainless-steel towers honors the victims of 9/11.

Former World's Largest Cedar Bucket

979 Mississippi Highway 6 West, Oxford, MS
662-234-8202

For a brief time, a bucket in front of the Cedar Bucket Furniture Company reigned as the world's largest. The seven-foot-tall bucket with a six-foot circumference held the title from 2005 until 2011 after one in Murfreesboro, Tennessee, burned by arson. The Murfreesboro bucket, which was six feet tall and nine feet around at its top, was built in 1887 and went to two World's Fairs before finding a home at Cannonsburgh Pioneer Village. In 2011, a new bucket was built in Murfreesboro. The new bucket is nearly six feet tall, and it is six feet wide at its base and seven and a half feet wide at the top, making it the new world's largest.

Lunar Lander Exhibit

Interstate 10 exit at Highway 607, Pearlington, MS
228-533-5554

A thirty-foot-tall replica of the Lunar Lander is located outside the Mississippi Welcome Center in Hancock County. It was used for training by the Apollo 13 astronauts. The space-boot prints and signature of astronaut Fred Haise, a Mississippi native, can be seen in the concrete at the base.

Moonshine–Running Submarine

Grand Gulf Military State Park
12006 Grand Gulf Road, Port Gibson, MS
601-437-5911

Outside the Grand Gulf Military State Park, visitors can see a submarine reportedly built during Prohibition to run moonshine from Davis Island to the Mississippi River. The sub, the only one of its kind to survive, was powered by the engine from a Model T Ford.

Ruins of Windsor

15095 Rodney Road, Port Gibson, MS

Windsor was the home of Smith Coffee Daniell II, situated on a 2,600-acre plantation. The ornate four-story mansion took two years to build, and

The ruins of Windsor plantation in Port Gibson, Mississippi. *Photo by Wil Elrick.*

Daniell died not long after its completion. The cupola atop the mansion was used during the Civil War by both Confederate and Union troops, and the house served as a Union hospital after the Battle of Port Gibson in 1863.

According to Atlas Obscura, Mark Twain would later use the cupola "to observe the nearby Mississippi River, and his description of Windsor appears in his memoir 'Life on the Mississippi.'" The home burned in 1890, leaving only the twenty-three columns, the staircase and a few wrought-iron decorations. The ruins are open to the public in daylight hours. From Port Gibson, go west on Rodney Road for about ten and a half miles until you see the entrance sign.

Hot and Cold Water Towers

Western Line Avenue, Ruleville, MS

Ruleville is one of several towns across the United States to use the municipal water tower joke, where one is labeled "hot" and the other "cold."

Hot and Cold water towers in Ruleville, Mississippi. *Courtesy of Magnolia677/ Wikimedia Commons.*

Giant Watermelon

248 U.S. Highway 49, Seminary, MS

An oversized melon that once marked the site of a fruit stand is now used for photo ops.

MISSISSIPPI OUTSIDER ART

This unique kind of roadside oddity comes in many forms. Some collections are indoors; some are outdoors. A few charge admission; others request donations. But the work never fails to astound and entertain.

The Frog Farm

186 Old Highway 61, Fayette, MS
601-493-3420; Admission fee

Self-taught folk artist Louise Cadney Colemen loves frogs. She creates frog sculptures of all shapes and sizes and decorates her yard with them. Her garden is open to the public.

Larry Grimes's Yard

5110 U.S. Highway 49, Tutwiler, MS
Private residence; Drive-by only

The work of Larry Grimes is visible from Highway 49 West, about halfway between Parchman Penitentiary and Rome, Mississippi. Grimes, born in Greenville in 1952, makes sculptures from car parts and found objects such as shovels, pipes and even sinks. The figures are lined up along his fence. Grimes's work is not for sale, but the unique sculptures are sure to bring a smile.

Margaret's Grocery

4535 North Washington Street, Vicksburg, MS
601-668-9611

This onetime store no longer sells groceries, but it is a local landmark filled with the art of the Reverend H.D. Dennis. The store was operated for many years by Dennis's wife, Margaret Rogers Dennis. The Reverend Dennis was born in 1916 in Rolling Fork, Mississippi, and began preaching at nineteen. He considered his art part of his ministry, according to the Mississippi Folklife Folk Art Directory, which says the site "is crowded with signs, gates, towers, and other items created by Dennis." Sometimes called the "Bible Castle," the site was left abandoned after Dennis's death, but the Mississippi Folk Art Foundation hopes to save it.

MISSISSIPPI'S LEGENDARY LOCALES

This list describes places you will need to park your car and get out, including quirky museums, unusual historic homes and whimsical places to eat or stay overnight.

Blue Front Café

107 East Railroad Avenue, Bentonia, MS
662-528-1900

This tiny juke joint that opened as a café in 1948 is now part of the Mississippi Blues Trail. "In its heyday the Blue Front was famed for its buffalo fish, blues, and moonshine whiskey," according to the Mississippi Blues Trail history. In the 1970s, it became "an informal, down-home blues venue that gained international fame among blues enthusiasts.…The café offered hot meals, groceries, drinks, recreation, entertainment, and even haircuts." It is owned by Jimmy "Duck" Holmes, a blues musician and son of the original owners.

Sleep in a Sharecropper's Shack

Shack Up Inn
001 Commissary Circle, Clarksdale, MS
662-624-8329

Since 1998, the owners of Shack Up Inn have been saving old shacks from farms and bringing them to their Clarksdale property to create an experience of authentic Delta living. The website says that "blues fans from around the world can still experience the unique history of the Delta Blues....With the exception of the addition of electricity, indoor plumbing, and AC/Heat, they are pretty much the real deal. While we do not claim to be the epitome of luxury, we do know that those who truly appreciate and respect our region's history will enjoy the experience we provide."

Clarksdale is home to the legendary crossroads where blues legend Robert Johnson supposedly sold his soul to the devil in exchange for his musical talent. Numerous other sites on the Mississippi Blues Trail are located nearby. The property includes a wide variety of shacks for lodging and the Juke Joint Bar.

Borroum's Drug Store

604 East Waldron Street, Corinth, MS
662-286-3361

Borroum's Drug Store, the oldest in Mississippi, opened in Corinth more than 150 years ago. The Encyclopedia of Mississippi says, "The store was established in 1865 by Andrew Jackson Borroum, a doctor who had

Historic Borroum's Drug Store in Corinth, Mississippi. *Courtesy of KevinMagee1/ Wikimedia Commons.*

obtained his degree from Louisiana Medical School and served as an assistant surgeon in Company C of the 34th Mississippi Infantry in the Civil War." He moved the store to its current location in 1916. It is still operated by one of Borroum's descendants, his great-granddaughter Camille Borroum Mitchell, who was one of the first two female students to obtain pharmacy degrees from the University of Mississippi. The store remains a working drugstore and soda fountain.

Petrified Forest

124 Forest Park Road, Flora, MS
601-879-8189; Admission fee

This privately owned forest is open to the public. It is an area filled with massive trees that were petrified into stone as much as one thousand years ago. The Petrified Forest website says, "The existence of this Petrified Forest has been known since the middle 1800s, but only within the past four decades has it been developed and opened for the public....The size of the petrified logs indicates that as living trees, these stone giants were over one hundred feet tall, and perhaps a thousand or more years old."

They were created by a torrential flood that ripped them from the ground and tossed them along the river until they eventually sank into the ooze and petrified. The site features nature trails, a museum that explains the petrifaction process, a gem-mining flume, a campground and a gift shop.

Riverboat Welcome Center

1512 U.S. Highway 82, Greenville, MS
662-332-2378

The state's welcome center in Washington County is located inside a building shaped like a paddlewheel riverboat. Set in a pond, the building gives the experience of being on a vintage riverboat. A small museum about riverboat history is located upstairs.

Sleep in River Shack

Tallahatchie Flats
58458 County Road 518, Greenwood, MS
662-453-1854

This unique getaway offers lodging in real farm tenant houses located on the banks of the Tallahatchie River. The small houses, each with porches in front and back, have from two to four rooms. The Tallahatchie Flats website says the homes "are preserved examples of the small rural homes that once dotted the Delta countryside where so many great blues artists were born and raised and wandered." The site claims, in fact, that blues great Robert Johnson may have died inside one of the homes. An old tavern on the property is available for events. Activities include fishing, canoeing, cycling, cotton picking for a souvenir, a nightly bonfire, nature trails and throwing a game of muleshoes.

Abandoned Mississippi River Basin Model

Buddy Butts Park
6615 McRaven Road, Jackson, MS
601-960-0471; Free

The Mississippi River Basin Model in Jackson. *Photo by Kelly Kazek.*

A two-hundred-acre scale model of the Mississippi River has been abandoned for decades, but local groups are working to preserve it. The model, used to research ways to mitigate flood damage, was begun in 1943 by the U.S. Army Corps of Engineers using prisoners of war for labor. Parts of the model were completed and in use by 1949, but it wasn't fully completed until 1966, according to Friends of the Mississippi River Basin Model.

The model was used until 1973. During that time, engineers ran seventy-nine simulations, including one in 1952 credited with preventing $65 million in flood damages in Omaha. When computer modeling made the site obsolete, it became a tourist attraction. The corps gave it to the City of Jackson in 1990, but the city could not afford to maintain it. The model is open to the public, but many areas are severely overgrown.

Eudora Welty's House

The Eudora Welty House in Jackson, Mississippi. *Courtesy of Michael Barera/Wikimedia Commons.*

1119 Pinehurst Street, Jackson, MS
601-353-7762

The home where Pulitzer Prize–winning author Eudora Welty spent seventy-six years of her life is open as a museum. The Tudor Revival home was built by Welty's parents in 1925 when she was sixteen years old. She wrote all of her books in an upstairs bedroom of the home. It was restored and is maintained by the Mississippi Department of Archives and History.

The Unfinished Octagonal Mansion

Longwood House Museum
140 Lower Woodville Road, Natchez, MS
601-442-5193; Admission fee

If it had been completed, Longwood Mansion would have thirty-two thousand square feet of living space over six floors. Instead, its owner, Dr. Haller Nutt, died in 1864, with only the exterior and the interior of the first floor completed and all work stopped. The home was deeded to the Pilgrimage Garden Club in 1970 and preserved in its unfinished state. Visitors can tour the mansion and see its lush first floor and stark upper floors. Longwood is listed in the National Register of Historic Places.

Longwood Mansion in Natchez, Mississippi. *Courtesy of Carol M. Highsmith/Library of Congress.*

Birthplace of the Teddy Bear

Towns of Onward and Rolling Fork

The residents of Rolling Fork and Onward celebrate being the "birthplace of the teddy bear" because the incident that inspired the world's most popular plush toy occurred in Sharkey County. It was 1902, near Smedes farm, when President Theodore Roosevelt was invited to go bear hunting with a group of prominent businessmen and politicians. A man hired as a guide trapped a bear, rendered it unconscious and tied it to a tree. He then sent word to Roosevelt to come shoot the bear. The president thought shooting the defenseless bear would be unsportsmanlike and refused to kill it. An editorial cartoon about the incident showed Roosevelt freeing a cute-faced, grateful bear. That gave a toy maker the idea to make stuffed bears, and well, you know the rest.

At 6693 U.S. Highway 61 in the tiny community of Onward, a historical marker was erected at the site of the hunt. Nearby Rolling Fork hosts the Great Delta Bear Affair each fourth Saturday in October. The event includes live music, children's activities, actors portraying Teddy Roosevelt and Teddy Bear Roosevelt, vendors, woodcarving artists and much more. For festival information, call 662-873-1685.

Faulkner's Writing on the Wall

Rowan Oak
916 Old Taylor Road, Oxford, MS
662-234-3284; Admission fee

Rowan Oak was the home of William Faulkner from the 1930s until his death in 1962. The primitive, Greek Revival–style house was built in the

Rowan Oak, home of William Faulkner, in Oxford, Mississippi. *Courtesy of FredlyFish4/Wikimedia Commons.*

1840s. It features the outline of Faulkner's Pulitzer Prize–winning novel *A Fable* written in graphite and red grease pencils on the plaster wall of his study. Faulkner's funeral was held in the parlor of the home. In 1972, Faulkner's daughter, Jill Faulkner Summers, sold the home to the University of Mississippi, which maintains it as a museum.

The Iron Boat that Sank in Twelve Minutes

USS Cairo Gunboat and Museum
3201 Clay Street, Vicksburg, MS
601-636-0583; Admission fee

The USS *Cairo* was one of seven shallow-draft river ironclads prowling the waters of the Mississippi River as part of the Union army's Western Gunboat Flotilla during the Civil War. It was commissioned in January 1862 and participated in battles in May and June, but by the end of the year, the *Cairo* would be gone. On December 12, *Cairo* was clearing mines ahead of an attack when one was detonated by unseen foes stationed behind a riverbank. "*Cairo* has the dubious distinction as the first warship in history to be sunk by an electrically detonated torpedo/mine," a museum display notes.

The USS *Cairo* sank in twelve minutes, but all of the crew survived. They were not able, however, to retrieve any belongings, so they landed in the Mississippi River mud and stayed there for more than one hundred years. The *Cairo* was raised in 1966. The boat and more than one hundred artifacts inside are on display in the museum.

World's Largest Apron Museum

110 West Eastport Street, Iuka, MS
662-279-2390; Free

The Apron Museum in Iuka, Mississippi, is the "world's largest" for a reason—it's the *only* apron museum. Carolyn Terry opened the museum after she amassed a collection of nearly four thousand aprons that covers decades of history.

The world's only apron museum, in Iuka, Mississippi. *Photo by Wil Elrick.*

Birthplace of Kermit the Frog

Jim Henson's Delta Boyhood Exhibit
415 Deer Creek Drive SE, Leland, MS
662-686-7383; Donations

Jim Henson's formative years were spent playing along Deer Creek, where he fed his imagination and love of nature. An original Kermit the Frog and other Muppet memorabilia are on display inside the city's chamber of commerce. According to BirthplaceoftheFrog.org, "The exhibit was given by Jane Henson and the Jim Henson Legacy as a gift to the people of Leland, featuring a tableau honoring Kermit the Frog's beginnings on Deer Creek."

Waveland Ground Zero Hurricane Museum

335 Coleman Avenue, Waveland, MS
228-467-9012; Donations

Waveland, a picturesque waterfront town, was defined as "ground zero" of Hurricane Katrina's landfall. The small town was virtually destroyed when a thirty-two-foot-high wall of water swept across it, and thirty-eight people were killed. Historic Waveland Elementary School, built in 1927 and the only building left standing on Coleman Avenue after the storm, was renovated to house the museum. Exhibits show the extent of the damage and the resilience of the residents.

Ground Zero Hurricane Museum in Waveland, Mississippi. *Courtesy of Emily Cotton/Wikimedia Commons.*

Elvis's Birthplace

306 Elvis Presley Drive, Tupelo, MS
662-841-1245; Admission fee

The humble two-room home where
Elvis Presley was born was preserved
and moved to the grounds of the
Elvis Presley Museum. The website
says, "In 1934, Vernon Presley
borrowed $180 for materials to build
a small frame house in East Tupelo.
It was in this little house on January
8, 1935, that the King of Rock 'n
Roll was born." While there, visitors

Elvis's birthplace in Tupelo, Mississippi.
Photo by Wil Elrick.

can also tour the one-room white clapboard Assembly of God Church Elvis
attended as a child and where he was first exposed to gospel music.

Mammy's Cupboard

555 U.S. Highway 61 Business, Natchez, MS
601-445-8957

This restaurant was built in 1940 in the figure of a mammy, which was
a popular stereotype after the theatrical release of *Gone with the Wind* the
year before. The figure is twenty-eight feet tall, and a café and gift shop are
located in the hoop skirt. The café serves lunch and desserts and is known
for its pies.

Mammy's Cupboard in
Natchez. *Photo by Wil Elrick.*

The Simmons & Wright Company Store

5493 Highway 11/80, Toomsuba, MS
601-632-1884

Established in 1884, the Simmons & Wright Company general store opened in the busy cotton community of Kewanee. The interior is much like it was in its early days. The store, listed in the National Register of Historic Places, still operates today, selling antiques, hardware, feed and seed and a few grocery items.

MISSISSIPPI TOMBSTONE TALES

This section lists just a few of the state's intriguing headstones and the stories behind them. Most cemeteries are open during daylight hours only. Many do not have street numbers in their addresses, but those listed are as close as possible.

The Lady in Red

Odd Fellows Cemetery
Rockport Road, Lexington, MS

A simple headstone in Odd Fellows Cemetery marks the grave of a woman whose identity has been a mystery for fifty years. The woman's body was found in 1969, buried on Egypt Plantation along a bank of the Yazoo River, when her coffin was unearthed by a backhoe.

A February 14, 2019, article in the *Clarion-Ledger* said the body "was preserved by alcohol in a metal-and-glass coffin. Her red velvet dress, cape and buckled shoes indicated she died in the mid-1800s." When no one was able to identify the woman, she was reinterred in Odd Fellows Cemetery beneath a stone giving an estimated year of birth and the year she was discovered. It says, "Lady in Red Found on Egypt Plantation, 1835–1969."

The Turning Angel

Natchez City Cemetery
2 Cemetery Road, Natchez, MS
601-445-5051

In Natchez City Cemetery, an angel statue watches over the graves of five young women who were killed in a tragic incident in the city's past. In 1908, a massive gas explosion caused the five-story Natchez Drug Company building to collapse, killing the employees inside, the youngest of whom was twelve.

A March 24, 1908 article in the *Cedar Falls Gazette* in Iowa stated, "The explosion tore away the rear wall of the building, which in falling crushed an adjoining tenement building. Immediately following the explosion, the wreckage caught fire, a stiff wind which was blowing carrying huge sparks to the north and west, setting fire to eighteen residences, ten of which were destroyed." In addition to the drug company employees, five others were killed in the blast.

The owner of the company bought a plot in Natchez City Cemetery to bury five workers. The young women's markers bear only their last names. The grief-stricken owner also bought a statue of an angel to mark the graves.

The grave of Florence Irene Ford in Natchez City Cemetery. *Photo by Kelly Kazek.*

According to legend, the statue "turns to look at cars driving by," Atlas Obscura says. "This effect is said to be most noticeable at night, when the cars' headlights shine on the statue around the bend of the road." While you're in the cemetery, check out the grave of Florence Irene Ford, the little girl who was afraid of storms and died at age ten. Florence was buried in a coffin with a viewing window, and her mother built a stairway down to the level of her casket so she could visit the cemetery and be with her daughter when it stormed.

Unknown Soldiers on Natchez Trace

Mile Marker 270, Natchez Trace Parkway, Tupelo, MS

Hidden in the woods along a patch on the old Natchez Trace are the graves of thirteen unknown Confederate soldiers. Visitors can stop at a sign near mile marker 270 and walk a short distance to the graves, which are marked with traditional military headstones.

According to the National Park Service, much of the original trace, called Old Trace, had already been abandoned by the start of the Civil War. Its website says, "However, the war did leave its mark on the Trace as it did upon the rest of the South. The soldiers marched, camped and fought along portions of this historic old road.…[Their graves are] a mute reminder of bygone days and of the great struggle out of which developed a stronger nation." Who the men are, how they died and why they are buried along the Old Trace are unknown.

Confederate graves on the old Natchez Trace near Tupelo. *Photo by Kelly Kazek.*

The Gypsy Queen Grave

Rose Hill Cemetery
701 Fortieth Avenue, Meridian, MS

In January 1915, a Romany gypsy clan camping in Alabama was in a state of panic. Their queen, Kelly Mitchell, was dying. She was in childbirth without aid of a doctor, as was custom, but it would be her fifteenth birth and her health was failing. In an unprecedented move, her husband, King Emil Mitchell, sent for the town physician and offered him $10,000 if he could save the queen's life. It was to no avail.

The grave of the Gypsy queen in Meridianville, Mississippi. *Courtesy of Natalie Maynor/Wikimedia Commons.*

Kelly, sometimes written "Callie," Mitchell, died on January 31, 1915, at the age of forty-seven in Sumter County. Her funeral, held twelve days later to allow gypsies to travel to the event, was an extravagant festival that would be described in newspapers across the country and lead to tales of a golden, or perhaps silver, casket and gold coins that would result in several grave-robbing attempts.

The gypsy camp in Coatopa was located near the Mississippi line, and King Emil chose to bury his beloved wife in the town of Meridian. A history of the Mitchell family on gypsyjib.com says her body was taken to Horace C. Smith Undertaking Company, now known as Webb Funeral Home, "because it was the closest place with proper funeral facilities, including refrigeration."

According to a February 7, 1915 article in the *Meridian Dispatch*, more than twenty thousand gypsies crowded into the town to witness the service held at St. Paul's Episcopal Church. Today, Emil Mitchell and others from the clan are buried near Kelly Mitchell. Visitors to their graves leave gifts of beads and other trinkets.

Douglas the Confederate Camel Grave

Cedar Hill Cemetery
326 Lovers Lane, Vicksburg, MS
601-634-4513

The grave of Old Douglas, the Confederate camel. *Courtesy of Natalie Maynor/Wikimedia Commons.*

The Forty-Third Mississippi Infantry had a mascot during the Civil War, a camel named Douglas, who was killed in 1863. Douglas was a member of the Camel Corps, a failed army experiment begun in the 1850s. His headstone proclaims Douglas "a favorite of both beasts and men," who was "intentionally killed by Yankee sharpshooters" during the siege of Vicksburg in June 1863. Reportedly, old Douglas had wandered to look for food when he was shot.

The Hermit of Deer Island

Old Biloxi Cemetery
1166 Irish Hill Drive, Biloxi, MS

In the 1950s, a Frenchman named Jean Guilhot made his home in a Mississippi shack and became known as the Hermit of Deer Island. Guilhot (1877–1959) is buried in Old Biloxi Cemetery beneath a marker that bears his photo and story. The oyster farmer with a mysterious past became a tourist attraction during his years on the island. His shack was a stop on tours, and shops sold postcards bearing his image.

Monument to the Burning Woman

Old Aberdeen Cemetery
21 Whitfield Street, Aberdeen, MS

The story of Mary Points is a tragic one and one that may have been forgotten if not for her unusual headstone. Mary burned to death in 1852 when her dress caught fire. Her husband, Jacob G. Points, had a relief carved of a woman whose dress is on fire. Etched below the figure ingulfed in flames are the words "To my Mary in Heaven."

The Witch of Yazoo

Glenwood Cemetery
Potters Field Road, Yazoo City, MS

The story surrounding this grave is pure legend, yet it continues to lure visitors to Glenwood Cemetery. A woman thought to be a witch is reportedly interred in a plot surrounded by chain links, which led to a legend printed in 1971 in the book *Good Old Boy*, written by local Willie Morris, who died in 1999 and is buried thirteen steps south of the witch's grave. No name or dates are given for the "witch."

VisitYazoo.org says, "According to the legend, the old woman lived on the Yazoo River, and was caught torturing fishermen who she lured in off the river. The sheriff is said to have chased her through the swamps where she was half drowned in quicksand by the time the sheriff caught up with her. As she was sinking, she swore her revenge on Yazoo City and on the town's people. 'In 20 years, I will return and burn this town to the ground!' No one thought much of it at the time. Then came May 25, 1904.…The Fire of 1904 destroyed over 200 residences and nearly every business in Yazoo City—324 buildings in total."

Memorials to Robert Johnson

Mount Zion Missionary Baptist Church, Phillipston Road/Leflore County Road 511, Morgan City, MS
Payne Chapel Memorial Baptist Church Cemetery, 32830 County Road 167, Itta Bena, MS, 662-254-9650
Little Zion Missionary Baptist Church Cemetery, 58458 Leflore County Road 518, Greenwood, MS

No one knows where the legendary blues musician Robert Johnson (1911–1938) is buried. What is known is that he died in Greenwood in 1938 when he was only twenty-seven years old. His talent and early death led to the tale that Johnson had sold his soul to the devil. According to legend, Johnson was told by a mysterious presence to go to the crossroads near Dockery Plantation at midnight, where he traded his soul for the musical expertise that made him famous. The legend is retold in the 1986 movie *Crossroads*.

A marker for Robert Johnson on the Mississippi Blues Trail. *Courtesy of Chillin662/ Wikimedia Commons.*

The three markers are unique, and each gives insight into Johnson's life. The headstone at Little Zion in Greenwood, etched to replicate his handwriting, are words he wrote not long before his death:

> *Jesus of Nazareth, King of Jerusalem*
> *I know that my Redeemer liveth and*
> *that He will call me from the Grave.*

North Carolina

What kid (including aging ones) doesn't like to come across a dinosaur on the roadside? North Carolina has plenty of those. You can also find a replica of the town of Mayberry from *The Andy Griffith Show*, a western-themed town movie set and a tiny burg where no cars are allowed. And then there's the house covered entirely in ceramic coffee mugs.

If size matters to you, check out the World's Largest Real Tire or the giant statue of the pirate Blackbeard. And then there's the furniture. In a state known for its furniture production, you can check out the World's Largest Chest of Drawers and the World's Largest Duncan Phyfe Chair. Die-hard fans of vintage theme parks should visit the long-abandoned Land of Oz, now open twice a year, for a walk along the yellow brick road with some familiar characters. Here are ways to have fun in the Tar Heel State.

NORTH CAROLINA ROADSIDE ATTRACTIONS

This section includes objects you can see from the road, often free of charge.

Giant Blackbeard

Downeast Marine
455 U.S. Highway 70, Beaufort, NC
252-728-5817

A statue of the pirate Blackbeard, about twenty feet tall, is a popular photo op for travelers.

World's Largest Real Tire

Hester Tire
13442 Highway 131 North, Bladenboro, NC
910-863-314

Owner Reynold Hester says a display at his shop is the world's largest real tire. It is fifty-nine by eighty inches with a radius of sixty inches. It is made by Michelin and fits only the largest dump truck in the world.

World's Largest Tire at Hester Tire. *Courtesy of Hester Tire.*

Uniroyal Gals and Critters

Grahamland Fiberglass
24605 U.S. Highway 74, Bolton, NC
910-655-0978; Admission fee

Drivers can pay at the gate to drive through this property with more than 250 fiberglass figures.

Bigfoot Statue

Cove Creek Road, Cataloochee, NC

A giant wooden Sasquatch is located at the head of the Bigfoot Trails in the Smoky Mountains. The statue is located 4.4 miles down Cover Creek Road.

Giant Hand

South McDowell and East Fourth Streets, Charlotte, NC

An oversized outstretched hand invites people to come lie down in it.

Monument to Old Man Traffic

Providence Road, Charlotte, NC

From the 1950s until his death in 1976, a local man named Hugh McManaway—who lived in a nearby mansion—directed, unbidden, traffic at one of Charlotte's busiest intersections. No one was sure why he did it, but locals began calling him Old Man Traffic. A likeness of Hugh, sculpted by Elsie Shaw, was erected in a median on Providence Road in 2000.

Monument to the Writer

ImaginOn
300 East Seventh Street, Charlotte, NC

A 2005 sculpture by Larry Kirkland pays tribute to former *Charlotte Observer* publisher Rolfe Neill. A bronze quill pen sticks up from an inkwell atop a stack of books, surrounded by typewriter keys, pencils and hand stamps.

Monuments to Books and Kids

Downtown Charlotte, NC

A stack of bronze sculpted books is located in a park in downtown Charlotte. Another sculpture, made of bricks by Brad Spencer, depicts children climbing on a brick book.

Tinkerbell Sign

The iconic Tinkerbell sign at Pink Motel. *Photo by Kelly Kazek.*

Pink Motel
1306 Tsali Boulevard, Cherokee, NC
828-497-3530

Since this iconic neon sign featuring Tinkerbell and her wand was erected in 1953, travelers have stopped to take photos with it.

Rock Police Officer

Clayton Police Department
201 South Barbour Street, Clayton, NC

Cornerstones, by artist Christian Karkow, shows the devastation left in the wake of an officer's death. On the exterior wall, the stones are pushed forward to create a silhouette, while they form a void on the other side.

Giant Black Widow

Innovative Pest Management
6596 Campground Road, Denver, NC

This realistic sculpture of a black widow spider was commissioned by owners of the pest control company. The sculpture was created by Dave Simpson.

Bronze Camel and His Human

Science Drive, Durham, NC

The life-sized statue of a camel stands alongside a statue of Knut Schmidt-Nielson on the campus of Duke University. Created by Jonathan Kingdon in 1995, the camel is eight feet high and weighs about two tons. Nielson was a noted professor of zoology at Duke.

Bull Statue

City Center Plaza
201 Corcoran Street, Durham, NC

In 2007, a massive work of art was commissioned to honor one of Durham's most respected businessmen, George Watts "Major" Hill. The ten-foot-high statue by Leah Foushee and Michael Waller depicts a bull named Major. Bulls have been used to symbolize Durham since the 1800s.

Dinosaur Trail

Museum of Life and Science
433 West Murray Avenue, Durham, NC
919-220-5429; Admission fee for museum

A beloved local brontosaurus that was vandalized in 2009 has been fully restored and now heads up the Dinosaur Trail at the Museum of Life and Science. These days, the vintage seventy-seven-foot-long creation made of concrete and plywood can be found frolicking among other critters of its era.

Eiffel Tower Replica, North Carolina

1740 Owen Drive, Fayetteville, NC

This 1/12-scale replica of the Eiffel Tower in Paris was built in 1971 to advertise the Bordeaux Shopping Center.

K9 Memorial

100 Bragg Boulevard, Fayetteville, NC

Artist Lena Toritch sculpted this bronze likeness of a Belgian Malinois wearing a combat vest to honor all soldier-dogs who serve in the military.

Futuro House in Frisco

52186 Morriss Lane, Frisco, NC
Private residence; Drive-by only

Frisco is home to one of the few surviving Futuros, prefabricated houses manufactured in the shape of spacecraft in the late 1960s. The homes were designed by Finnish architect Matti Suuronen. About sixty remain worldwide.

World's Second–Largest Chest of Drawers

508 North Hamilton Street, High Point, NC

This chest, built in 1926 by the High Point Chamber of Commerce, is not as large as the one in Jamestown, but it has more whimsy: two oversized socks hang from its drawers.

World's second-largest chest of drawers in High Point, North Carolina. *Courtesy of Carol M. Highsmith/Library of Congress.*

World's Largest Chest of Drawers

Furnitureland South
5635 Riverdale Drive, Jamestown, NC
336-841-4328; Free

This eighty-foot-tall highboy chest marks the entrance to a local furniture store.

Giant Milkshake

Dairi-O
365 East Dalton Street, King, NC
336-983-5560
A thirty-foot-tall milkshake creates an entrance to the Dairi-O restaurant, which has been in business since the 1940s. The milkshake was added in 2011.

Giant Moose

546 East Plaza Drive, Mooresville, NC
704-663-1222

This fifteen-foot-high fiberglass moose in front of Bucko's restaurant makes for a fun photo op.

King Neptune

713 Shepard Street, Morehead City, NC

This oversized King Neptune, complete with merman tail, is located on a dock beside the Olympus Dive Center.

World's Largest Ten Commandments

Fields of the Wood
10000 Highway 294, Murphy, NC
828-494-7855; Free

Positioned on the side of a large hill in Murphy, this tribute to the biblical commandments certainly commands attention. Visitors can walk to the top of the site and read each of the Ten Commandments. The site is part of the Fields of the Wood, which features oversized Christian attractions.

Giant Plunger

4850 U.S. Highway 70, New Bern, NC

How many times could you have used a giant plunger at your house? Just sayin'. The oversized implement was built by a local plumber.

World's Largest Working Frying Pan

102 South Sycamore Street, Rose Hill, NC

Yep, it's big, and, yep, it works. This 15-foot pan covering 176 square feet was created in 1963 by the Ramsey Feed Company as a tribute to the area's poultry industry—although is the threat of being fried really a tribute? The huge pan weighs two tons. It can be placed on forty propane burners and fry up 365 whole chickens, according to AtlasObscura.com.

Movie Scene Train Wreck from The Fugitive

973 Haywood Road, Sylva, NC

A train wreck created for the 1993 movie *The Fugitive* remains in the woods of the Great Smoky Mountains. The train's collision with a prison bus allows Harrison Ford, the titular fugitive, to escape and set out to prove his innocence.

According to AbandonedExplorers.com, "Filmmakers simply placed a full-size bus in the path of an oncoming freight train, and let physics do the rest. The bus was nearly torn in half by the impact, and the train was made to derail after the collision leaving nothing but mangled wrecks in its wake."

World's Largest Duncan Phyfe Chair

Main and Salem Streets, Thomasville, NC

This giant chair is the only one in the Duncan Phyfe design and the only one sat on by a future president, Lyndon Johnson. The thirty-foot-high chair was built in 1948, and Johnson visited it when he was campaigning in 1960.

World's Largest Duncan Phyfe Chair. *Courtesy of Carol M. Highsmith/Library of Congress.*

Giant Coffee Pot

Old Salem Museums and Gardens
600 South Main Street, Winston-Salem, NC
336-721-7300

A shiny, seven-foot-three-inch coffee pot makes a great selfie op in the restored Moravian village of Old Salem. The pot was made in 1858 by tinsmiths and brothers Julius and Sam Mickey. According to RoadsdieAmerica.com, the pot could hold "11,840 cups of brew."

NORTH CAROLINA OUTSIDER ART

This unique kind of roadside oddity comes in many forms. Some collections are indoors; some are outdoors. A few charge admission; others request donations. But the work never fails to astound and entertain.

Marvin Johnson's Gourds

Angier Municipal Building
28 North Raleigh Avenue, Angier, NC
919-639-4413; Tours by appointment

Marvin Johnson was well known in the area for his gourd art. He and his wife, Mary, opened the Gourd Museum on their property in 1965. Since Marvin's death, the collection has been housed at the local municipal building. It includes gourds made into a variety of objects such as lamps, teapots and musical instruments.

Marvin Johnson's gourds in Angier, North Carolina. *Courtesy of Carol M. Highsmith/Library of Congress.*

Kayak Ranch

Southwestern Community College
60 Almond School Road, Bryson City, NC
Free

This local artists' version of Texas's Cadillac Ranch features a row of colorful kayaks half buried in the ground.

Cup House of Collettsville

Old Johns River Road, Collettsville, NC
Free

This home isn't easy to find, but if you have some extra mugs lying around, you might want to make the trip so you can help decorate the Cup House of Collettsville. The property includes a modest home and a second small building—all covered with coffee mugs hung on small nails. The fence is also covered.

The Cup House of Collettsville, North Carolina. *Photo by Wil Elrick.*

The home was the project of Avery and Doris Sisk. According to Atlas Obscura, the collection began fifteen years ago when Avery bought a box-lot of fifteen mugs and decided to display them on the home. Since then, hundreds of mugs have been added, both by the Sisks and by people who come to see the house. Avery welcomes people to leave mugs—if they can find an empty nail. Directions: Follow North Carolina Highway 90 northwest out of Collettsville for about half a mile and turn left onto Old Johns River Road. Follow for about two and a half miles to a gravel road on the right. Follow the gravel road all the way to the end.

Clyde Jones's Critter Crossing

137 Bynum Hill Road, Pittsboro, NC
Free

Since 1982, local chainsaw artist Clyde Jones has created wooden animals to paint in bright colors and display in his yard. Small Museum of Folk Art says, "Before you even get to the Critter Crossing, you will see critters of all shapes and sizes in the yard of almost every resident of Bynum....But you cannot miss the Critter Crossing when you finally get to it—the tin roof is painted with sea creatures, penguins march across the walls, and the yard is filled with critters of all shapes and sizes."

Gene Dillard Mosaic House

2706 Elgin Street, Durham, NC
Private residence; Visible from the road

For years, artist Gene Dillard has been creating mosaics on his house and in his yard. The result is a sparkling work of art where he lives with his family.

Gene Dillard's mosaic house in Durham, North Carolina. *Courtesy of Gene Dillard.*

Roadside Metal Dinosaurs

Benton & Sons Fabrication Company
1921 North Carolina Highway 581, Pikeville, NC
919-734-1700; Visible from the road

Ben Benton Jr. was looking for a way to keep his workers occupied during lulls and also lure customers to his business. The result was an eighteen-foot-tall metal T-rex. Since then, a stegosaurus and brachiosaurus have joined the menagerie.

Shangri-La Village

11535 North Carolina Highway 86, Prospect Hill, NC
Free

This village filled with miniature structures made of stones is the work of Henry L. Warren, who began building them when he retired in the 1960s. When he died in 1977, he had completed twenty-seven structures, including a theater, hotel, water tower and more. They are still on display.

Mary's Bottle House

2431 Holden Beach Road SW, Supply, NC
910-842-9908; Donations

Folk artist Mary Paulsen started creating artwork in her yard in the 1980s and covering her house with bottles in 2008. Her creative and colorful art can be seen throughout the yard.

NORTH CAROLINA'S LEGENDARY LOCALES

This list describes places you will need to park your car and get out, including quirky museums, unusual historic homes and whimsical places to eat or stay overnight.

Largest Home in the Nation

Biltmore Estate
One Lodge Street, Asheville, NC
800-411-3812; Admission fee

Built in 1895 for George and Edith Vanderbilt, Biltmore is the nation's largest privately owned home. The public can tour three of the floors and the basement. Portions of the house are still lived in by Vanderbilt descendants. The eye-popping home features:

- 135,280 square feet of living space
- Thirty-five bedrooms and forty-five bathrooms
- Art by Pierre-Auguste Renoir and John Singer Sargent
- Sixteenth-century tapestries
- A ten-thousand-volume library
- A formal banquet hall with a 70-foot ceiling
- Sixty-five fireplaces
- An indoor pool
- A bowling alley

These days, the estate is like the Disney World of house museums, featuring inns, restaurants, shops, a winery, an equestrian center and more.

The Country Doctor Museum

7089 Peele Road, Bailey, NC
252-235-4165; Admission fee

This museum is the "oldest museum in the United States dedicated to the history of America's rural health care," its online history says. It was founded in 1967 in the home of a real local doctor by an organization that wanted to "build a lasting memorial for rural physicians." The museum's collection includes more than five thousand medical artifacts and equipment, as well as reproductions of examination rooms. The property includes a gift shop and carriage house with exhibits of early transportation.

Abandoned Land of Oz Theme Park

1007 Beech Mountain Parkway, Beech Mountain, NC
800-514-3849; Admission fee

From 1970 to 1980, the Land of Oz was a family attraction located at the top of Beech Mountain, the highest point in the state. The park, built by Grover and Harry Robbins, was closed following a fire and remained abandoned for decades. Today, it is opened two weekends per year, in spring and fall, for families to experience the park as it was in its heyday. The original yellow brick road was refurbished, along with numerous attractions, such as

Land of Oz in Beech
Mountain, North Carolina.
Photo by Wil Elrick.

Dorothy's house, the Witch's Mansion and the poppy field. Along the road, visitors will meet characters dressed as Dorothy, Glinda, the Scarecrow, Tin Man, Cowardly Lion, the Wicked Witch, the Wizard and more.

Belhaven Memorial Museum

Belhaven Town Hall
315 East Main Street, Belhaven, NC
252-943-3055; Admission fee

What happens to the hoardings of an eccentric woman after she dies? The collection becomes a one-of-a-kind museum, of course. In this case, the oddities gathered over the course of Eva Blount Way's ninety-two years are on display in the Belhaven Memorial Museum. She died in 1962, and some of her collection is now on display in city hall.

The objects include, according to Roadside America: Tumors in jars, carcasses of animal oddities, "a dress worn by a local 700-pound woman (she died in bed and had to be craned out the window)," a "German W.W.I half-boot (looks like it was amputated along with the foot)" and "a flea bride and groom (may be viewed with a magnifying glass)."

The Blowing Rock

432 The Rock Road, Blowing Rock, NC
828-295-7111; Admission fee

The Blowing Rock is a wave-shaped cliff that hangs over Johns River Gorge. It is known as the Blowing Rock because, on certain days, lightweight items such as leaves or blades of grass thrown over the edge at four thousand feet above sea level will blow back to the person who threw them via strong wind currents. Because of this, Ripley's Believe It or Not dubbed it "the only place in the world where snow falls upside down."

The legendary Blowing Rock. *Photo by Wil Elrick.*

The site includes a small cottage filled with historical photos, signs and advertisements from the Blowing Rock, and an observation deck with majestic Grandfather Mountain visible across the gorge. Visitors can actually climb on the rocks and have their photos made overlooking the gorge.

Tweetsie Railroad

300 Tweetsie Railroad Lane, Blowing Rock, NC
828-264-9061; Admission fee

Tweetsie Railroad is a family-oriented Wild West theme park located between Boone and Blowing Rock. The centerpiece of the park is a three-mile ride on a train pulled by one of Tweetsie Railroad's two historic narrow-gauge steam locomotives. Activities include train rides, a petting zoo, amusement rides, carnival games, shows and more.

America's Tallest Lighthouse

Cape Hatteras
46379 Old Lighthouse Road, Buxton, NC
252-473-2111; Admission fee

Cape Hatteras is one of the coast's most recognizable lighthouses. The 193-foot-high lighthouse was built in 1871 to warn sailors of the danger of Diamond Shoals. Cape Hatteras is painted in a black-and-white barber pole design. The National Park Service opens the Cape Hatteras Lighthouse from late April to October.

Mac's Indian Village Cabins

160 Teepee Drive, Cherokee, NC
828-497-5161

At one time, there were faux teepee fronts at the entrance to each rustic cabin, but these have dwindled to a handful. The motel, one of the oldest in the area, was featured in the 1998 Kevin Bacon movie *Digging to China*. It has been renamed Qualla's Cabins and Motel.

Santa's Land Fun Park & Zoo

571 Wolfetown Road, Cherokee, NC
828-497-9191; Admission fee

One of the few remaining small roadside theme parks still in operation, Santa's Land has all the kitschy attractions families have loved for generations, including rides like a Rudolph rollercoaster, live animals, shows, candy stores and, of course, Santa. Opens for the season each May.

Santa's Land Fun Park and zoo in Cherokee, North Carolina. *Photo by Kelly Kazek.*

Andre the Giant Memorabilia

Rankin Museum of American Heritage
131 Church Street, Ellerbe, NC
910-652-6378; Admission fee

The Rankin Museum of American Heritage in Ellerbe features exhibits dedicated to Andre the Giant, a famous wrestler who lived in the area until his death. Visitors will see such artifacts as Andre's size 26 wrestling boots.

Hunger Games *Ghost Town*

4255 Henry River Road, Hickory, NC
828-471-4768; Admission fee

The site that served as the setting for District 12 in the *Hunger Games* movies is now a preserved ghost town. The small mill village of Henry River was abandoned in the 1970s, and numerous mill homes and buildings survive. The village is open for tours and events.

Town with No Cars Allowed

133 Henry Martin Trail, Love Valley, NC
919-349-3541

This is yet another western-themed town built in the North Carolina mountains, but this one has a twist: It is a real town and no one is allowed to drive cars through it. The town was built in 1954 by Andy Barker and includes a saloon, a general store, hitching posts, a church and rodeos. People must park their cars outside of town and either walk or ride horses or buggies into town. The surrounding Brushy Mountains also offer numerous riding trails.

Brown Mountain Lights

Brown Mountain lookout near Morganton, North Carolina. *Photo by Wil Elrick.*

Various, Pisgah National Forest

People have claimed to see the spooky Brown Mountain Lights at numerous points in the Pisgah National Forest. BrownMountainLights.com says: "For perhaps 800 years or more, ghostly lights have been seen flaring and creeping along, and below, the ridge at night. Some of the earliest reports came from Cherokee and Catawba Indians, settlers, and Civil War soldiers. Thousands have witnessed the spectacle, which is ongoing to this day."

The site also claims the lights have been investigated by the federal government, but no source was found. Some overlooks to try:

- Wiseman's View overlooking Linville Gorge with a view of Table Rock and Hawksbill Mountains.
- Brown Mountain Overlook, North Carolina Highway 181, twelve miles north of Morganton.
- Lost Cove Overlook, Blue Ridge Parkway, Mile Marker 310.

Wright Brothers National Memorial

1000 North Croatan Highway, Kill Devil Hills, NC

A tower memorializes the experiments in flight conducted by brothers Orville and Wilbur Wright here. From 1900 to 1903, the brothers worked at the site, chosen because of its steady winds, until they finally succeeded in flying. The tower was designed by Rodgers and Poor and erected in the 1930s.

Cryptozoology and Paranormal Museum

328 Mosby Avenue, Littleton, NC
631-220-1231

Located inside a reportedly haunted home, this is an unusual version of the more typical cryptid museums popping up across the country. This facility was opened by cryptozoologist Stephen Carcelo, who displays his collection of artifacts, including casts of Bigfoot prints found in the area, a haunted doll and ghost hunting equipment.

Mayberry Courthouse & Jail

625 South Main Street, Mount Airy, NC
336-786-6066; Various admission fees

Fans of *The Andy Griffith Show* know that the show's locale was inspired by his own hometown of Mount Airy, North Carolina. These days, the town makes the most of its connection to the beloved show. Fans can tour the Mayberry Courthouse & Jail, take photos with a statue of Andy and Opie, stay in Andy's boyhood home or visit the Andy Griffith Museum. The town also features replicas of Floyd's Barber Shop and Wally's Service Station.

Movie Set Western Town

494 Bonnie Avenue, Smithfield, NC
919-300-1981

In 1997, former actor Bill Drake decided to move into set design and began building his own western town. Today, the site is used as a movie set, photography background, wedding venue, entertainment and more.

Seashell-Shaped Service Station

East Sprague Street, Winston-Salem, NC

In the 1930s, Joe Glenn and Bert Bennett built several Shell stations shaped like actual seashells as a way to promote the gasoline brand. Today, only one remains. It was listed in the National Register of Historic Places. It is not open, but it has been preserved so visitors can stop for photos.

The last shell-shaped Shell station in Winston-Salem, North Carolina. *Courtesy of Carol M. Highsmith/Library of Congress.*

NORTH CAROLINA TOMBSTONE TALES

This section lists just a few of the state's intriguing headstones and the stories behind them. Most cemeteries are open during daylight hours only. Many do not have street numbers in their addresses, but those listed are as close as possible.

Rum Keg Girl Grave

Old Burying Ground
400 Ann Street, Beaufort, NC
252-728-5225

The land for the Old Burying Ground was deeded to the town in 1731, making it one of the area's oldest cemeteries. One of the most visited graves in the cemetery is that of the Girl in the Barrel of Rum. According to the Beaufort Historical Association, "In the 1700s an English family, including an infant daughter, came to Beaufort. The girl grew up with a desire to see her homeland, and finally persuaded her mother to allow her to make the voyage. Her father promised his wife he would return the girl safely. The girl enjoyed her visit to London but died on the voyage home. She would have been buried at sea, but her father could not bear to break his promise. He purchased a barrel of rum from the captain, placed her body in it, and brought it to Beaufort for burial."

Grave of the Rum Keg Girl in Beaufort, North Carolina. *Courtesy of Gerry Dincher / Wikimedia Commons.*

Standing British Officer Grave

Old Burying Ground
400 Ann Street, Beaufort, NC
252-728-5225

An unnamed British naval officer killed before the American Revolution reportedly wanted to be buried standing, in full uniform. A small sign at the grave says, "British Naval Officer buried standing in salute to His Majesty King George Third."

Tom Dooley Grave

Tom Dula Road, Ferguson, NC
State Highway 1134/Tom Dula Road, 1.1 miles from the intersection of State Highway 268

Thanks to a popular folk song, Tom Dooley is one of the nation's most legendary convicted murderers. Dooley, born Thomas Dula (the surname was likely pronounced with a long A and eventually corrupted into "Dooley), was hanged at the age of twenty-two in 1868 for the murder of Laura Foster, although he went to the gallows protesting his innocence.

The grave of Tom Dooley in Ferguson, North Carolina. *Courtesy of Jan Kronsell/ Wikimedia Commons.*

To find the cemetery, go to the bluff about twelve feet above the road from the sign, and you'll find an entrance about three hundred feet east of the cemetery. According to FindaGrave.com, "The gravesite is on privately owned property but accessible to the public."

World's Heaviest Twins Graves

Crab Creek Baptist Church
72 Jeter Mountain Road, Hendersonville, NC

In life, Benny and Billy McCrary earned the title World's Heaviest Twins from Guinness World Records. They are buried side by side in Crab Creek Baptist Church Cemetery. They were known for riding motorcycles, and an image of them riding together is etched on their headstone. Billy died in a motorcycle crash in 1979. Benny died in 2001. According to Guinness, Billy weighed 743 pounds and Benny weighed 723. Their waists were eighty-four inches around. Their size was attributed to a pituitary gland abnormality they sustained after getting German measles as children.

Spaghetti the Carny Mummy Grave

Hillside Cemetery
426 Hillside Avenue, Laurinburg, NC

A carnival worker named Cancetto Farmica, known as "Spaghetti," became a sideshow act after his death. Cancetto died in a fight in 1911 and was taken to a local funeral home for embalming. After Farmica's father didn't return to claim the body, the funeral director decided to keep the mummified remains, just in case. For sixty-two years, they were on display at McDougald Funeral Home until finally being buried in 1973.

Siamese Twins, Chang and Eng, Graves

White Plains Baptist Church Cemetery
614 Old U.S. Highway 601, Mount Airy, NC

Twins Chang and Eng Bunker were born conjoined in Siam in 1811, which led to the condition being known as "Siamese twins." With no other way to make a living, the men became sideshow entertainers. The men married a pair of sisters; Chang fathered 10 children and Eng fathered 11. In January 1874, Chang contracted bronchitis and died. Although Eng's family begged him to allow doctors to cut him from his brother, he refused, dying hours later. They are buried in a single grave.

The grave of Siamese twins Chang and Eng Bunker. *Courtesy of Shadle/ Wikimedia Commons.*

Gentleman Giant Grave

Old Smithville Burying Ground
401 East Moore Street, Southport, NC

A simple headstone marks the burial site of Elias Gerthal Gore (1906–1944), known as Southport's Gentleman Giant. Gore, nicknamed "Nehi," was reportedly seven feet, eleven inches tall and weighed four hundred pounds.

South Carolina

Every southerner needs to visit the World's Largest Sweet Tea at least once, if you want my opinion. While you're in South Carolina, you can also visit the Kazoo Factory and Museum or the Atalaya Castle. The adventurous might visit the UFO Welcome Center or Agnes of Glasgow's haunted grave. Lovers of art must stop in Columbia, where they can see a realistic tunnel mural painted on the side of a building and the World's Largest Fire Hydrant. The quirky-but-loveable South of the Border provides a true history lesson in roadside tourist stops so be sure to put it on your list when visiting the Palmetto State.

SOUTH CAROLINA ROADSIDE ATTRACTIONS

This section includes objects you can see from the road, often free of charge.

Giant Sundial

Barnwell County Courthouse
141 Main Street, Barnwell, SC

This free-standing, vertical sundial is the only one of its kind in the world. It was installed in downtown Barnwell in 1858 after being donated by Captain Joseph D. Allen. Reportedly, it has kept time within two minutes of standard time since it was installed.

Neverbust Chain in Columbia, South Carolina. *Photo by Teresa Caldwell.*

Neverbust Chain

1500 Main Street, Columbia, SC

This giant chain was installed in 2000 by local artist Blue Sky. The massive links that span an alley between two buildings are made of steel.

Tunnel Vision in Columbia, South Carolina. *Photo by Teresa Caldwell.*

Tunnelvision

1550 Marion Street, Columbia, SC

A realistic mural that looks like the entrance to a tunnel confuses and entertains visitors to downtown Columbia. Painted on the wall of the Federal Land Bank Building, it was created by local artist Blue Sky in 1975.

World's Largest Fire Hydrant in Columbia, South Carolina. *Photo by Teresa Caldwell.*

World's Largest Fire Hydrant

1400 Taylor Street, Columbia, SC
803-779-4242

Another creation by local artist Blue Sky, Busted Plug Plaza is billed as the World's Largest Fire Hydrant. The fireplug is forty feet tall and weighs about 675,000 pounds. It was purposely made to look cattywampus and, for many years, sprayed water from its base.

Spaceship House in South Carolina

1574 South Waccamaw Drive, Garden City Beach, SC
Private residence; Drive-by only

The Spaceship House is a disc-shaped home built along the beach at Murrell's Inlet in the 1970s. It was reportedly built to withstand hurricane winds.

Luke Skywalker's House

2851 Marshall Boulevard, Sullivan's Island, SC

A unique dome-home that looks a lot like it belongs on the fictional planet of Tatooine, this private home is located on the beach. Visible from the road.

Statue of Peg-Legged Vaudeville Dancer

Fairview Street, Fountain Inn, SC

Clayton Bates was born in Fountain Inn, where he lost his leg in a cotton mill accident. He wore a wooden leg and went on to become a famous vaudeville tap dancer. A marker at his statue says, "Just watch me peg it, you can tell by the way I leg it, I'm Peg-Legged Bates, the one-legged dancing man."

World's Largest Crab

9597 North Kings Highway, Myrtle Beach, SC
843-449-1097

Tommy, the World's Largest Crab, keeps watch over the appropriately named Giant Crab Seafood Restaurant. Tommy is twenty-five feet tall and thirty-five feet wide.

Civitas Statues

Dave Lyle and Gateway Boulevards, Rock Hill, SC
803-329-5620

Four bronze verdigris Civitas statues tower over a four-way intersection, one on each side. Each statue is about twenty-two feet tall. They are holding objects that symbolize the themes of Rock Hill: Gears of Industry, Flame of Knowledge, Stars of Inspiration and Lightning Bolt of Energy.

World's Largest Sweet Tea

200 South Main Street, Summerville, SC

A fifteen-foot-tall Mason jar holds 2,524 gallons of tea, earning it the Guinness World Record as the World's Largest Sweet Tea in 2010. The oversized jar is affectionately named Mason.

SOUTH CAROLINA OUTSIDER ART

This unique kind of roadside oddity comes in many forms. Some collections are indoors; some are outdoors. A few charge admission; others request donations. But the work never fails to astound and entertain.

Pearl Fryar's Topiary Gardens

145 Broad Acres Road, Bishopville, SC
803-484-5581; Donations

Pearl Fryar, the subject of a 2006 documentary called *A Man Named Pearl*, created an incredible garden filled with astonishing topiary art and folk sculptures. Born in Clinton, North Carolina, Fryar settled in Bishopville in 1976 and built a home in 1980. He learned to grow and sculpt trees and bushes and began creating a one-of-a-kind garden—one with a message. Fryar says on his website, "I want people to leave with that message....Life

Pearl Fryar's Topiary Garden in Bishopville, South Carolina. *Courtesy of Judson McCranie/ Wikimedia Commons.*

is about choices, about love and peace, and if you accomplish them in that order, life is going to be good."

His garden has been featured in numerous publications and has won a variety of beautification and art awards. He requests that visitors call only during daytime.

Biblical Tree Carvings

Mepkin Abbey
1098 Mepkin Road, Moncks Corner, SC
843-761-8509; Various admission

Roman Catholic monks who live on the property have sculpted biblical scenes from the life of Christ into fallen oak trees. They are located in a beautiful and serene formal garden. The grounds include the abbey church, cemetery, gardens and a gift shop in the reception center. Open to the public for limited hours.

Kingdom of Oyotunji African Village

56 Bryant Lane, Seabrook, SC
843-846-8900; Admission fee

This village near Sheldon is based on the culture of the Yoruba and Dahomey tribes of West Africa. People live and work in the village, originally founded in the 1970s, but it is also filled with concrete African monuments, including an elaborate fountain and a mausoleum where the remains of Orisamola Awolowo, one of its founding fathers, are interred. The village has a "palace," a marketplace and temples. Its mission, according to its website, is to share "the depth of culture, beautiful art, grandeur of customs and resilient history of the New World Yoruba." Tours can be booked online.

Great Wall of China (The Dishes Kind)

Bob Doster's Backstreet Studios
217 East Gay Street, Lancaster, SC
803-285-9190; Free

Bob Doster, an award-winning sculptor, has created dozens of works of art that are on public display around the state. One of his well-known folk-art creations is a wall outside his studio made of found objects with the help of local art students. It is a popular place for photos.

The Great Wall of China at Bob Doster's Backstreet Studios in Lancaster, South Carolina. *Courtesy of Cherry Doster.*

SOUTH CAROLINA'S LEGENDARY LOCALES

This list describes places you will need to park your car and get out, including quirky museums, unusual historic homes and whimsical places to eat or stay overnight.

The Kazoobie Kazoo Factory

12 John Galt Road, Beaufort, SC
843-982-6387; Admission fee

At this location, visitors not only learn how kazoos are made, but get to tour one of the largest ever collections of the musical instruments. Guests can also make a custom kazoo and visit the gift shop for kazoos and "kazoo accessories."

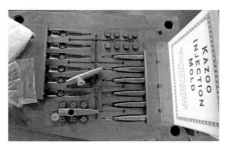

The Kazoo Factory museum and gift shop in Beaufort, South Carolina. *Courtesy of Bobistraveling/Wikimedia Commons.*

Macauley Museum of Dental History

Enter through Waring Library
175 Ashley Avenue, Charleston, SC
843-792-2288; Free

Learn the history of the dental profession at this museum established by Dr. Neill W. Macauley in 1975. The museum includes a collection of historical tools and instruments, a nineteenth-century dental office display and a traveling Civil War–era dentist's chest.

South of the Border. *Courtesy of Carol M. Highsmith/Library of Congress.*

South of the Border

3346 U.S. Highway 301, Hamer, SC
843-774-2411

Built in 1950 as a quirky stop for tourists to rest, eat or fuel up, South of the Border soon became a tourist destination unto itself. The complex features lodging, dining, shopping and attractions, such as a Reptile Lagoon and Pedroland, a kiddie amusement park. The Sombrero Tower, a two-hundred-foot-high observation platform, has a glass elevator that offers great views of the surrounding countryside.

Last Covered Bridge in SC

Campbell's Covered Bridge
171 Campbells Covered Bridge Road,
   Landrum, SC
Free

This picturesque span is the state's last surviving covered bridge. Located near the town of Gowensville, it crosses Beaverdam Creek. The bridge, closed to motor traffic in the 1980s, was listed in the National Register of Historic Places in 2009.

Campbell's Covered Bridge in Greenville County, South Carolina. *Photo by Teresa Caldwell.*

Atalaya Castle

Huntington Beach State Park
Atalaya Road, Murrells Inlet, SC
843-237-4440; Admission fee

Built in the 1930s as a private home, Atalaya Castle is now open as an event venue and for tours. A festival featuring artisans and food vendors is also held on the grounds each September. Atalaya Castle was built by Archer Huntington, a New York philanthropist, for his wife, Anna, as a winter residence in hopes of helping her tuberculosis. The thirty-room manor was inspired by Spanish, or Moorish architecture. Anna, an artist and sculptor, designed wrought-iron grills to provide hurricane protection for all the windows. The castle also included animal enclosures where the couple kept bears, horses, monkeys and a leopard. The castle was listed in the National Register of Historic Places in 1984.

Tiny Police Stations

160 North Palmer Street/U.S. Highway 21, Ridgeway, SC
U.S. Highway 321, Olar, SC

One of the world's smallest police stations, in Ridgeway, South Carolina. *Photo by Teresa Caldwell.*

The former Ridgeway Police Station is about the size of a home bathroom. It is billed as the "world's smallest," but there is a smaller one in the town of Olar, South Carolina, and an even smaller one in Florida. The Ridgeway station was used until 1990, when a new station was built next door. (Note: It's still pretty tiny.) The Olar station is about the size of a shed.

Old Sheldon Church Ruins

Old Sheldon Church Road, Yemassee, SC
843-525-8500; Free

The ruins of a beautiful Greek Revival church lie in a wooded area near Beaufort. The original building was constructed as Prince Williams Parish Church in the mid-1700s and burned during the Revolutionary War. It was rebuilt in 1826 and was destroyed during the Civil War, leaving only its columns and brick walls. The beautiful ruin is surrounded by trees dripping with Spanish moss. The tranquil setting is popular with photographers.

Ruins of Old Sheldon Church in Yemassee, South Carolina. *Courtesy of Carolyn Elizabeth Heath/ Wikimedia Commons.*

Teapot Museum in Teapot-Shaped Building

2734 West Cleveland Street, Elloree, SC
803-596-4275; Admission fee

A collection of more than five thousand teapots, acquired by Sybil and Julian Boland, is exhibited in a building with a blue teapot-shaped façade.

Gullah Geechee Cultural Heritage Corridor

Various sites
Headquarters: 2817 Maybank Highway, Johns Island, SC
843-818-4587

The Gullah Geechee Cultural Heritage Corridor is a federal National Heritage Area. It was created by Congress to recognize the unique culture of the Gullah Geechee people and includes coastal areas of North Carolina, South Carolina, Georgia and Florida.

Last Yogi Bear Honey Fried Chicken Restaurant

514 South Fifth Street, Hartsville, SC
843-332-7031

Yogi Bear Honey-Fried Chicken was a chain of restaurants founded in the mid-1960s by Gene Broome, who had a specialized formula for making honey-flavored chicken. It was bought by Hardee's and eventually all of the stores closed except the one in Hartsville. It still has its retro neon sign featuring Yogi Bear.

Boneyard Beach

Bull's Island
489 Bill's Island Road, Awendaw, SC

This unique spot on Bull's Island, a six-and-a-half-square-mile parcel, can be reached only by ferry or private boat. It is named for the salt-bleached oak scattered along the sand like bones, remnants of a maritime forest. The beach is also known for an abundance of seashells.

Old Charleston City Jail

21 Magazine Street, Charleston, SC
843-722-8687; Admission fee

The fortress-like walls of Charleston's first jail once held the notorious Lavinia Fisher (1793–1820), described by some as the nation's first female serial killer. Although she was a member of a local gang, who she murdered—and if she did—is up for debate. She and her husband, John, owned a local inn from which numerous people were reported missing.

She and John were found guilty of highway robbery and imprisoned in the jail from 1819 to 1820, when they were hanged. Legends of Lavinia's ghost haunting the old jail have led to its history being featured on TV shows such as *Ghost Hunters* and *Ghost Adventures*. The jail, which housed prisoners from 1802 to1939, is open limited times for ghost tours.

The Patriot *Movie Bridge*

Cypress Gardens
3030 Cypress Gardens Road, Moncks Corner, SC
843-553-0515; Admission fee

A bridge built by filmmakers for the 2000 movie *The Patriot* can be visited at Cypress Gardens, a preserve and cypress swamp.

Chapel of Ease Ruins

St. Helena Parish Chapel
17 Lands End Road, St. Helena Island, SC

The Saint Helena Parish Chapel of Ease was built circa 1740 by local planters who were unable to travel all the way to Beaufort each week. Instead, they could worship at the chapel. Only the church walls and a small cemetery remain; locals say the site is haunted.

Ghost Town of Dorchester

Dorchester State Park
300 State Park Road, Summerville, SC
843-873-1740; Admission fee

This town, abandoned at the start of the Revolutionary War, is now a historic site featuring an original brick bell tower and a tabby fort. South Carolina Parks says, "From 1697 until the beginning of the Revolutionary War, the trading town of Dorchester flourished along the Ashley River, inland from colonial Charleston. Today, Colonial Dorchester State Historic Site's remarkably preserved archaeological remains give visitors a peek into the early history of colonial South Carolina."

UFO Welcome Center

4004 Homestead Road, Bowman, SC
Donations

The UFO Welcome Center, located in the back yard of Jody Pendarvis, is home to a handmade, forty-two-foot-wide flying saucer. The wood, fiberglass and plastic saucer features a ramp that can be raised and lowered for entry. Nearby, he constructed a smaller saucer. Built in 1994, the structures have been featured on *The Daily Show* and in numerous publications.

SOUTH CAROLINA TOMBSTONE TALES

This section lists just a few of the state's intriguing headstones and the stories behind them. Most cemeteries are open during daylight hours only. Many do not have street numbers in their addresses, but those listed are as close as possible.

Agnes of Glasgow's Haunted Grave

Bethesda Presbyterian Church
502 East DeKalb Street, Camden, SC

Agnes of Glasgow (1760–1780), a native of Scotland, reportedly stowed away on a ship and came to the colonies to be with her lover, a British army officer. She arrived in Camden and wandered the countryside looking for him. Before she could locate him, Agnes died and was buried near this little church. Legend says her lonely ghost haunts the area.

Grave of Agnes of Glasgow in Camden, South Carolina. *Photo by Teresa Caldwell.*

Trapdoor Grave

Willowbrook Cemetery
212 Church Street, Edgefield, SC

When he died, Dr. James Adams Devore (1816–1884) left specific requests for his grave: He wanted a tunnel dug leading to his body, which was to be enclosed, sitting in a chair, behind a wall of glass. The entire grave was to be topped with a steel door. Reportedly, the orders were carried out to the letter.

Woman Who Lived as a Union Soldier

Florence National Cemetery
803 East National Cemetery Road, Florence, SC

Florena Budwin is buried beneath a traditional Union headstone. The only date on the stone is January 25, 1865. Her birth date is unknown. According to FindAGrave.com, Florena went to war with her husband, Captain John Budwin. Both were captured and sent to Andersonville, Georgia, as prisoners of war. She was transferred to the Florence Stockade in 1864 and eventually died while imprisoned. The fate of her husband, or whether "Florena Budwin" was her real name, is unknown.

233

Poor Alice Flagg Grave

All Saint's Church Cemetery
3560 Kings River Road, Pawley's Island, SC
843-237-4223

According to legend, Alice Flagg (circa 1834–1849) died as a teenager of a broken heart after her wealthy family prevented her from marrying someone beneath her social position. The grave is often covered with flowers, seashells or other trinkets in her memory.

Reportedly, Alice had become secretly engaged to the young man, but she was sent to boarding school in Charleston. She fell ill and returned home to be nursed but she soon died, some say from heartache.

The Rich Man's Pyramid

Magnolia Cemetery
70 Cunnington Avenue, Charleston, SC
843-722-8638

William Burroughs Smith (1815–1892) was billed the "richest man in Charleston" in his death announcement in the newspaper. According to FindaGrave.com, Smith's body was kept in the Magnolia Cemetery receiving tomb for two years while his special mausoleum was being designed and built. The pyramid was designed by local architect Edward C. Jones and completed in 1894. The pyramid features a Tiffany stained-glass window. Smith, his wife, their daughter and grandchildren are buried in the tomb.

The Little Boy Grave

Graniteville Cemetery
Gregg Highway, Graniteville, SC

The story behind this mysterious headstone is filled with supposition with very few facts behind it. But the indisputable fact remains that a headstone marked simply "The Little Boy" and the date "October 1855" is located in Graniteville Cemetery.

The legend, according to the *Aiken Standard* newspaper, says that the child was traveling by train alone from Charleston to Hamburg when he fell unconscious from an unknown illness. He was taken off the train and moved to a bed in the Graniteville Hotel. Attempts to revive the child, whose name and age were unknown, failed.

Townspeople, saddened at the loss of the boy with no identity, ensured he was buried in a nice casket in a plot in the city cemetery. The headstone, the article said, is a replacement for the original. Visitors to the boy's grave leave trinkets, including small toy cars, pinwheels and even a crocheted blanket.

Tennessee

You know you're in Tennessee when you see the words "a bust of Minnie Pearl made from chicken wire." The Volunteer State has plenty of other tributes to country artists, as well as fun stops such as the World's Largest Cedar Bucket and a giant mosaic dragon.

Billy Tripp's Mindfield is just that—a trip—and Millennium Manor will have you marveling at the ingenuity of the human mind. Those who prefer more thrills to their amusements can tour the Bell Witch Cave, visit Backyard Terrors Dinosaur Park or stop at a gorgeous marble mausoleum to look for the legendary bloodstains.

The cuteness factor reaches almost unbearable levels with the march of the Peabody Ducks and each Mule Day in Columbia. This list provides day and weekend trips for all ages.

TENNESSEE ROADSIDE ATTRACTIONS

This section includes objects you can see from the road, often free of charge.

Minnie Pearl Chicken Wire Bust

104 College Avenue, Centerville, TN

Minnie Pearl was born Sarah Ophelia Colley in 1912 in the tiny town of Centerville. Using the stage name "Minnie Pearl," she became a comedian who entertained fans for decades on the Grand Ole Opry and on the TV show *Hee Haw*. A bust in her likeness was created from chicken wire in 2016 by artist Ricky Pittman. It is located on the grounds of the Hickman County Courthouse.

Mills Darden, the Giant of Tennessee

1415 Midway Road, Darden, TN

At a time when the average male was five feet, six inches tall, one man stood out: Mills Darden, who was seven feet, six inches tall and weighed more than one thousand pounds. Born in North Carolina in October 1799 to John and Mary Darden, his name was often misspelled "Miles." He came with his family to Lexington, Tennessee. Mills was married and had several children with his wife, Mary, who was only four feet, eleven inches tall and weighed less than one hundred pounds.

According to the book *Every Day in Tennessee History* by James Jones, "a typical Miles Darden breakfast consisted of a dozen eggs, two quarts of coffee, a gallon of water, and 30 buttered biscuits."

A historical marker about him says, "Born in North Carolina in 1799, Darden settled in Henderson County about 1830s. He was an innkeeper and farmer, and physically one of the heaviest men ever to live in the world. At the time of his death, Darden weighed in excess of 1,000 pounds. He and his first wife are buried 1.7 miles north." The coffin he was buried in was reportedly eight feet long, thirty-five inches deep and thirty-two inches across at its widest.

Airplane Wing Sundial

3788 Central Pike, Hermitage, TN

In 2001, sculptor Joe Sorci erected an artwork made of two airplane wings embedded in the ground. The wings were positioned to form a sundial. The sculpture is located in a public park with a picnic area.

The Mom Who Swayed the Vote for Women's Rights

601 South Gay Street, Knoxville, TN

A statue in downtown Knoxville depicts the woman behind the man who helped pass the Nineteenth Amendment allowing women to vote. It shows Phoebe "Febb" Burn with her hand on the shoulder of her son, twenty-four-year-old Tennessee legislator Harry T. Burn. The monument was sculpted by Nashville artist Alan LeQuire and erected just a few steps from the Woman Suffrage Memorial, also sculpted by LeQuire. They were commissioned to celebrate the centennial of the passage of the amendment in 2020.

Here's the backstory: By the spring of 1920, thirty-five of the forty-eight states had ratified the Nineteenth Amendment granting women the right to vote. Thirty-six were needed. All hopes lay with Tennessee. The Tennessee Senate approved the amendment, but the first vote in the House ended in a tie: 48–48. When another vote was called, it was time for Harry Burn to make history. In his pocket, he carried a letter from his mother advising him to "be a good boy" and put the "rat" in ratification. Burn voted yes, and the vote was 49-48. On August 26, 1920, the Nineteenth Amendment to the Constitution became law.

Former World's Largest Rubik's Cube

Holiday Inn
525 Henley Street, Knoxville, TN
Free

Former world's largest Rubik's Cube in Knoxville, Tennessee. *Photo by Kelly Kazek.*

An oversized version of the iconic Rubik's Cube toy was created by Hungarian architecture professor Erno Rubik himself. It was built to be displayed at the 1982 World's Fair in Knoxville. It had mechanisms to make it move, but it no longer works. After the fair, it languished and was nearly discarded. The Holiday Inn on Henley Street in downtown Knoxville rescued it and put it on display. Visitors can walk into the lobby and see it.

Guinness World Records has since declared another cube as the world's largest, but the Holiday Inn still sells T-shirts for its unusual attraction. Just outside the Holiday Inn is the Sunsphere, also built for the 1982 World's Fair. Visitors can ride to the observation deck for stunning views of the city.

Giant Burger and Frenchie Fries

Pal's Sudden Service
Kingsport and various locations

Driving through northeastern Tennessee, travelers are likely to suddenly slow their cars to gawk at the giant food along the highway. The giant hot dog, hamburger, drink and "Frenchie" fries set atop a small building signal motorists that they have arrived at one of Tennessee's unique creations, a Pal's Sudden Service drive-through restaurant.

Pal's was the brainstorm of Fred "Pal" Barger, who opened his first Pal's in 1956 in Kingsport. It's still in business today. Barger decided on a clever marketing scheme when he built the second Pal's on Lynn Garden Drive in Kingsport. In 1962, he purchased a twenty-foot-tall Muffler Man holding a burger and installed it on the restaurant's roof. In 1984, Pal was discussing plans for a drive-through-only restaurant with artists Karen and Tony Barone. They sketched a building with a tiered front. On each "step" would be a giant food item—a burger, then a hot dog, then a drink and an order of Pal's specialty, Frenchie fries. The special facility was built by architect Tony Moore.

Pal's Sudden Service in Kingsport, Tennessee. *Photo by Kelly Kazek.*

Barger continued to expand his empire. The chain now includes twenty-two restaurants in northeastern Tennessee and southern Virginia, eighteen of which have giant food on the buildings.

World's Largest Cedar Bucket

Cannonsburgh Pioneer Village
312 South Front Street, Murfreesboro, TN

The World's Largest Cedar Bucket reigned in Murfreesboro from 1887 and 2005, when it was burned by arson. The bucket, which went to two world's fairs, was an impressive six feet high, nine feet around at the top and six feet around at the base. When it burned, a bucket in Oxford, Mississippi, became the world's largest. In 2011, a new bucket was built at Murfreesboro's Cannonsburgh Pioneer Village, and it reclaimed the title. The replacement is nearly six feet tall and it is six feet wide at its base and seven and a half feet wide at the top.

Mystical Mosaic Dragon

Fannie Mae Dees Park
2400 Blakemore Avenue, Nashville, TN

This colorful artwork by artist Pedro Silva was restored in 2018. Officially called *Sea Serpent*, the sculpture resembles the Loch Ness Monster.

Whisk for Biggest Omelet Ever

131 Twenty-First Avenue S, Nashville, TN

A sixteen-foot-tall whisk is one of about twenty artsy bicycle racks scattered throughout Nashville. The whisk is called *Good Eats* and was created by Memphis artist Wayne Henderson.

Eiffel Tower Replica, Tennessee

1020 Maurice Fields Drive, Paris, TN

The City of Paris, Tennessee, celebrates its connection to the French city with a sixty-foot-tall replica of the Eiffel Tower. It was donated to the city in 1992 by Christian Brothers University in Memphis, where it was built as an engineering project. It was erected in what is now called Eiffel Tower Park.

Airplane Filling Station

6829 Clinton Highway, Powell, TN
865-771-1174

A service station was built in 1931 in the shape of a plane, a relatively new form of transportation at the time. It was built by brothers Henry and Elmer Nickle to capitalize on the fascination with flight. It was abandoned for many years. In 2004, it was placed in the National Register of Historic Places, and in 2018, it was renovated and reopened as a barbershop. A historical marker was erected in the parking lot.

Giant Crane That's a Bird

2107 Frank Bird Boulevard, Rockford, TN

What do you do with a derelict warehouse crane? You could scrap it—or you could make it into a, well, crane. A crane of the feathered kind. In the field across from Axis Fabrication, a crane was turned into a giant yellow bird that lights up at night, thanks to solar panels on its wings.

Spaceship House in Tennessee

1408 Palisades Road, Signal Mountain, TN
Private residence; Drive-by only

The famous Spaceship House on Signal Mountain above Chattanooga was built in 1973 by Curtis King.

The two-thousand-square-foot, three-bedroom home is made of steel and cement and has a retractable staircase entry. The interior has a modern, space-age feel.

TENNESSEE OUTSIDER ART

This unique kind of roadside oddity comes in many forms. Some collections are indoors; some are outdoors. A few charge admission; others request donations. But the work never fails to astound and entertain.

Millennium Manor

500 North Wright Road, Alcoa, TN
Private residence; Drive-by only

William Andrew "W.A." Nicholson and his wife, Fair, moved to Tennessee in 1937 so he could take a job at the Alcoa plant. On land across the street, the couple began building Millennium Manor by hand, without use of machines. It was built to withstand Armageddon, William said. The Nicholsons lived in a home built from a kit until they completed the manor in 1946 and moved in. Fair died in 1950 and William in 1965. The manor fell into disrepair, but the current owner is reportedly renovating it.

Backyard Terrors Dinosaur Park

Backyard Terrors and Dinosaur Park in Bluff City, Tennessee. *Photo courtesy of Backyard Terrors.*

1065 Walnut Grove Road, Bluff City, TN
423-391-7017; Donations

What do you do when you dream of owning a life-sized dinosaur? If you're Chris Kastner, you build one…or forty. He built his first in 2007, and when passersby enjoyed stopping for photos, he built more and more and more until he had an entire herd of creatures. These days, Kastner's yard is a six-acre park he opens daily to the public. People come for picnics or to hold birthday parties or just to take photos. Currently, no admission is charged, but donations are welcomed. Kastner also operates a haunted house attraction called the Funhouse. Admission is charged for the haunted house.

Billy Tripp's Mindfield

8 South Monroe Avenue B, Brownsville, TN
731-772-0901

This amazing site has been an ongoing project for artist Billy Tripp since 1989. "Included in the network of steel are individual pieces representing various events and periods of Billy's life," according to the Mindfield website. He even salvaged a water tower from a Kentucky factory, brought it to the Mindfield and reconstructed it as a memorial to his parents. The works at the site illustrate Tripp's "belief in the inherent beauty of our world, and the importance of tolerance in our communities and governmental systems." Tripp plans to continue working on the site until his death and then hopes to be interred there.

Billy Tripp's Mindfield in Brownsville, Tennessee. *Courtesy of Thomas R Machnitzki/ Wikimedia Commons.*

Fortress of Faith

250 Lee Shirley Road, Greenback, TN
Donations

Junior Banks began building a castle on his property in 1993 at the age of forty-six. Since then, it has grown into a massive structure embedded with found objects, including some that Banks says contain messages from God. He's done all the work himself using salvaged building materials and claims to have spent only about $2,000 on the castle. After years of building, Banks noticed images that showed in the concrete or building materials that looked like faces or beasts, which he feels are messages from God.

E.T. Wickham Stone Park

3915 Oak Ridge Road, Palmyra, TN

Enoch Tanner Wickham (1883–1970) left behind a legacy of more than forty life-sized statues made of concrete. From 1950 until his death, Wickham built statues of famous figures and displayed them on concrete pedestals in a roadside park known as Wickham Stone Park.

Since his death, vandals destroyed many of the statues, removing many of their heads and limbs. In an effort to preserve them, some of the works were moved to the Trahern Art Building at Austin Peay State University in nearby Clarksville, and another was moved to Soldier's Chapel in Fort Campbell, Kentucky. Some can still be seen along Oak Ridge and Buck Smith Roads.

Headless statues of E.T. Wickham in Palmyra, Tennessee. *Photo by Kelly Kazek.*

TENNESSEE'S LEGENDARY LOCALES

This list describes places you will need to park your car and get out, including quirky museums, unusual historic homes and whimsical places to eat or stay overnight.

Bell Witch Cave

430 Keysburg Road, Adams, TN
615-696-3055; Admission fee

The legend of the Bell Witch is known as the most documented haunting in the nation and marked the only time in history a man's death was attributed to a spirit. The "haunting" of the Bell family began in the early 1800s on their farm in rural Robertson County along the Red River. Because the strange occurrences began not long after John Bell had a dispute with a neighbor

The Bell Witch Cave in Adams, Tennessee. *Photo by Kelly Kazek.*

named Kate Batts, the haunting was believed to have been instigated by Kate, who was labeled a witch.

Beginning in 1817, a sinister entity tormented the Bells, but particularly John and his daughter Betsy, one of his eight children. Until 1821, the attacks continued—pulling hair, kicking, slapping, yanking off bed covers—witnessed by many people in the community and recorded in affidavits and journals. John, born in 1750, would die in 1820.

The many eyewitness accounts and testimonials led a famed parapsychologist of the early twentieth century, Dr. Nandor Fodor, to label the legend "America's Greatest Ghost Story."

The Bell Witch Cave, which is near the property where the Bell farmhouse once stood, is open for tours. The owners built a cabin like the one thought to be used by the Bell family, and it houses some artifacts from the home, such as a chimney stone and an iron kettle. According to the cave's owners, Kate Batts haunted this cave and strange occurrences happen there to this day.

Home of Buford "Walking Tall" Pusser

342 Pusser Street, Adamsville, TN
731-632-4080; Admission fee

This home is a creepy yet educational memorial to the man whose story is told in the 1973 film *Walking Tall*. Buford Pusser was the real-life sheriff of McNairy County who became famous for his war against moonshiners, gamblers and prostitution. During that time, Pusser was stabbed, shot and run down by a car and his wife was murdered. He survived all that, but his car mysteriously crashed and burned in 1974, killing him.

His home was preserved as a memorial to the man who literally carried a big stick. Many of the family's possessions and furnishings remain in the home and the burned-out car in which Buford died is on display. Oh, and don't forget to buy a replica big stick in the gift shop on your way out.

Castle Gwynn

Home of the Renaissance Festival
2124 Newcastle Road, Arrington, TN
615-395-9950; Tours with admission to festival

This replica of a twelfth-century Welsh castle is actually a private home. But owners Mike and Jackie Freeman make it the centerpiece of the annual Tennessee Renaissance Festival each May. During the festival, which the Freemans began in 1986, the castle is open for tours. The castle also appeared in Taylor Swift's music video *Love Story*. The festival includes entertainers dressed in Renaissance clothing, jousting tournaments, artisans and food vendors.

Tina Turner Museum

121 Sunny Hill Cove, Brownsville, TN
731-779-9000; Free

The one-room elementary school Tina Turner attended now houses a museum in her honor. Flagg Grove School was built in the 1880s as one of the first schools for African Americans in the South. The building was originally located in the small town of Nutbush, where Turner grew up. The museum includes a collection of photographs, outfits from some of her most famous performances, gold and platinum records and old yearbooks. The museum is part of the West Tennessee Delta Heritage Center, which also includes the childhood home of blues musician Sleepy John Estes, located next door, and exhibits dedicated to the area's heritage and blues history.

Johnny Cash "One Piece at a Time" Cadillac

Storytellers Hideaway Farm and Museum
9347 Old Highway 46, Bon Aqua, TN
931-996-4336; Admission fee

Housed in a farmhouse Johnny Cash used to get away from it all, this museum tells about Cash's life as well as the history of the region. The centerpiece of the collection is a "one piece at a time" Cadillac built by Bill Patch of Welch, Oklahoma, in honor of Cash's humorous hit about a man working on an assembly line who smuggled parts out one by one until he had a Cadillac. Patch's stunning black Caddy has the requisite misfit pieces. The car has moved around some over the years, so check before going to be sure it's still there.

Sleep in a Pullman Car

Chattanooga Choo Choo
1400 Market Street, Chattanooga, TN
423-266-5000

Housed in the historic 1909 Terminal Station, the Chattanooga Choo Choo Historic Hotel offers overnight stays in Pullman train cars, as well as lodging in the terminal itself. The station was headed for demolition in 1973 when it was saved and turned into a hotel. The terminal, owned by the Southern Railway, is listed in the National Register of Historic Places. It was built in the Beaux Arts style, and its domed lobby ceiling gives it a grand feel. The property includes restaurants, bars, music venues and retail stores.

Mule Capital of the World

Columbia, TN
West Seventh Street, Columbia, TN
931-381-9557

The time to visit Columbia is for the annual Mule Day festivities each April. Events include a mule parade, crowning of a Mule Day queen, a mule pull and a liar's contest. In other months, Columbia offers quaint shops in its picturesque historic downtown, with the main attractions being the home of President James Polk and the historic 1835 Athenaeum Rectory, which showcases Gothic and Moorish architecture.

Hidden Hollow

1901 Mount Pleasant Road, Cookeville, TN
931-526-4038; Admission fee

In the 1970s, Arda E. Lee created the eighty-six-acre Hidden Hollow park on her family's farm. Lee claimed he had a vision from God instructing him to build a park where families could enjoy time together. The self-made theme park includes a fifty-foot-tall illuminated cross, gem mining, miniature golf, paddle boats, a pond for fishing and swimming, a petting zoo, playgrounds and picnic areas.

Bush's Beans Museum

3901 U.S. Highway 411, Dandridge, TN
865-509-3077; Free

Located in A.J. Bush & Company general store, where Bush's Beans began in 1897, this museum dedicated to all things beany is entertaining and tasty. It is free to tour the visitor center—which includes seeing a film and walking through a giant can of beans while learning the history of the company—but tours are also offered with lunch for a fee. The meal, of course, includes beans. A gift shop sells all kinds of souvenirs, including a plush version of the company's popular spokes-dog, Duke.

Sir Goony's Family Fun Center

10925 Kingston Pike, Farragut, TN
865-675-3262; Admission Fee

Lovers of old-time miniature golf courses should visit Sir Goony's, which has an original Goonysaurus. The handmade orange dinosaur has glowing eyes and a bone for a cane. Goony Golf was E.K. "Dutch" Magrath's version of Florida's Goofy Golf chain. He opened the first course in Chattanooga in 1960.

Gathering of Synchronous Fireflies

Great Smoky Mountains National Park
Sugarlands Visitors Center
1420 Fighting Creek Gap Road, Gatlinburg, TN
865-436-1200; Free

Smoky Mountains National Park is one of the few places in the nation where a special type of firefly gathers and lights in unison each spring as part of a mating ritual. The lightning bugs can be seen at a viewing area in Elkmont Campground, and the park offers shuttle service from the Sugarlands Visitor Center.

According to the Great Smoky Mountains National Park website, the fireflies "take from one to two years to mature from larvae, but will live as adults for only about 21 days. While in the larval stage, the insects feed on snails and smaller insects. Once they transform into their adult form, they do not eat."

The lighting patterns are part of their mating ritual. "Each species has a flash pattern that helps male and female recognize each other," the website says. The males flash while flying, and the females usually flash while stationary.

Salt and Pepper Shaker Museum

461 Brookside Village Way, Gatlinburg, TN
865-430-5515; Admission fee

Who hasn't dreamed of seeing more than twenty thousand sets of salt and pepper shakers all in one locale? This quirky museum—the only other one like it in the world is its sister museum in Spain—is the place to see shaker sets from a variety of eras made from all kinds of materials. From shakers that look like headstones or skulls to monks and cartoon characters, visitors have plenty to see.

Deadly Safe of Jack Daniel

Jack Daniel's Distillery
280 Lynchburg Highway, Lynchburg, TN
931-759-6357; Admission fee

Jack Daniel's safe in his office at Jack Daniel Distillery in Lynchburg, Tennessee. *Photo by Kelly Kazek.*

Jack Daniel is one of the most well-known names in the country, but not as many know Jasper Newton Daniel, which was Jack's birth name. Jack was famous for the whiskey he created, and even today his distillery is a popular tourist destination.

Jack's method of death would only add to the distiller's legend. The oft-repeated story, which is told on distillery tours, states that Jack arrived at work early the morning of October 10, 1911, and attempted to open his office safe. He had problems with the combination and could not manage to open it. In frustration, he kicked the solid metal safe, breaking his toe.

An infection set in, causing gangrene. After several years, Jack succumbed to blood poisoning. The offending safe remains at the distillery and is shown on tours. The running joke is that the moral of Jack's story is "Never go to work early." According to legend, his last words were "One last drink, please." This unusual death was portrayed on Spike TV's show *1,000 Ways to Die*. Jack is buried in Lynchburg City Cemetery.

Crystal Shrine Grotto

5668 Poplar Avenue, Memphis, TN
901-767-8930; Free

Crystal Shrine Grotto in Memorial Park Cemetery in Memphis. *Courtesy of doxtxob/Wikimedia Commons.*

This unusual oasis is located inside a man-made cave on the grounds of Memorial Park Cemetery. Known as the Crystal Shrine Grotto, it was created by artist Dionicio Rodriguez in the 1930s after he was hired by Elliott Clovis Hinds, the owner of the cemetery. According to the Memorial Park Cemetery history, Dionicio dug the cave sixty feet into a hill so he could create the grotto.

Dionicio "decorated the interior with faux crags made of cement and quartz crystals," the Memorial Park Cemetery website said. "Beautiful crystals are exposed to the sunlight on the exterior end to create gorgeous glowing effects. The stonework around the grotto showcases a series of biblical tableaus with two-dimensional figures depicting the life of Jesus Christ."

He created many of the scenes in the grotto but did not create figural art for the niches before leaving the project. Nearly half a century later, artist David Day added biblical figures. The grotto was listed in the National Register of Historic Places in 1991.

Peabody Ducks

Peabody Hotel
118 South Second Street, Memphis, TN
901-529-4000; Free

The Peabody is likely the only luxury hotel in the world known first and foremost for its daily duck parade. Visitors, including those who aren't staying at the hotel, flock to the lobby to watch the ducks who live on the roof be brought down to the fountain for a swim.

The tradition began in the 1930s when manager Frank Schutt and a friend, Chip Barwick, returned from a weekend hunting trip to Arkansas.

The ducks at the
Peabody Hotel in
Memphis, Tennessee.
*Courtesy of Enoch Lai/
Wikimedia Commons.*

The hotel's online history explains: "The men had a little too much Tennessee sippin' whiskey, and thought it would be funny to place some of their live duck decoys (it was legal then for hunters to use live decoys) in the beautiful Peabody fountain. Three small English call ducks were selected as 'guinea pigs,' and the reaction was nothing short of enthusiastic. Thus began a Peabody tradition which was to become internationally famous."

It was a bellhop who created the duck march, however. In 1940, former circus animal trainer Edward Pembroke taught the fowl the now-famous Peabody Duck March. Pembroke served as the Peabody Duckmaster for fifty years until his retirement in 1991.

Ducks visit the lobby fountain each day at 11:00 a.m. and 5:00 p.m. They ride the elevator from their rooftop perch, known as the Royal Duck Palace, to the lobby. Each duck serves only three months as a marcher before being returned to the wild, so the staff takes care not to domesticate them. Of course, duck souvenirs are also available to guests.

Walk the Mississippi River

Mud Island River Park
125 North Front Street, Memphis
901-576-7241; Free

In Memphis, you can see the entire Mississippi River, the fourth-longest river in the world, in one short outing. The River Walk is a five-block replica of the lower Mississippi River, from Cairo, Illinois, to New Orleans, Louisiana. According to its online history, "Each 30-inch stride is equivalent to one

Mud Island River Park in Memphis. *Courtesy of Thomas R Machnitzki/Wikimedia Commons.*

mile on the actual river. Along your journey, you'll revisit historical events and learn about geographical transformations. The '1,000-mile' journey concludes at the Gulf of Mexico, a one-acre enclosure that holds 1.3 million gallons of water. There, visitors can enjoy a leisurely pedal boat ride around the Gulf area with the Memphis skyline in the background." The park is closed in winter months, as is the adjoining Mississippi River Museum.

Birthplace of Rock and Roll

Sun Studio
706 Union Avenue, Memphis
901-521-0664; Admission fee

Sun Studio in Memphis, Tennessee. *Courtesy of David Jones/Wikimedia Commons.*

Sun Studio is best known as the place where eighteen-year-old Elvis Presley recorded his first song, but Elvis was only one of many people who became stars under the tutelage of Sam Phillips at Sun Studio. When it opened in 1950, the business was called Memphis Recording Studio. In the early days of rock and roll, artists recording at Sun included B.B. King, Johnny Cash,

254

Carl Perkins, Jerry Lee Lewis and Roy Orbison. Today, visitors can tour the studio and stand in the footsteps of these larger-than-life legends, as well as see memorabilia from that era.

Cannonsburgh Village

312 South Front Street, Murfreesboro, TN
615-890-0355; Free

This pioneer village includes numerous buildings that represent Tennessee life from the 1830s to the 1930s. The village includes a school, a gristmill, a museum, a caboose, a telephone operator's house, the University House, the Leeman House, the Wedding Chapel, a doctor's office, a general store and a blacksmith's shop, a well and other points of pioneering interest.

Cooter's Place Store and Museum

2613 McGavock Pike, Nashville
615-872-8358

Ben Jones, who portrayed Cooter on *The Dukes of Hazzard*, runs a souvenir business and museum for fans of the TV show. Enthusiasts can have photos made with the iconic car known as the General Lee, as well as view photos, props, costumes and memorabilia from the show. Several other cars are displayed, including Cooter's Tow Truck, Daisy's Jeep and Rosco's patrol car. Cooter's Place also sells every kind of *Dukes of Hazzard* souvenir imaginable. He has three other stores, located in Gatlinburg, Pigeon Forge and Luray.

Nashville's Parthenon

2500 West End Avenue, Nashville, TN
615-862-8431; Admission fee

A full-scale replica of Greece's Parthenon is the centerpiece of Nashville's Centennial Park. The replica was constructed of plaster, wood and brick as a temporary exhibit for Tennessee's 1897 Centennial Exposition. The

Parthenon replica in Nashville, Tennessee. *Courtesy of Mayur Phadtare/Wikimedia Commons.*

building was so popular, and the cost of demolishing it so high, that it was left standing after the fair. In 1920, crews began reconstructing the replica, this time using concrete. The exterior was completed in 1925, the interior in 1931. Inside the Parthenon, now used as a tourist attraction and art gallery, stands a forty-two-foot replica of the statue of Athena, just like the one in ancient Greece.

The Secret Atomic City

Oak Ridge City Hall
200 South Tulane Avenue, Oak Ridge, TN
865-425-3411

The city of Oak Ridge, Tennessee, was once a huge secret project created by the U.S. government. The entire town was developed in 1942 so that the United States and its allies could work secretly on the Manhattan Project with the purpose of building an atomic bomb.

According to the Atomic Heritage Foundation, Oak Ridge was the home of the uranium enrichment plants K-25 and Y-12; the liquid thermal diffusion plant S-50; and the pilot plutonium production X-10 Graphite Reactor.

People working on the project lived in prefabricated homes or dorms. The project ended after World War II, and the "secret" town was officially placed on maps as Oak Ridge.

Today, the Oak Ridge National Laboratory and the Y-12 National Security Complex still operate there. The town acknowledges its history with the Manhattan Project National Historical Park, which includes tours of the 1943 X-10 nuclear reactor, which is the oldest in the world, and other buildings used in the project. Visitors can also tour the American Museum of Science and Industry and see the four-ton bronze International Friendship Bell sent from Japan to celebrate peace between the nations.

The Lost Sea

140 Lost Sea Road, Sweetwater, TN
423-337-6616; Admission fee

The Lost Sea is located deep inside a mountain in East Tennessee. The body of water, listed by the Guinness Book of World Records as America's largest underground lake, is part of a cave system called Craighead Caverns.

The trip into the caverns starts with a walking tour followed by a ride in a glass-bottomed boat along the Lost Sea.

Although the cave system was used by Native Americans, the lake wasn't discovered until 1905, when a thirteen-year-old boy named Ben Sands wiggled through a small hole and found it, according to the Lost Sea's online history. The size of the lake is still unknown since its edges have not been found.

Trenton Teapot Museum

309 South College Street, Trenton, TN
731-855-2013; Free

The World's Largest Collection of Porcelain Veilleuses-Theieres (night-light teapots) is located adjacent to the Trenton, Tennessee Police Department. Visitors can view 526 small teapots, equipped with a matching porcelain stand or oil vessel to light as a warmer. The collection of pots from around the world, including Asia, Europe and Africa, is valued at more than $3 million. The pots date from 1750 to 1869 and were collected by Dr. Frederick Freed. Call to set up a guided tour or enter through the police department.

TENNESSEE TOMBSTONE TALES

This section lists just a few of the state's intriguing headstones and the stories behind them. Most cemeteries are open during daylight hours only. Many do not have street numbers in their addresses, but those listed are as close as possible.

Old Isham the War Horse Grave

French Brantley Road, Beech Grove, TN
Located behind a wooden fence between Interstate 24 and Highway 41

Just outside of Beech Grove is a lonely grave, once forgotten, that bears the remains of Old Isham, known as the Rebel war horse. Isham was the horse of Confederate general Benjamin Franklin Cheatham. The horse was named for Isham Harris, Confederate governor of Tennessee. Old Isham's date of death is unknown, but it was in the 1880s, a few years before Cheatham's death in 1886. Cheatham buried Isham with full military honors.

The grave was left unattended for decades but was rediscovered in the early 2000s. In 2002, a unit of the Sons of Confederate Veterans placed a tombstone on the grave, built a wooden fence around it and installed a Confederate flag. His marker is inscribed: "Old Isham, CSA, Honored Mount of Gen. Cheatham."

Dammit the Dog

Ninth Street, Cookeville, TN
Near the intersection with Dixie Avenue

A small marker flush with the ground on the campus of Tennessee Tech University marks the grave of Dammit the Dog, a beloved campus companion who died in 1954. Nearby is a red fire hydrant, supposedly for Dammit's use in the afterlife. The stray wandered onto campus in 1950 and reportedly got his name when a student said "Damn it" and, to cover his lapse in manners, said it was the dog's name. The grave and fire hydrant are on the lawn across from Derryberry Hall.

The Blood-Stained Crypt of Nina Craigmiles

320 Broad Street NW, Cleveland, TN

The beautiful and historic St. Luke's Episcopal Church is a landmark in Cleveland that has been the site of many happy events, but its origins lie with one of the city's most tragic families. The church was a gift to the city from John Henderson and Myra Adelia Thompson Craigmiles in 1872 in memory of their daughter, Nina.

On October 18, 1871, when Nina was seven years old, she went on a ride with her grandfather and their buggy crashed, killing the little girl. Nina's tragic death shocked the town's residents, but it is said no one grieved as deeply as her father, who adored his little girl. John Craigmiles decided to build an Episcopal church in Nina's memory. No expense was spared. In the churchyard, the Craigmileses constructed a mausoleum of Carrara marble that cost as much as $50,000, or nearly as much as the cost of building the church. It would house Nina's remains and be available for future Craigmiles family burials.

Upon its completion, the church was named St. Luke's Memorial Episcopal Church. Historians say the building is one of the few Oxford Movement Gothic churches in the world to maintain its integrity. The only additions over the decades have been electricity, air conditioning and heating.

The mausoleum also is an architectural prize with its Gothic spires and statues of angels holding lambs and crosses. Above the metal doors is etched: "J.H. Craigmiles." On the doors themselves are the words: "Nina, October 1871." Nina's remains lie inside in a marble sarcophagus etched with the words, "Fell asleep October 18, 1871." Her parents are also interred in the

The red-stained marble on the mausoleum of Nina Craigmiles in Cleveland, Tennessee. *Photo by Kelly Kazek.*

mausoleum, which is often visited by photographers and the curious because of the eerie mystery surrounding it.

At some point following Nina's entombment, red stains appeared on the white marble exterior of the mausoleum. Efforts to remove the stains failed. According to legend, the stained marble blocks were replaced several times, but the red stains always returned. Reddish tints can be seen in parts of the marble to this day.

Casey Jones Hero Train Engineer Grave

The grave of hero Casey Jones in Mount Calvary Cemetery in Jackson, Tennessee. *Courtesy of Wikimedia Commons.*

Mount Calvary Cemetery
419 Hardee Street, Jackson, TN

The grave of John Luther "Casey" Jones (1864–1900) is marked by a monument etched with the words: "This memorial was erected in 1947 to perpetuate the legend of American Railroading and the man whose name became its symbol of daring and romance." Jones was the engineer of the Illinois Central No. 1, or the Cannonball Express, when it became a runaway train on April 30, 1900. He stayed with the train until the end, attempting to slow it as much as possible before impact. He was the only one who died in the ensuing crash, and his actions are thought to have saved many lives. Jones's story has been the subject of songs, books and movies.

Dorothy Marie's Playhouse Grave

Hope Hill Cemetery
Hope Hill Cemetery Road, Medina, TN

The small playhouse looks more suited to a child's backyard than a cemetery. The unusual monument marks the grave of Dorothy Marie Harvey, who died in 1931 when she was only five years old.

According to local lore, Dorothy Marie, who was born on February 4, 1926, was traveling north with her parents, who were looking for work. But while passing through Medina, the child contracted measles and died. Legend says Dorothy Marie loved dolls so much that the playhouse was built over her tombstone. The interior of the house is filled with dolls and toys. The house has been replaced several times over the years after it deteriorated or was vandalized.

Builder of Parthenon Replica Buried in a Pyramid

Mount Olivet Cemetery
1101 Lebanon Pike, Nashville, TN
615-255-4193

Eugene Lewis was a dreamer but one who tended to make dreams a reality. When he was named director general of the Tennessee Centennial Exposition held in Nashville in 1897, the chief civil engineer for the Nashville, Chattanooga and St. Louis Railroad had an idea: Build a replica of the Parthenon to showcase Nashville's reputation as the "Athens of the South."

The Tennessee Centennial Exposition opened on May 1 and entertained 1.8 million visitors over six months. The Parthenon was the centerpiece of the exhibit, which also included a pyramid, but unlike the Parthenon, the pyramid was meant to be temporary, to last only as long as the exposition.

Following the Exposition, the grounds were converted to Centennial Park, a permanent city park with the Parthenon at its center. The wood-and-plaster replica remained until 1920, when it was rebuilt with concrete. Lewis, born in 1845, also was a force behind Nashville's Union Station, built in 1900. When Lewis died in 1917, he was buried in a pyramid-shaped crypt guarded by stone sphinxes in Nashville's Mount Olivet Cemetery.

Wade Bolton's Eternally Crossed Fingers

Elmwood Cemetery
824 South Dudley Street, Memphis, TN
901-774-3212

Prominent Memphis citizen Wade Hampton Bolton was known for his philanthropy. He was a benefactor to the Bolton School and Stonewall

Two views of the statue of Wade Bolton in Elmwood Cemetery in Memphis. *Photo by Kelly Kazek.*

Jackson's widow. But in life, Bolton was, by all accounts, a man who earned little affection.

The Bolton family was embroiled in a notorious ongoing feud with the Dickens family. On July 14, 1869, Wade H. Bolton was shot and killed by Tom Dickens at Memphis's court square. Dickens was arrested and put on trial, but he was found not guilty. A year later, Dickens, too, was murdered. Wade Bolton's true nature is evident in the terms of his will, in which family members were left mostly with harsh words. He did, however, leave $10,000 "to the widow of Gen. T.J. Jackson, who fell at the battle of Chancellorsville," and an endowment that was used to found Bolton College, which is now Bolton High School.

The terms of Bolton's will also stated he wanted a statue on his grave that depicted him as he was in life. His family complied. On the beautiful grounds of Memphis's historic Elmwood Cemetery stands a life-sized statue of a man, scowling down at visitors, with his fingers crossed behind his back, his vest buttoned incorrectly and his shoes untied.

Napoleon Tomb Replica

Mt. Olivet Cemetery
1101 Lebanon Pike, Nashville, TN
615-255-4193

In Nashville's Mt. Olivet Cemetery, visitors come across a stately looking sarcophagus made of black marble at the top of a set of steps. The sarcophagus bears the name "Vernon King Stevenson" and is a replica, with the exception of the material, of Napoleon Bonaparte's tomb in Paris, which is made of red porphyry. Inside that tomb, Bonaparte's body lies within five other coffins: one of iron, one of mahogany, two of lead and another of ebony.

Stevenson's tomb may give the impression that Stevenson was a prominent citizen, which he was, and that he was loved by Nashvillians, which he wasn't. Known as the "Father of Tennessee Railroads," Stevenson helped put Nashville on the map by building the Nashville and Chattanooga Railroad in 1848 when he was thirty-six years old. Of course, as he had purchased land along the route in the years leading up to its completion, the railroad made Stevenson a wealthy man.

He was named a major in the Confederate army's Quartermaster Department, but his reputation was tarnished when he abandoned his duties and fled the city on one of his trains during the Great Panic of 1862.

He moved his family and belongings south but left behind many of the army's supplies. He moved to New York in 1864.

Fifteen years after war's end, Stevenson earned the ire of Nashvillians once again when he sold the Louisville and Nashville Railroad and it was no longer headquartered in the city. He died in 1884. No explanation is given for the extravagant monument, and one can only assume that, like Bonaparte, Stevenson considered himself a conqueror.

Vernon King Stevenson is buried in Nashville's Mt. Olivet Cemetery in a replica of Napoleon Bonaparte's tomb. *Photo by Kelly Kazek.*

Beautiful Jim Key Grave

110 Himesville Road, Shelbyville, TN

A 1904 advertisement invited the public to see Beautiful Jim Key at the World's Fair in St. Louis. Price of admission was fifteen cents, a fair amount considering visitors would get to see a horse who, according to the ad, "Reads, Writes, Spells, Counts, Figures, Changes Money Using a National Cash Register, Even Gives Bible Quotations."

Jim Key was a stallion foaled in Shelbyville in 1889. He was owned by a former slave known as Dr. William Key, a self-trained veterinarian. The horse was purported to have the IQ of a human sixth grader and could tell time, sort mail, use a telephone and more. He and his owner became renowned in 1897 and performed across the country.

Jim Key was billed as the "smartest horse in the world" and was valued at $1 million. He spelled his name using alphabet blocks and solved math problems using numbered blocks.

Doc trained Jim Key from a foal and traveled the world giving performances. He would insist on giving special performances for black audiences at a discount and convinced planners of the world's fair in Charleston, South Carolina, to have a day exclusively for black audiences.

Dr. Key died in 1909, three years before his beloved horse. He is buried in Willow Mount Cemetery. The remains of the horse were moved from Key's property in 1967 to a field three miles south of the Shelbyville courthouse on Highway 130.

Strolling Jim Grave

Walking Horse Hotel
101 Spring Street, Wartrace, TN
931-389-7050

Near the stables of the Walking Horse Hotel in Wartrace is a granite monument to a horse that defined a breed. Strolling Jim was the first world champion Tennessee Walking Horse, a show breed.

Strolling Jim won twelve straight walking horse sweepstakes before winning the first Tennessee Walking Horse National Celebration in 1939. The next year, he again won twelve straight stakes and also was crowned grand champion at the Tennessee State Fair Show in Nashville. He would continue to win shows and astound audiences throughout his life.

Strolling Jim died at age twenty-one on April 23, 1957, in Wartrace and was buried near the hotel stables. The restaurant at the hotel is named Strolling Jim Restaurant and houses what the owner claims is the world's largest collection of Tennessee Walking Horse photos and art. Visitors can watch films of Strolling Jim on video monitors and purchase Strolling Jim hats and T-shirts in the gift shop.

Texas

exas is big. We got that. So we know there are plenty of world's largest things to see there, including a Bowie knife, longhorn steer, killer bee, rattlesnake, cowboy boots, caterpillar and pecan, among others. But you can also visit the World's Smallest Active Catholic Church and a scale replica of China's Terra Cotta Army.

The Lone Star State also has lots of fun western and pioneer sites, such as the historic Fort Worth Stockyards, which holds daily cattle drives, ghost towns and tributes to Davy Crockett. In Grapevine, visitors can see a daily shootout between animatronic cowboys who come out of a giant cuckoo-type clock.

Texans also love their junk—there's actually a Cathedral of Junk, as well as junked Cadillacs wedged into the earth and a house covered in beer cans. It might take years to see all the weirdness Texas has to offer, but it will be worth it.

TEXAS ROADSIDE ODDITIES

This section includes objects you can see from the road, often free of charge.

Dr. Seuss Park & Storybook Town

Abilene, TX

Abilene, billed the Storybook Capital of America, is home to "the largest collection of public Storybook Sculptures of its kind in America, if not the world," according to the city's website. The statues feature characters from classic children's stories, as well as from Dr. Seuss's books. The city is also home to the National Center for Children's Illustrated Literature and host to the Children's Art & Literacy Festival the second weekend of each June.

Midpoint of Route 66 Museum

301 Route 66, Adrian, TX

Thousands of motorists driving along Route 66 stop to take photos with a sign in Adrian, Texas, announcing the highway's midpoint. There are photo ops at the sign on the side of the road and a Route 66 emblem and a midpoint line painted on the road itself. (Just be safe and don't selfie in the road, y'all.) You can also stop for a bite at the Midpoint Café. Call 806-538-6215 for information.

Statue of Bevo, World's Largest Longhorn

22298 San Antonio Street, Austin, TX
512-476-7211

This statue named for the University of Texas mascot is located behind the University Co-op, a campus book and supply store.

Giant Taco Goddess

Maria's Taco Xpress
2529 South Lamar Boulevard, Austin, TX
512-444-0261

The larger-than-life sculpture of Maria Corbalan on the roof of Taco Xpress is known as the "Taco Goddess."

Nessy the Lakeness Dragon

4550 Mueller Lake Park
Simond Avenue, Austin, TX

Nessy, a creature covered in shimmery, handmade tiles, delights visitors to Austin's Mueller Lake Park. The sixteen-foot-high, thirty-foot-long sculpture is the creation of renowned artist Dixie Friend Gay.

World's Largest Bowie Knife

1600 block of East Wise Street, Bowie, TX

In 2016, this huge knife was unveiled next to the Welcome to Bowie sign. It was certified by Guinness World Records in 2017.

Hygieostatic Bat Roost

109 Farm-to-Market Road 473, Comfort, TX
Private residence; Drive-by only

A historic structure located beside the road in Kendall County piques the curiosity of passersby. The name raises more questions than it answers—it is a Hygieostatic Bat Roost. In 1918, Albert Steves, a mayor pro tempore of San Antonio, asked a local health officer, Dr. Charles A.R. Campbell, to design a structure to help control the spread of malaria by encouraging bats to come into the area to eat the disease-carrying mosquitoes.

The special roost is a thirty-foot-high raised tower with a pyramid-shaped roof. A concrete base was built seven feet from the ground to allow wagons to drive beneath it to collect the bats' guano.

Campbell patented the bat roost design, and more than a dozen were built worldwide. One other survives on private property in Orange, Texas, while a second one in Sugarloaf Key, Florida, survived until it was toppled by Hurricane Irma in 2017.

Not One, but Two Popeye Statues

City Hall
101 East Dimmit Street, Crystal City, TX

Thanks to the *Popeye* comic strip, business in Crystal City was booming in the 1930s. Its spinach factory was turning out ten thousand cans a day after Popeye made the vegetable popular. Crystal City, billed as the World Spinach Capital, holds an annual Spinach Festival and erected a Popeye statue in front of city hall in 1937. A second statue was erected inside the chamber of commerce.

Giant Bowler Hat

Griffin Street E, Dallas, TX

A two-ton, twenty-foot-wide bowler hat created by artist Keith Turman is located in a vacant lot off Griffin Street between Browder and South Ervay Streets.

Giant Eyeball

1607 Main Street, Dallas, TX

A thirty-foot-high bloodshot eyeball created by artist Tony Tassert arrived in Dallas in 2013 after initially being displayed in Chicago, then Wisconsin.

Giant Rooftop Jackalope

5925 Camp Bowie Boulevard, Fort Worth, TX

In 1982, artist Nancy Lam added antlers to an eight-foot-high bunny statue to create a likeness of the legendary cryptid the Jackalope.

Paisano Pete, Giant Roadrunner

Intersection of Highway 290 and Main Street, Fort Stockton, TX

When he was built in 1979, Pete was the World's Largest Roadrunner at twenty-two feet long and eleven feet high. One was built of metal and other found objects in Las Cruces, New Mexico, that is twenty feet high and forty feet long, but Pete still proudly represents his species as the mascot of Fort Stockton.

World's Largest Rattlesnake

Freer Chamber of Commerce
5344 Texas Highway 44, Freer, TX
361-394-6891

A giant rattlesnake is coiled outside the Freer Chamber of Commerce to commemorate the town's annual Rattlesnake Round Up.

Roadside Giants of Glenn Goode

1651 Farm-to-Market Road 371, Gainesville, TX

The late Glenn Goode collected oversized fiberglass statues on his property in Gainesville and was known as the "Fiberglass Man." His collection includes a Big John Grocery Man, Muffler Man, Cowboy Muffler Man and Uniroyal Tire Gal. They can still be seen on his property, but time may be running out: He requested the statues remain for five years following his death on March 14, 2015, before being sold.

Galveston Great Storm Memorial

4800 Seawall Boulevard, Galveston, TX

In 1900, a massive hurricane swept across Galveston, killing more than six thousand people. The Galveston Commission for the Arts commissioned a memorial statue by artist David W. Moore. It was erected in 2000, the year before Moore's death.

Galveston Giant

2627 Avenue M, Galveston, TX

A statue honors Jack Johnson, the Galveston Giant, the first African American heavyweight boxing champion. The statue, however, is not "giant." It is much smaller than the six-foot, two-inch Johnson.

Statue of "Three-Legged" Texas Ranger

Williamson Museum on the Georgetown Square
716 South Austin Avenue, Georgetown, TX
512-943-1670

Robert McAlpin Williamson (circa 1804–1859) was an important man in Texas history—he was a lawmaker, newspaper editor and supreme court justice for the Republic of Texas and was responsible for organizing the Texas Rangers. In Williamson County, which is named for him, a statue was erected in his honor, but it is his unusual physical feature that draws people to the site. Williamson contracted tuberculosis arthritis at the age of fifteen, and it left his right leg bent at a ninety-degree angle. To enable him to walk, doctors attached a wooden leg at the knee, leaving the bent portion, which resulted in the nickname "Three-Legged Willie." It didn't seem to diminish his accomplishments. The statue was erected in 2013.

Glockenspiel Clock Tower Shootout

Grapevine Convention & Visitors Bureau Headquarters
636 South Main Street, Grapevine, TX
817-410-3185

A 127-foot-high Glockenspiel Clock Tower stands sentry over Main Street with the aid of two nine-foot-tall characters known as the "Would-Be Train Robbers." The figures, known locally as Nat and Willy, emerge from the tower each day, every two hours, from 10:00 a.m. to 8:00 p.m. The Grapevine, Texas website says, "Visitors gather each day to see this exciting glockenspiel experience. Just as glockenspiels in Europe are rooted in history, Grapevine's Clock Tower figures reflect the Western lore that many visitors from outside Texas find interesting and entertaining."

Leaning Water Tower of Britten

Exit 114, Interstate 40 (Route 66), Groom, TX

Ralph Britten, owner of a Route 66 truck stop and diner, wanted to find a way to lure travelers off the road and into his wallet. According to an article on the Texas Hill Country website, "An intentional display that deliberately grabs your attention…the Britten Leaning Water Tower was set on a lean as a marketing tool. And it worked. Motorists passing by this Texas roadside oddity would often pull off Route 66 (now Interstate 40) to make sure their eyes weren't deceiving them, and wind up at Ralph Britten's truck stop and restaurant."

The leaning water tower of Groom, Texas. *Courtesy of Carol M. Highsmith/ Library of Congress.*

World's Largest Killer Bee

Hidalgo City Hall
704 East Texano Drive, Hidalgo, TX
956-843-2286

People of a certain age recall the Killer Bee invasion of the 1990s, when some African Queen bees escaped a lab in South America and made their way to Hidalgo. To commemorate the event, city officials erected a ten-foot-high, twenty-foot-long bee statue, which has been featured in *Time* and the *Guinness Book of World Records*, among others.

World's Largest Killer Bee in Hidalgo, Texas. *Courtesy of Carol M. Highsmith/ Library of Congress.*

Thirty-Six-Foot-Tall Fab Four

8th Wonder Brewery
2202 Dallas Street, Houston, TX
713-581-2337

An impressively large tribute to the Beatles by well-known local sculptor David Adickes is currently on display in the parking lot at 8th Wonder Brewery.

Eiffel Tower Replica, Texas

18608 Ranch Road 1431, Jonestown, TX

This 1/50-scale replica of the Eiffel Tower was built in France and was located in Austin from 1998 to 2013. The twenty-one-foot-high tower has been in Jonestown since 2018.

An Eiffel Tower replica in Texas. *Courtesy of Carol M. Highsmith/ Library of Congress.*

Marfa Lights Viewing Area

U.S. Highway 90, Marfa, TX

For more than a century, people have claimed to see mysterious orbs of light that dance along the horizon southeast of Marfa. Known as the Marfa Lights, they are typically red, blue or white. People have seen the lights from many different places, but there is an official Marfa Lights Viewing Area located nine miles east of town on U.S. Highway 90, toward Alpine.

Davy Crockett Statue

Ozona City Park
Eleventh Street, Ozona, TX

A statue erected in honor of Davy Crocket, hero of the Alamo, is located in downtown Ozona in Crockett County, which holds an annual Davy Crockett Festival. The thirteen-foot-tall granite statue was erected in 1939.

Janis Joplin's Childhood Home

4330 Thirty-Second Street, Port Arthur, TX

The home where Janis Joplin lived as a child is a private residence, but photos can be made from the street of the house and the historical marker out front.

World's Smallest Active Catholic Church

3490 Texas Highway 237, Round Top, TX
979-378-2277

The tiny St. Martin's Catholic Church holds about twenty people and still hosts services. According to an article on FayetteCountyHistory.org, the reason for the tiny church was a noble one: "By 1915 most of the Catholics had died or moved away. They needed a new school building in Fayetteville and the Catholic Bishop gave them permission to demolish St. Martin's Church and use the lumber to build the school at Fayetteville. There was enough lumber left over to build the small chapel at the original site of St. Martin's Church."

World's Largest Cowboy Boots

North Star Mall
7400 San Pedro Avenue, San Antonio, TX

A pair of fiberglass boots looms over the mall, posing a perfect photo op.

World's Largest Pecan

Texas Agricultural and Heritage Center
390 Cordova Road, Seguin, TX
830-379-0933

The town of Seguin, billed as the Pecan Capital of Texas, is nutty about its claim to fame—so much so that when a town in Missouri had the nerve to create a pecan larger than Seguin's World's Largest

The world's largest pecan in Seguin, Texas. *Courtesy of Lezlie K. King /Wikimedia Commons.*

Pecan, Seguin built another, larger pecan. It is sixteen feet long and eight feet wide. Currently, Seguin is also home to the former title holder, billed as the World's Oldest Largest Pecan (lots of qualifiers there) and the World's Second Largest Mobile Pecan, a ten-footer on wheels that stands in front of Pape's Nutcracker Museum.

Oversized Armadillo

Bussey's Flea Market
18738 Interstate 35 North, Schertz, TX
210-651-6830

A huge roadside armadillo draws customers to the flea market.

Prada Marfa

U.S. Highway 90, 1.4 miles west of Valentine, TX

Driving through rural Texas, visitors come upon a Prada store. But like many desert mirages, this store is not real. It's an installation created in 2005 by artists Elmgreen and Dragset. The "store" was quickly looted of its "merchandise," so the artists stocked it with purses without bottoms and pairs with two right shoes. They also installed security cameras.

Giant Books Library Façade

Waskom Public Library
103 Waskom Avenue, Waskom, TX
903-687-3041

In 2018, the Waskom Public Library was looking for ways to make the small facility more visible. Artist Chris Opp created a façade lined with twenty-two-foot-high books and a ruler. An apple is set atop the building.

The unique Waskom, Texas Public Library façade. *Courtesy of Waskom Public Library.*

J.R. Ewing Statue

Doss Heritage and Culture Center
1400 Texas Drive, Weatherford, TX

Larry Hagman, the actor who so famously portrayed oil baron J.R. Ewing on *Dallas*, attended high school in Weatherford. A statue of Hagman in character as Ewing was erected in 2014, two years after Hagman's death.

Peter Pan Statue

Weatherford Public Library
1014 Charles Street, Weatherford
817-598-4150

Weatherford native Mary Martin was a renowned Broadway actress and the mother of actor Larry Hagman. A statue of the petite Martin (1913–1990) portraying Peter Pan is located in front of the library.

Woodlands Lake Monster

3030 Woodlands Parkway, The Woodlands, TX

Rising from the lake in South Shore Park, a colorful version of the Loch Ness Monster greets visitors. The steel serpent sculpture by artist Marc Rosenthal was erected in 1985.

TEXAS OUTSIDER ART

This unique kind of roadside oddity comes in many forms. Some collections are indoors; some are outdoors. A few charge admission; others request donations. But the work never fails to astound and entertain.

Cadillac Ranch

Exit 60, Interstate 40, Amarillo, TX
Free

In 1974, three members of the artist group Ant Farm—Chip Lord, Hudson Marquez and Doug Michels—had the urge to create a head-turning installment. More than thirty-five years later, people are still talking about the Cadillac Ranch, so the group was certainly successful.

The art project is made up of ten half-buried Cadillacs placed nose-first in the ground. The car models range from 1949 to 1963. The land was owned by Stanley Marsh III, a millionaire who was a patron of the project.

Cadillac Ranch in Amarillo, Texas. *Courtesy of Carol M. Highsmith/Library of Congress.*

Not far away, at Exit 96 on I-40 in Panhandle, Texas, a copycat art installation is rapidly decaying. Five Volkswagen Beetles are buried in the ground, but they have been largely left to the elements and vandals.

Cathedral of Junk

The Cathedral of Junk in Austin, Texas. *Courtesy of Jennifer Morrow/Wikimedia Commons.*

4422 Lareina Drive, Austin, TX
512-299-7413; Donations

Vince Hannemann created his Cathedral of Junk from more than sixty tons of cast-off items, many of them donated by helpful supporters. He began building it in 1989. The art garden is located behind Hannemann's private home. Tours by appointment only.

Sparky Park

3701 Grooms Street, Austin, TX
512-974-6797; Free

This park was once the site of an electrical substation, built in 1930. When it was replaced with a new substation, residents thought the abandoned site was an eyesore. Artist Berthold Haas constructed an art wall to hide the building and machinery so local families could play in the park. Neighbors helped him use found objects to create the fence, which Atlas Obscura describes as being influenced by "Antonio Gaudi's Parq Guell (and perhaps other Spanish Art Nouveau creations), 60's psychedelia, the Wonder Cabinets of 1700's Germany, the early 20th century Midwestern Grotto Culture, and the more conventional grottos seen in stately English gardens."

Gene Cockrell's Yard Art

Marshall Drive, Canadian, TX
Private residence; Visible from the road

Folk artist Gene Cockrell makes all kinds of figures from concrete and metal to populate his yard, from lions and horses to aliens and a Dallas Cowboys cheerleader. He began making his creations in the 1990s. Go east one and a half miles past the four-way stop at Main and Cheyenne, and the yard will be on the left.

House of Sugar

4301 Leavell Avenue, El Paso, TX
Visible from road

In 1973, retired Levi's employee Rufino Loya Rivas began building his "Casa de Azucar," a folk-art creation he made from cement and found objects. Much of the art was inspired by the Catholic religion and by Mexican art.

The Sugar House in El Paso, Texas. *Courtesy of Susan Barnum/Wikimedia Commons.*

Art Car Museum

140 Heights Boulevard, Houston, TX
713-861-5526; Admission fee

See some of the colorful, decorated cars that make up the annual Art Car Parade in Houston in this museum nicknamed the Garage Mahal.

Beer Can House

222 Malone Street, Houston
713-926-6368; Admission fee

This famous landmark covered with beer cans and tabs was made by John Milkovisch, a retired upholsterer for the Southern Pacific Railroad, beginning in 1968. In addition to the cans, the house is adorned with marbles, rocks and scrap metal pieces. It took him eighteen years to cover the house in flattened aluminum beer cans. According to the website OrangeShow.org, Ripley's Believe It or Not estimated the home is covered in more than fifty thousand cans.

The Orange Show

2402 Munger Street, Houston, TX
713-926-6368; Admission fee

The Orange Show is a monument to the favorite fruit of late folk artist Jeff McKissack. The Houston postal worker built the maze of artwork by hand from 1956 to 1979.

The three-thousand-square-foot outdoor environment is now part of the Orange Show Center for Visionary Art. Its website says the site includes "an oasis, a wishing well, a pond, a stage, a museum, a gift shop, and several upper decks. It is constructed of concrete, brick, steel and found objects including gears, tiles, wagon wheels, mannequins, tractor seats and statuettes. Each piece of the Orange Show Monument was hand-placed and hand-painted by McKissack....[It] is one of the most important folk art environments in the United States."

Smither Park

2441 Munger Street, Houston, TX
713-926-6368; Free

The art in this park is contributed by more than three hundred artists. Stephanie Smither hired artist Dan Phillips to create the park, located next to the Orange Show, in honor of her late husband, John H. Smither. The Smithers were supporters of folk art.

Eclectic Menagerie Park

2330 Holmes Road, Houston, TX
800-233-8736
Private residence; Visible from service road

Artist Ron Lee created twenty-six oversized scrap-metal artworks on the property of Texas Pipe & Supply. The company does not allow visitors on the property, but the critters—including spiders, dragons, birds, an armadillo and a rhino—can be seen from the service road that runs parallel to Texas Highway 288 at the first exit after crossing Interstate 610.

Stonehenge II and Easter Island Heads

Hill Country Arts Foundation
120 Point Theatre Road South, Ingram, TX
830-367-5120

The late Alfred Shepperd built this 3/5-scale replica of Stonehenge using "stones" made of plaster over wire mesh. Two replica Easter Island heads stand nearby.

Stonehenge in Odessa

East University Boulevard, Odessa, TX
Free

A Stonehenge replica at the University of Texas in Odessa. *Courtesy of Carol M. Highsmith/ Library of Congress.*

Unlike its counterpart in Ingram, this Stonehenge replica is made of actual stones—thirty to forty thousand pounds worth. The replica, built in 2004, is open to the public.

World's Largest Virgin Mary Mosaic

1301 Guadalupe Street, San Antonio, TX
210-271-3151; Free

This forty-foot-tall mosaic of the Virgin Mary is made to resemble a prayer candle. It was created in 2004 outside the Guadalupe Cultural Arts Center.

World's largest mosaic of the Virgin Mary in San Antonio, Texas. *Courtesy of Carol M. Highsmith/ Library of Congress.*

TEXAS LEGENDARY LOCALES

Unlike roadside attractions, this list of locales describes places you will need to park your car and get out, including quirky museums, unusual historic homes and whimsical places to eat or stay overnight.

Four-Hundred-Year-Old Home

Steinbach House
100 Karm Street, Castroville, TX
830-538-9838; Free

The seventeenth-century Steinbach House that was shipped to Castroville from France and rebuilt. *Courtesy of Carol M. Highsmith/Library of Congress.*

When the residents of Alsace, France, offer your town a gift, you graciously accept. When they give you a four-hundred-year-old home, it complicates matters but, in the end, leaves you with one heck of an unusual tourist attraction.

The Steinbach House was built using wooden pegs between 1618 and 1648 in the village of Walbach. The villagers dismantled it and shipped it to Texas in 1998. Some villagers volunteered to come to Castroville to reassemble the home, and they also donated period furniture to decorate the house. It now serves as a welcome center and museum and is open for tours.

Bronze Casts of Famous Hands

George W. Truett Memorial Hospital
3501 Junius Street, Dallas, TX
214-820-0111; Free

Surgeon Adrian E. Flatt's hobby was casting the hands of celebrities in bronze. His collection of more than one hundred pairs of hands is on display at the hospital and includes Dr. Seuss, Walt Disney, Charles Schultz, Winston Churchill, Joe DiMaggio, Louis Armstrong, Andre the Giant and more.

Real-Life Cattle Drive

Fort Worth Stockyards
2501 Rodeo Plaza, Fort Worth, TX
817-624-4741; Various fees

A visit to the Fort Worth Stockyards immerses you in the cowboy life. The ninety-eight-acre livestock market had been used since 1866 and now houses a variety of venues for shopping, dining, adult and family-friendly entertainment, museums and lodging. But that's not all—while enjoying modern amenities, visitors can witness a real cattle drive, as cattle are moved from one end of the stockyards to the other, and watch rodeos that are held regularly in the historic coliseum. Lodging includes a 1908 western hotel with a room where Bonnie and Clyde stayed in the 1930s.

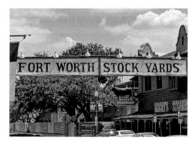

Historic Fort Worth Stockyards.
Photo by Wil Elrick.

The Kettle House

1410 Miramar Drive, Galveston, TX
Visible from the road; Fee for lodging

A home that was originally created as a spherical metal storage tank was purchased in the 1960s and taken to Miramar Drive. The owner, welder Clayton E. Stockley, hoped to make it into an unusually shaped convenience store. He never completed the project, however. In 2018, the structure was sold and renovated by Michael and Ashley Cordray for the HGTV show *Big Texas Fix*. The interior is a Mid-Century Modern–lover's dream, with a spiral staircase leading to the top floor. These days, the home can be rented from Airbnb. It sleeps ten.

Dinosaur Valley State Park

1629 Park Road 59, Glen Rose, TX
254-897-4588; Admission fee

This park not only offers camping, picnicking, hiking and fishing but it also lets visitors walk in the footsteps of dinosaurs. The *actual footsteps*! They can be found in the bed of Paluxey River, which was once "at the edge of an ancient ocean," the Texas Park Service says. To be sure Glen Rose lives up to its billing as the Dinosaur Capital of Texas, dinosaur statues were erected at the park.

Ruins of Saint Dominic's Church

440 County Road 5226, Hondo, TX
Free

The stone ruins of a church and its adjoining cemetery are the only reminder of the original town of D'Hanis, which was moved to be closer to a railroad stop when the old town was bypassed. The church burned in 1912, and its remains were left abandoned. Look for the ruins

Ruins of Saint Dominic's Catholic Church in D'Hanis, Texas. *Courtesy of Larry Moore/ Wikimedia Commons.*

east of the D'Hanis Independent School District high school, a quarter of a mile south of Highway 90.

Replica of Terra Cotta Army

Lucky Land
8625 Airline Drive, Houston, TX
281-447-3400; Admission fee

A replica of the famed Terra Cotta Army in China can be viewed at Lucky Land, an attraction park and garden space. The two-acre property is meant to give visitors a glimpse of ancient Asian history through replicas of Chinese villages, kung fu statues, koi ponds and panda statues.

World's Longest Car Wash

Buc-ee's
27700 Katy Freeway, Houston, TX
Fee charged for car wash

The car wash at this Buc-ee's, a chain of massive convenience stores, was officially certified by Guinness World Records as the world's longest. At 255 feet long, taking your car through it is like driving nearly the length of a football field. The Buc-ee's in New Braunfels, Texas, is unofficially the World's Largest Convenience Store.

Buc-ee's bills its New Brauffels, Texas location as the "world's largest convenience store." *Courtesy of Larry Moore/Wikimedia Commons.*

Ghost Town of Terlingua

Terlingua, TX
432-371-2234; Free

This authentic ghost town is situated in Brewster County, nearly to the Mexican border. It was a small boomtown when there was plenty of cinnabar to be mined for its mercury. Today, it is a unique combination of modern conveniences and Old West flavor. GhostTownTexas.com says: "This is not some abandoned movie set or a fabricated tourist trap. This was a real mining town that went bust and the miners walked away, leaving their homes behind. Today you'll find a ghost town made up of decaying buildings, mine shafts, tall tales, ruins, crotchety old-timers, a three-legged dog, too much cactus, and semi-friendly rattlesnakes. It's been slightly revitalized with rustic Texas lodgings (graciously updated), world famous chili fixins, an internationally acclaimed restaurant…and—perhaps most importantly—a fully operational saloon/bar."

Metal art in the ghost town of Terlingua, Texas. *Courtesy of Carol M. Highsmith/ Library of Congress.*

Ace of Clubs House

420 Pine Street, Texarkana, TX
903-793-4831; Admission fee

The intriguing name for this house comes from the fact that it is shaped like a club, with three octagonal wings and a rectangular wing. Built in 1885 for

James Harris Draughon, the Italianate Victorian home is listed in the National Register of Historic Places and is a Recorded Texas Historical Landmark. It is open as a museum. According to the Texas Forest Trail website, "Legend has it a lucky card drawn in a poker game inspired its cloverleaf shape. Inside, its rooms provide a glimpse of Texarkana high society between 1880 and 1940."

The Ace of Clubs House in Texarkana, Texas. *Photo by Wil Elrick.*

World's Largest Spring-Fed Swimming Pool

Balmorhea State Park
9207 Texas Highway 17, Toyahvale, TX
432-375-2370; Admission fee

A pool in Balmorhea State Park covers 1.3 acres and holds 3.5 million gallons of water, according to the Texas Parks and Wildlife Service. It is fed by San Solomon Springs, which pushes more than 15 million gallons of water into the pool each day. The water is up to 25 feet deep and stays at a temperature in the mid-70s year 'round.

Texas Chainsaw Massacre *House*

Grand Central Café
1010 King Court, Kingsland, TX
325-388-6022

Initially, the structure used as the setting for the creepy family home in the original *Texas Chainsaw Massacre* was located in Round Rock, Texas. In 1998, it was moved to Kingsland and restored. Since 2002, it has been home to the Grand Central Café. The restaurant's website says, "Built in the early 1900s, this Queen Anne style cottage…[was] quite grand for its time with fish scale roofing and its chamfered corners with gingerbread trim."

Devil's Rope Museum and Route 66 Museum

100 Kingsley Street, McLean, TX
806-779-2225; Free

Opened in 1991, this museum in McLean was the first one dedicated to Route 66 memorabilia. Located in the same building, the Devil's Rope Museum has been teaching people about the ins and outs of barbed wire. Limited hours.

Devil's Rope Museum in McLean, Texas. *Courtesy of Carol M. Highsmith/Library of Congress.*

Southfork Ranch

3700 Hogge Drive, Parker, TX
972-442-7800; Admission fee

A trip to Southfork Ranch is a must for fans of the TV show *Dallas*, which ran for thirteen years beginning in 1978. The real home that served as the Ewing Ranch is open for tours, which includes the Dallas Legends exhibit with memorabilia from the series. The website says, "See the gun that shot J.R., Lucy's wedding dress, the Dallas family tree and Jock's Lincoln Continental." The grounds include Miss Ellie's Deli and two retail shops with gifts and collectibles.

Ice Cream Cone Building

Tasty Pfreeze Ice Cream 'N Stuff
2700 West Pecan Street, Pfulgerville, TX
517-819-4760

This building, originally a Twistee Treat, was seen in the film *Friday Night Lights*. It has held a variety of businesses over the years, and the "ice cream" roof has recently been painted blue. Currently, the business is open only in summer.

Concrete Shipwreck

Pelican Island, TX

The SS *Selma* was an oil tanker built of concrete in 1919 by F.F. Ley and Compny of Mobile, Alabama. It was one of twelve concrete vessels constructed with the approval of President Woodrow Wilson. Its partially submerged wreck lies along the Houston Ship Channel, a mile from Galveston Island, where it was scuttled in 1920 following a collision. The wreck is visible from the historic marker on Pelican Island.

Texas Ranger Hall of Fame and Museum

100 Texas Ranger Trail, Waco, TX
877-750-8631; Admission fee
Reservations required

Texas Ranger Hall of Fame, Waco, Texas. *Courtesy of Wikimedia Commons.*

The Hall of Fame and Museum tell the story of the legendary Texas Rangers. The museum opened in 1968, and the Hall of Fame was founded in 1976 for the American Bicentennial. The site is supported by the City of Waco.

The museum not only houses uniforms, artifacts and displays related to the Texas Rangers but also acts as the official repository for records. The website at texasranger.org says, "The Texas Ranger is one of the most cherished symbols of the Lone Star State, a positive and enduring icon of Texas and America. Many families take immense pride in having a relative who was, or is, a Texas Ranger."

Munster Mansion

3636 Farm-to-Market Road 813, Waxahachie, TX
Admission fee; Tours by appointment

Built by Sandra and Charles McKee in 2002, this mansion is a replica of the mansion from the TV show *The Munsters*, both inside and out. The couple even has a Muntser Koach that is typically parked outside the home. In the past, the McKees opened the home for an annual charity event but have recently stopped the practice. Now, they open their home only for pre-booked tours for groups of four or more. Register for tours at the website or leave a message on the Munster Mansion Texas Facebook page. Visitors are asked not to simply show up at the home, especially because of its location on a dangerous road the McKees describe as a "country highway."

Teepee Motel and RV Park

4098 East Business 5R, Wharton, TX
979-282-8474

This motel, unrelated to the Wigwam Villages, features teepee-shaped rooms. It was built in 1942 and renovated and reopened in 2006.

The Tee Pee Motel in Wharton, Texas, is pictured here in 1977. *Courtesy of John Margolies/Library of Congress.*

Western Town

7A Ranch
333 Wayside Drive, Wimberley, TX
512-847-2517

This replica western town is part of 7A Ranch, a family-owned destination with cabins and lodges. The town, which was originally built in 1956, provides family entertainment. The 7A website says, "Imagine a day when desperadoes faced off with the local law and decent citizens rubbed shoulders with card sharps and fancy ladies. In Pioneer Town, located at 7A, you can spend the day and weave your way through the Opera House, Cowboy Museum, Game Room, Bottle House, Print Shop, Ice Cream Parlor, Log Cabins and Storefronts. Take a few pictures of your kiddos in the shoe-shining seat, on the life-sized plastic horse or behind the Wanted poster."

Professional Wrestling Hall of Fame

712 Eighth Street No. 100, Wichita Falls, TX
940-264-8123; Admission fee

This museum that preserves the history of professional entertainment wrestling was moved from New York. It is filled with costumes, photos, trophies and all kinds of wrestling memorabilia.

Roy Orbison Museum

213 East Hendricks Boulevard, Wink, TX
432-527-3743; Free, Tours by appointment

A small collection of Roy Orbison artifacts for die-hard fans, including the Wink High School yearbook featuring his photo. Some items belonged to Orbison, while some displays are dedicated to memorabilia donated by fans.

TEXAS TOMBSTONE TALES

This section lists just a few of the state's intriguing headstones and the stories behind them. Most cemeteries are open during daylight hours only. Many do not have street numbers in their addresses, but those listed are as close as possible.

Rope Walker Grave

Hebrew Cemetery
2100 Block of West Second Avenue, Corsicana, TX

A simple headstone in the Hebrew Cemetery in Corsicana, Texas, is marked with the words "Rope Walker" and the year "1884." The mysterious grave has led to years of supposition about the true identity of the man buried there. According to legend, an acrobat born in Russia in 1829 was in town to perform a tight-rope act. He wasn't just any acrobat, but a one-legged one who walked the rope with a notched peg-leg and who carried an iron stove on his back to add drama. The story says he fell two stories and was crushed by the stove. Before he died, he was able to tell doctors he was Jewish. Recently, some researchers claim to have identified the man as the "Great Professor Berg." Others, however, disagree.

"Machine Gun" Kelly Grave

Cottondale Cemetery
Wise County Road 3571, Cottondale, TX

Infamous gangster George "Machine Gun" Kelly (1895–1854) died at age of fifty-eight or fifty-nine, depending on the source, in Leavenworth Federal Penitentiary, where he was transferred after serving time in Alcatraz. He was buried under a simple slab with his name misspelled "Kelley."

Graves of Bonnie and Clyde

Dallas, TX

In one of the most famous poems penned by outlaw Bonnie Parker before she and lover Clyde Barrow were gunned down, she wrote:

> *Some day they'll go down together*
> *they'll bury them side by side.*
> *To few it'll be grief,*
> *to the law a relief*
> *but it's death for Bonnie and Clyde.*

Their families had other ideas and the young lovers were not even buried in the same cemetery, although both are buried in Dallas. Bonnie Parker (1910–1934) is buried in Crown Hill Memorial Park at 9178 Webb Chapel Road beneath a small marker etched with the words: "As the flowers are all made sweeter by the sunshine and the dew, So this old world is made brighter by the lives of folks like you."

The grave of Clyde Barrow and his brother, Buck Barrow, in Western Heights Cemetery. *Photo by Wil Elrick.*

Clyde (1909–1934) is buried in Western Heights Cemetery at 1617 Fort Worth Avenue beside his brother and gang member Marvin "Buck" Barrow (1903–1933). The marker says only: "Gone but not forgotten."

The Alamo Cats Graves

300 Alamo Plaza, San Antonio, TX
210-225-1391
Fee for guided tours

People go to the Alamo to hear tales of history and revolution and maybe to walk where John Wayne once walked. Some visitors are surprised to find the graves of two cats who made their homes at the famous site and are buried on the grounds. Ruby and C.C. were strays who were fed and cared for by the staff. Ruby came in 1981 and died in 1986. C.C. showed up in 1996 and died in 2014. Plaques in their honor are attached to a stone in a courtyard.

Morafic the Horse

188535 Champion Forest Drive, Spring, TX

When Morafic, a champion Arabian show horse, died in 1974 at the age of eighteen, he was buried in a pasture and a life-size statue placed on his grave. Today, the grave is located in the median on Champion Forest Drive across from a Walgreen's.

Shorty the Squirrel Grave

North Broadway Avenue, Tyler

Shorty was a squirrel who lived outside the Smith County Courthouse in Tyler, Texas. He was adopted by the townspeople, who reportedly spoiled him with treats. When he died in 1963, he was buried in a nearby park. Although his true birth date is unknown, the dates he lived outside the courthouse until his death are etched on his gravestone: 1948–1963. Shorty's story was aired on Paul Harvey's radio show, adding to his fame.

List of Sites by City

ALABAMA

Abbeville
The Legend of Huggin' Molly, Huggin' Molly's Restaurant

Andalusia
Big White Dress Shirt, Andalusia Chamber of Commerce

Anniston
Hitler's Tea Service, Berman Museum of World History
World's Largest Office Chair, Miller Furniture

Birmingham
African Village in America
Mary Anderson Grave, Elmwood Cemetery
Negro Southern League Museum
Paul "Bear" Bryant Grave, Elmwood Cemetery
Quinlan Castle
Sloss Furnaces and Fright Furnace
World's Largest Cast-Iron Statue, Vulcan Park and Museum

Boykin
Gee's Bend Quilts, Gee's Bend Quilters Collective

Carrollton
Face in the Courthouse Window, Pickens County Courthouse

Cherokee
Key Underwood Coon Dog Cemetery

Clanton
The Big Peach Water Tower

Clayton
Victorian Octagonal House, Petty-Roberts-Beatty House Museum
Whiskey Bottle Tombstone, Clayton City Cemetery

Cullman
Ave Maria Grotto

Daphne
Malbis Plantation

Dora
Tim Hollis' Pop Culture Museum

Dothan
World's Smallest City Block

Elberta
Dinosaur Herd, Barber Marina
Lady in the Bay, Barber Marina
Roadkill Café
Alabama's Stonehenge Replica, Barber Marina

Enterprise
World's Largest Boll Weevil

Eufaula
Tree That Owns Itself in Eufaula

Fairhope
  The Hermit Hut
  Fairhope Storybook Castles

Florence
  The Rosenbaum House by Frank Lloyd Wright

Gulf Shores
  Enter Through Shark's Mouth, Souvenir City
  Giant Purple Octopus, Purple Octopus Souvenirs and Gifts

Huntsville
  Eggbeater Jesus, First Baptist Church
  Salem Witch House Replica
  Miss Baker, the Monkeynaut Grave

Irondale
  The Original Whistle Stop, Irondale Café

Lanett
  Little Nadine's Playhouse Grave, Oakwood Cemetery

Leeds
  World's Largest Collection of Motorcycles, Barber Motorsports Park and
    Vintage Museum

Lincoln
  Ricky Bobby Movie Setting; Talladega Superspeedway
  Last Confederate Veteran, Refuge Baptist Church Cemetery

Lowndesboro
  Ruins of Dicksonia Plantation

Mentone
  The Rock Pulpit, Sallie Howard Memorial Chapel

Millbrook
  Film-set Town of Spectre, Jackson Lake Island

Mobile
Africatown
Fort Conde Historic Site
USS Alabama Battleship Memorial Park

Monroeville
To Kill a Mockingbird setting, Old Monroe County Courthouse
Ruins of Capote's Childhood Home

Montevallo
Spirit Trees of Tinglewood Trail, Orr Park

Montgomery
Hank Williams's Death Car, Hank Williams Museum
Lynching Memorial; Memorial for Peace and Justice
Hank Williams's Fake Grass, Oakwood Annex Cemetery

Muscle Shoals
Singing River Sculptures
Where the Stones and Aretha recorded, FAME Studios

Natural Bridge
Natural Bridge Park

Northport
Courtyard of Wonder, Kentuck Arts Center

Point Clear
The Civil War Hospital Hotel, Grand Hotel Marriott Resort, Gulf Club
and Spa

Prattville
The Bamboo Forest, Wilderness Park

Roanoke
The Alabama Baby, Randolph County Historical Museum

Robertsdale
Eat in a Train, Derailed Diner

Rockford
Fred, the Town Dog; Old Rock Jail

Scottsboro
Unclaimed Baggage

Seale
Museum of Wonder, Butch Anthony

Selma
Edmund Pettus Bridge
Grave of Elodie Todd Dawson, Old Live Oak Cemetery

Sheffield
Cher's Album-Cover Studio, Muscle Shoals Sound Studio
Singing River Sculpture

Spanish Fort
Giant Dental Pick, Dr. Barry Booth's office

Tuscaloosa
Ruins of Early State Capitol, Capitol Park

Tuscumbia
Dine in a Cave, Rattlesnake Saloon

Wagerville
The Faces of Mt. Nebo Cemetery, Mount Nebo Baptist Church

Wetumpka
Greek Temple Replica, Jasmine Hill Gardens
The Astrobleme, Wetumpka Impact Crater

Arkansas

Alma
Henry Humphrey: Victim of Bonnie and Clyde
Popeye Statue, Popeye Park

Beaver
Arkansas' Only Suspension Bridge, Beaver Bridge

Bentonville
Birthplace of Walmart, Walmart Museum
Sam Walton Grave, Bentonville Cemetery

Blytheville
Art Deco Greyhound Bus Station, Welcome Center and Transportation Museum

Calico Rock
Ghost Town of Peppersauce

Clinton
Arkansas' Natural Bridge

Dyess
Boyhood Home of Johnny Cash, Dyess Colony

Eureka Springs
America's Most Haunted Hotel, Crescent Hotel and Spa
Christ of the Ozarks
Great Passion Play, Holy Land
Magical Treehouse Castle, Oak Crest Cottages and Treehouses
Morris, the General Manager Cat, Crescent Hotel and Spa
Quigley's Castle
Sleep Near Lions and Tigers, Turpentine Creek Wildlife Refuge
Texaco Bungalow
Thorncrown Chapel

Fayetteville
Hogeye the Dancing Razorback statue
Castle at Wilson Park
Wizard's Cave and Labyrinth, Terra Studios Art Gallery and Park

Fort Smith
Chaffee Barbershop Museum
Giant Arrows Lawn Art

Legendary Gallows Replica, Fort Smith National Historic Site
Old-Timey Amusement Park, Park at West End
Planters' Mr. Peanut Sign

Fouke
The Fouke Monster, Peavy's Monster Mart

Gurdon
Gurdon Light Viewing Area
The Hoo Hoo Monument

Hope
Clinton's Birthplace Museum

Hot Springs
Al Capone's Hotel, Arlington Resort Hotel & Spa
Bathe in the Hot Springs, Bathhouse Row
Gangster Museum of America
Marker for Babe's (and Baseball's) First 500-Foot Homer
Maxwell Blade's Odditorium and Curiosities Museum

Lavaca
Giant Bud Light Can, Belle Point Ranch

Little Rock
All Aboard Restaurant and Grill
ESSE Purse Museum & Store

Louann
The Goat Woman of Smackover, Liberty Cemetery

Mammoth Springs
Mammoth Springs Frisco Depot

Marianna
Jones Bar-B-Q Diner

Mountainburg
Concrete Dinosaurs, Mountainburg City Park

Murfreesboro
Sleep in a Teepee, Diamond John's Riverside Retreat
Uncle Sam, World's Largest Diamond, Crater of Diamonds State Park

Norman
Caddo Indian Memorial

North Little Rock
The Old Mill, Pugh Park

Omaha
Lacey Michelle's Castle

Pine Ridge
Lum and Abner Jot 'Em Down Store and Museum

Redfield
Mammoth Orange, orange-shaped diner

Rogers
Daisy Airgun Museum
Ruins of Monte Ne

Texarkana
The Only Post Office in Two States, State Line Post Office

Twist
When B.B. King Named His Guitar Lucille

Van Buren
Mystery Grave of Arkansas, Fairview Cemetery

Walnut Ridge
Beatles-Themed Town

Yellville
Rush Ghost Town

Florida

Aventura
Ninety-Three-Foot Spiral Slide, Aventura Mall

Bradenton
Ruins of Braden Castle
The Flying Wallendas Grave, Manasota Memorial Park
Tootsie in a Patriotic Bikini, Uniroyal Gal

Brooksville
Boyett's Grove

Captiva
The Bubble Room

Carrabelle
Carrabelle Bottle House
World's Smallest Police Station

Cassadaga
Spiritualist Town of Cassadaga

Christmas
World's Largest Alligator, Jungle Adventures

Clearwater
Kapok Tree Inn

Daytona Beach
Drive-In Church
Memorial to Brownie the Town Dog; Riverfront Park

Doral
Jackie Gleason Grave, Our Lady of Mercy Catholic Cemetery

Dunedin
Mosaic House of Dunedin

Edgewater
Giant Wooden Indian Heads, Peter Wolf Toth Museum

Englewood
Boat-Shaped Grave, Lemon Bay Cemetery

Fort Lauderdale
Cruise-Ship Hotel: B Ocean Resort

Fort Walton
Oldest Surviving Goofy Golf

Gibstonton
Boot of Circus Giant

Homestead
The Coral Castle

Islamorada
Betsy the Giant Lobster

Jacksonville
Goofy Gator Statue
Baby Bridges: Cancer Survivors Park

Key Largo
Boat from *The African Queen*
Christ of the Deep
Jules' Undersea Lodge

Key West
She Really Was Sick, B.P. Roberts, Key West Cemetery
Hemingway's Six-Toed Cats, Hemingway Home and Museum

Kissimmee
Giant Mermaid on a Building, Mermaid Gift Shop
Monument of States: Lakefront Park
Orange-Shaped Building, Eli's Orange World
Tupperware Museum

Land o' Lakes
Dupree Gardens Ruins

Lake Wales
Ruins of St. Anne's Shrine

Madiera Beach
Memorial to Lost Seamen: John's Pass Village & Boardwalk
World's Largest Chicken Wing: Hooter's

Marathon
Dolphin from TV's *Flipper*, Dolphin Research Institute and Center

Miami
Parking Garage as Art

Miami Beach
Lichtenstein Mermaid

Mount Dora
Starry Night House

New Smyrna Beach
Grave in the Middle of the Road

North Fort Myers
The Shell Factory

Ochopee
Skunk Ape Research Center

Ona
Solomon's Castle

Orlando
Half-Buried Giant Woman: Lake Eola Park

Panama City Beach
Goofy Golf in Panama City Beach

Pensacola Beach
Futuro House in Pensacola Beach

Port Orange
Ruins of Bongoland

Port St. Lucie
Giant Conch Shell

Safety Harbor
Whimzeyland

Sanford
Mr. Imagination's Wall

Santa Rosa Beach
Truman Show Movie Town, Community of Seaside

Smyrna Beach
Sugar Mill Ruins

St. Petersburg
Tiny Town

Tampa
Hong Kong Willie's Creations
Two-Headed Alligator Statue

Vero Beach
Giant Kissing Sailor & Nurse, McKee Botanical Garden

Wausau
Monument to the Possum

Winter Haven
Twenty-Four-Foot-Tall Potty Chair

GEORGIA

Adairsville
Ruins of Barnsley Mansion, Barnsley Resort

Alpharetta
Cagle Castle

Andersonville
Prisoner-of-War Camp and Museum, Andersonville National
  Historic Site

Athens
R.E.M. Murmur Trestle
Tree That Owns Itself in Athens
World's Only Double-Barreled Cannon

Atlanta
The Autoeater Sculpture
The Great Fish, Atlanta Fish Market
"Hunger Games" Mansion of President Snow, Swan House
Lion of Atlanta, Oakland Cemetery
Sideways the Dog Grave, Georgia Tech
The Varsity, World's Largest Drive-In Restaurant
White House Replica
World's Longest Freestanding Escalator, CNN Center

Avondale Estates
Waffle House Museum

Ball Ground
Burger Bus

Blairsville
Sleepy Hollow Fairy Garden

Brunswick
"First" Brunswick Stew Pot

Buena Vista
Pasaquan

Calhoun
Airplane Stuck in Wacky House, Sam's Tree House

Cherry Log
Expedition: Bigfoot!

Clarkesville
SamG Land

Claxton
Fruitcake Capital of the World

Cleveland
Babyland General Hospital; adopt Cabbage Patch Kids

Columbus
Barbecue in a Bus, Country's Barbecue on Broadway
Circus Train Wreck Memorial, Riverdale Cemetery
Inventor of Coca-Cola Grave, Linwood Cemetery
World's Largest Lunchbox Museum, River Market Antiques

Dallas
Gaggle of Roadside Giants

Eastman
Site of World's First Stuckey's

Eatonton
Native Rock Eagle Effigy
Uncle Remus Museum, Joel Chandler Harris

Elberton
Georgia Guidestones

Fort Benning
Calculator the Dog Grave, Sacrifice Field

Gainesville
World's Largest Tiger Statue

Hartwell
Best Biskits by a Dam Site

Jekyll Island
Haunted Jekyll Island Millionaires Club

Juliette
Film Set Whistle-Stop Café

Macon
Allman Brothers Plot, Rose Hill Cemetery

Milledgeville
Central State Hospital: Abandoned Milledgeville State Lunatic Asylum

Morganton
Drive a Tank, Crush a Car, Tank Town USA

Moultrie
Statue of Life-Size Circus Elephant, Pleasant Grove Primitive Baptist Church Cemetery

Ochlocknee
Pope's Store Museum

Plains
Jimmy Carter Peanut

Rome
Headstone of "Human Bunny," Myrtle Hill Cemetery

Santa Claus
Town of Santa Claus

Savannah
Cracked Earth: A World Apart

Forrest Gump's Bench, Savannah History Museum, Visitor's Center
Little Gracie Watson Grave, Bonaventure Cemetery

Stone Mountain
Stone Mountain Park

Summerville
Paradise Garden

Thomasville
Home with Fifty Exits, Lapham-Patterson House

Vidalia
Vidalia Onion Museum, Fountain

Waynesboro
Millionaire's Bird Dog Cemetery, Di-Lane Wildlife Management Area

Woodstock
Monument to Bob, the Town Turkey

Kentucky

Bardstown
Giant Bourbon Barrel, Barton 1792 Distillery
Sleep in a Jail Cell, Jailer's Inn Bed and Breakfast

Blackberry
Hatfield and McCoy Feud Monument, Orrville Morris Park

Bowling Green
Bronze Big Red mascot, Augenstein Alumni Center
Duncan Hines's Kitchen, Western Kentucky University Museum
Ride a Boat Through a Cave, Lost River Cave

Brandenburg
Eat in the Jail Where Hank Williams Slept, Jailhouse Pizza

Burlington
Four-Legged Mayors of Rabbit Hash, Rabbit Hash General Store

Calvert City
Apple Valley Hillbilly Garden and Toyland

Cave City
Big Mike's Mystery House, Big Mike's Rock & Gift Shop

Clermont
Forest Giants in a Giant Forest, Bernheim Arboretum and Research Forest

Covington
Notre Dame Cathedral Replica, St. Mary's Cathedral Basilica of the Assumption

Falmouth
Punkyville

Florence
Florence Y'all Water Tower, Florence Mall

Fort Knox
The Car Where Patton Died, Gen. George Patton Museum

Fort Mitchell
Collection of Ventriloquist Dummies, Vent Haven Museum

Frankfort
Giant Floral Clock, Kentucky State Capitol
Daniel Boone Grave, Frankfort Cemetery
Memorial Sundial, Kentucky Vietnam Veterans Memorial

Greenville
9/11 Memorial

Harrodsburg
Woman Who Danced Herself to Death, Youngs Park

Hazard
  Mother Goose Building

Highland Heights
  The Stegowagenvolkssaurus, W. Frank Steely Library

Hopkinsville
  King Arthur's Round Table, Round Table Literary Park

LaGrange
  Trains Share Street with Cars, Trains on Main

Lexington
  Man o' War Memorial
  World's Largest Dixie Cup

Louisville
  Col. Harland Sanders Grave, Cave Hill Cemetery
  Finn's Flock, Waterfront Park
  Frito-Lay Magician, Cave Hill Cemetery
  The Haunted Hospital, Waverly Hills Sanitorium
  Jerry's Junk
  Patriotic House Façade, Heigold House
  Sleep in a Teepee, Wigwam Village No. 2
  World's Largest Baseball Bat
  World's Largest Vampire Bat
  World's Largest Bourbon Glass
  World's Largest Golden Replica of David

Mammoth Cave
  World's Longest Cave, Mammoth Cave National Park

Mayfield
  Wooldridge Statues, Maplewood Cemetery

Munfordville
  Kentucky Stonehenge

New Haven
Ride in a Steam Locomotive, Kentucky Railway Museum

Owensboro
World's Largest Burgoo Pot, Moonlite Bar-B-Q

Paducah
Speedy, the Mortuary Mummy, Maplewood Park Cemetery

Pikeville
McCoy Family Feud Cemetery, Dils Cemetery

Slade
Natural Bridge and Skylift

Smithland
Mantle Rock

Versailles
Kentucky Castle

Williamstown
Noah's Ark Encounter

LOUISIANA

Abbeville
Giant Cans of Syrup, C.S. Steen Syrup Mill Inc.

Abita Springs
Abita Mystery House

Angola
Louisiana State Penitentiary Museum

Baton Rouge
Old State Capitol Castle

Bossier City
Muffler Man Cowboy, Topps Western World

Chauvin
Kenny Hill's Sculpture Garden

Covington
World's Largest Ronald Reagan Statue

Darrow
Married Dogs Grave, Houmas House

Gibsland
Bonnie and Clyde Ambush Museum, marker at ambush site

Gray
Giant Rubber Shrimp Boots, Houma Area Visitors Center

Hammond
Charles Smith's African-American Heritage Museum

Kenner
Monument to the First Prize Fight

Lafayette
9/11 Memorial in Lafayette, Parc San Souci

Lake Charles
Mardi Gras Museum, Central School Arts & Humanities Center

Logansport
International Boundary Marker, Republic of Texas

Monroe
Grave of a Truly Married Man, Monroe Old City Cemetery

Moreauville
Pilot Who Vanished Chasing UFO, Sacred Heart Catholic Church Cemetery

Natchitoches
Steel Magnolias House

New Orleans
BMike's Studio BE
Body Parts Chapel, St. Roch Cemetery
Carousel Bar
The Doullut Steamboat Houses, Holy Cross neighborhood
Fisherman's Castle at Irish Bayou
Giant Safety Pin, Sydney and Walda Besthoff Sculpture Gardens
House of Broel Miniatures Museum
Mardi Gras World
Museum of the American Cocktail
Museum of Death
New Orleans Historic Train Garden, Botanical Garden
Nicolas Cage's Pyramid, St. Louis Cemetery No. 1
Scrap-House Katrina Memorial
Tomb of unknown slave, St. Augustine Catholic Church
Tomb of the Voodoo Priestess, St. Louis Cemetery No. 1
Voodoo Museum

Rodessa
Frog Guardians

Shreveport
Giant Light-Up Dalmatian, Central ARTSTATION

Thibodeaux
Arm of St. Valerie, St. Joseph Co-Cathedral

White Castle
Nottaway Plantation

MISSISSIPPI

Aberdeen
Monument to the Burning Woman, Old Aberdeen Cemetery

Bay St. Louis
Angel Tree

Bentonia
Blue Front Café, Mississippi Blues Trail

Biloxi
The Hermit of Deer Island, Old Biloxi Cemetery

Brookhaven
Coffee Pot on a Building

Charleston
Statue of Scissors the Twice-Champion Pig

Clarksdale
Devil's Crossroads, Robert Johnson
Sleep in a Sharecropper's Shack, Shack Up Inn

Corinth
Borroum's Drug Store

Fayette
The Frog Farm

Flora
Petrified Forest

Greenville
Riverboat Welcome Center

Greenwood
Sleep in River Shack, Tallahatchie Flats

Gulfport
Marshall Jesus Sculpture

Hattiesburg
9/11 Memorial in Hattiesburg

Iuka
World's Largest Apron Museum

Jackson
Abandoned Mississippi River Basin Model, Buddy Butts Park
Eudora Welty's house

Leland
Birthplace of Kermit the Frog, Jim Henson's Delta Boyhood Exhibit

Lexington
The Lady in Red, Odd Fellows Cemetery

Meridian
The Gypsy Queen Grave, Rose Hill Cemetery

Morgan City
Memorials to Robert Johnson, Mount Zion Missionary Baptist Church, Payne Chapel Memorial Baptist Church Cemetery, Little Zion Missionary Baptist Church Cemetery

Natchez
The Unfinished Octagonal Mansion, Longwood House Museum
Mammy's Cupboard
The Turning Angel, Natchez City Cemetery

Oxford
Former World's Largest Cedar Bucket
Faulkner's Writing on the Wall, Rowan Oak

Pearlington
Lunar Lander exhibit

Port Gibson
Moonshine-Running Submarine, Grand Gulf Military State Park
Ruins of Windsor

Rolling Fork
Birthplace of the Teddy Bear, Great Delta Bear Affair festival

Ruleville
    Hot and Cold Water Towers

Seminary
    Giant Watermelon

Toomsuba
    The Simmons & Wright Company Store

Tupelo
    Elvis's Birthplace
    Unknown Soldiers on Natchez Trace

Tutwiler
    Larry Grimes's Yard

Vicksburg
    Douglas the Confederate Camel Grave, Cedar Hill Cemetery
    The Iron Boat That Sank in 12 Minutes, USS Cairo Gunboat and
        Museum
    Margaret's Grocery

Waveland
    Waveland Ground Zero Hurricane Museum

Yazoo City
    The Witch of Yazoo, Glenwood Cemetery

NORTH CAROLINA

Angier
    Marvin Johnson's Gourds, Angier Municipal Building

Asheville
    Largest Home in the Nation, Biltmore Estate

Bailey
The Country Doctor Museum

Beaufort
Giant Blackbeard, Downeast Marine
Rum Keg Girl Grave, Old Burying Ground
Standing British Officer Grave, Old Burying Ground

Beech Mountain
Abandoned Land of Oz Theme Park

Belhaven
Belhaven Memorial Museum, Belhaven Town Hall

Bladenboro
World's Largest Real Tire, Hester Tire

Blowing Rock
The Blowing Rock
Tweetsie Railroad

Bolton
Uniroyal Gals and Critters, Grahamland Fiberglass

Bryson City
Kayak Ranch, Southwestern Community College

Buxton
America's Tallest Lighthouse, Cape Hatteras

Cataloochee
Bigfoot Statue

Charlotte
Giant Hand
Monuments to Books and Kids
Monument to Old Man Traffic, Hugh McManaway
Monument to the Writer, ImaginOn, Rolfe Neill

Cherokee
Mac's Indian Village Cabins
Tinkerbell Sign, Pink Motel
Santa's Land Fun Park & Zoo

Clayton
Rock Police Officer, Clayton Police Department

Collettsville
Cup House of Collettsville

Denver
Giant Black Widow, Innovative Pest Management

Durham
Bronze Camel and His Human, Knut Schmidt-Nielson
Bull Statue
Dinosaur Trail, Museum of Life and Science
Gene Dillard Mosaic House

Ellerbe
Andre the Giant Memorabilia, Rankin Museum of American Heritage

Fayetteville
Eiffel Tower Replica, North Carolina
K9 Memorial

Ferguson
Tom Dooley Grave

Frisco
Futuro House in Frisco

Henderson
World's Heaviest Twins Graves, Crab Creek Baptist Church

Hickory
Hunger Games Ghost Town

High Point
World's Second Largest Chest of Drawers

Jamestown
World's Largest Chest of Drawers, Furnitureland South

Kill Devil Hills
Wright Brothers National Memorial

King
Giant Milkshake, Dairi-O

Laurinburg
Spaghetti the Carny Mummy Grave, Hillside Cemetery

Littleton
Cryptozoology and Paranormal Museum

Love Valley
Town with No Cars Allowed

Mooresville
Giant Moose

Morehead
King Neptune

Mount Airy
Siamese twins, Chang and Eng, Graves, White Plains Baptist Church
    Cemetery
Mayberry Courthouse & Jail

Murphy
World's Largest Ten Commandments, Fields of the Wood

New Bern
Giant Plunger

Pikeville
Roadside Metal Dinosaurs, Benton & Sons Fabrication Co.

Pisgah National Forest
Brown Mountain Lights

Pittsboro
Clyde Jones's Critter Crossing

Prospect Hill
Shangri-La Village

Rose Hill
World's Largest Working Frying Pan

Smithfield
Movie Set Western Town

Southport
Gentleman Giant Grave, Old Smithville Burying Ground

Supply
Mary's Bottle House

Sylva
Movie Scene Train Wreck from *The Fugitive*

Thomasville
World's Largest Duncan Phyfe Chair

Winston-Salem
Giant Coffee Pot, Old Salem Moravian Village
Seashell-Shaped Service Station

SOUTH CAROLINA

Awendaw
Boneyard Beach, Bull's Island

Barnwell
Giant Sundial, Barnwell County Courthouse

Beaufort
The Kazoobie Kazoo Factory

Bishopville
Pearl Fryar's Topiary Gardens

Bowman
UFO Welcome Center

Camden
Agnes of Glasgow's Haunted Grave, Bethesda Presbyterian Church

Charleston
Macauley Museum of Dental History, Waring Library
Old Charleston City Jail
The Rich Man's Pyramid, Magnolia Cemetery

Columbia
Neverbust Chain
Tunnelvision
World's Largest Fire Hydrant

Edgefield
Trapdoor Grave, Willowbrook Cemetery

Elloree
Teapot Museum in Teapot-Shaped Building

Florence
Woman Who Lived as a Union Soldier, Grave of Florena Budwin, Florence National Cemetery

Fountain Inn
Statue of Peg-Legged Vaudeville Dancer

Garden City Beach
Spaceship House in South Carolina

Graniteville
The Little Boy Grave, Graniteville Cemetery

Hamer
South of the Border

Hartsville
Last Yogi Bear Honey Fried Chicken Restaurant

Johns Island
Gullah Geechee Cultural Heritage Corridor

Lancaster
Great Wall of China (the Dishes Kind), Bob Doster's Backstreet Studio

Landrum
Last Covered Bridge in S.C., Campbell's Covered Bridge

Moncks Corner
Biblical Tree Carvings, Mepkin Abbey
The Patriot Movie Bridge, Cypress Gardens

Murrells Inlet
Atalaya Castle, Huntington Beach State Park

Myrtle Beach
World's Largest Crab

Olar
Tiny Police Station

Pawley's Island
Poor Alice Flagg Grave, All Saint's Church Cemetery

Ridgeway
Tiny Police Station

Rock Hill
Civitas Statues

Seabrook
Kingdom of Oyotunji African Village

St. Helena Island
Chapel of Ease Ruins, St. Helena Parish Chapel

Sullivan's Island
Luke Skywalker's House

Summerville
Ghost Town of Dorchester
World's Largest Sweet Tea

Yemassee
Old Sheldon Church ruins

TENNESSEE

Adams
Bell Witch Cave

Adamsville
Home of Buford "Walking Tall" Pusser

Alcoa
Millennium Manor

Arrington
Castle Gwynn, Renaissance Festival

Beech Grove
Old Isham the War Horse Grave

Bluff City
Backyard Terrors Dinosaur Park

Bon Aqua
Johnny Cash "One Piece at a Time" Cadillac, Storytellers Hideaway Farm and Museum

Brownsville
Billy Tripp's Mindfield
Tina Turner Museum, Flagg Grove Elementary School

Centerville
Minnie Pearl Chicken Wire Bust

Chattanooga
Sleep in a Pullman Car, Chattanooga Choo Choo

Cleveland
The Blood-Stained Crypt of Nina Craigmiles

Columbia
Mule Capital of the World, annual Mule Day

Cookeville
Dammit the Dog, Tennessee Tech University
Hidden Hollow

Dandrige
Bush's Beans Museum, A.J. Bush & Company 1897 general store

Darden
Mills Darden, the Giant of Tennessee

Farragut
Sir Goony's Family Fun Center

Gatlinburg
Fortress of Faith
Gathering of Synchronous Fireflies, Great Smoky Mountains National Park
Salt and Pepper Shaker Museum

Hermitage
Airplane Wing Sundial

Jackson
Casey Jones Hero Train Engineer Grave, Mount Calvary Cemetery

Kingsport
Giant Burger and Frenchie Fries, Pal's Sudden Service

Knoxville
The Mom Who Swayed the Vote for Women's Rights, Women's Suffrage Memorial
Former World's Largest Rubik's Cube, Sunsphere Holiday Inn

Lynchburg
Deadly Safe of Jack Daniel, Jack Daniel's Distillery

Medina
Dorothy Marie's Playhouse Grave, Hope Hill Cemetery

Memphis
Birthplace of Rock and Roll, Sun Studio
Crystal Shrine Grotto
Peabody Ducks, Peabody Hotel
Wade Bolton's Eternally Crossed Fingers Elmwood Cemetery
Walk the Mississippi River, Mud Island River Park

Murfreesboro
Cannonsburgh Village
World's Largest Cedar Bucket, Cannonsburgh Pioneer Village

Nashville
Builder of Parthenon Replica Buried in a Pyramid, Mount Olivet Cemetery

Cooter's Place Store and Museum
Mystical Mosaic Dragon, Fannie Mae Dees Park
Napoleon Tomb Replica, Mt. Olivet Cemetery
Nashville's Parthenon
Whisk for Biggest Omelet Ever

Oak Ridge
The Secret Atomic City, Oak Ridge City Hall

Palmyra
E.T. Wickham Stone Park, Enoch Tanner Wickham's folk art

Paris
Eiffel Tower Replica, Tennessee

Powell
Airplane Filling Station

Rockford
Giant Crane That's a Bird

Shelbyville
Beautiful Jim Key Grave

Signal Mountain
Spaceship House in Tennessee

Sweetwater
The Lost Sea

Trenton
Trenton Teapot Museum, World's Largest Collection of Porcelain
Veilleuses-Theieres (night-light teapots)

Wartrace
Strolling Jim Grave, Walking Horse Hotel

TEXAS

Abilene
Dr. Seuss Park & Storybook Town

Adrian
Midpoint of Route 66 Museum

Amarillo
Cadillac Ranch

Arthur
Janis Joplin's Childhood Home

Austin
Statue of Bevo, World's Largest Longhorn
Cathedral of Junk
Giant Taco Goddess, Maria's Taco Xpress
Nessy the Lakeness Dragon, Mueller Lake Park
Sparky Park

Bowie
World's Largest Bowie Knife

Canadian
Gene Cockrell's Yard Art

Castroville
400-Year-Old Home

Chertz
Oversized Armadillo, Bussey's Flea Market

Comfort
Hygieostatic Bat Roost

Corsicana
Rope Walker Grave, Hebrew Cemetery

Cottondale
"Machine Gun" Kelly Grave, Cottondale Cemetery

Crystal City
Not One, But Two Popeye Statues, Crystal City Hall

Dallas
Graves of Bonnie and Clyde
Bronze Casts of Famous Hands, George W. Truett Memorial Hospital
Giant Bowler Hat
Giant Eyeball

El Paso
House of Sugar

Fort Stockton
Paisano Pete, Giant Roadrunner

Fort Worth
Giant Rooftop Jackalope
Real-Life Cattle Drive, Fort Worth Stockyards

Freer
World's Largest Rattlesnake, Freer Chamber of Commerce

Gainesville
Roadside Giants of Glenn Goode

Galveston
Galveston Giant
Galveston Great Storm Memorial
The Kettle House

Georgetown
Statue of "Three-Legged" Texas Ranger

Glen Rose
Dinosaur Valley State Park

Grapevine
Glockenspiel Clock Tower Shootout, Grapevine Convention & Visitors Bureau Headquarters

Groom
Leaning Water Tower of Britten

Hidalgo
World's Largest Killer Bee, Hidalgo City Hall

Hondo
Ruins of Saint Dominic's Church

Houston
Art Car Museum
Beer Can House
Eclectic Menagerie Park
The Orange Show
Replica of Terra Cotta Army, Lucky Land
Smither Park
Thirty-Six-Foot-Tall Fab Four, 8th Wonder Brewery
World's Longest Car Wash, Buc-ee's

Ingram
Stonehenge II and Easter Island Heads, Hill Country Arts Foundation

Jonestown
Eiffel Tower Replica, Texas

Kingsland
Texas Chainsaw Massacre House, Grand Central Café

Marfa
Marfa Lights Viewing Area

McLean
Devil's Rope Museum and Route 66 Museum

Odessa
Stonehenge in Odessa

Ozona
Davy Crockett Statue, Ozona City Park

Parker
Southfork Ranch

Pelican Island
Concrete Shipwreck

Pflugerville
Ice Cream Cone Building, Tasty Pfreeze Ice Cream 'N Stuff

Round Top
World's Smallest Active Catholic Church

San Antonio
The Alamo Cats Graves
World's Largest Cowboy Boots, North Star Mall
World's Largest Virgin Mary mosaic

Sequin
World's Largest Pecan, Texas Agricultural and Heritage Center
Pape's Nutcracker Museum

Spring
Morafic the Horse

Terlingua
Ghost Town of Terlingua

Texarkana
Ace of Clubs House

Toyahvale
World's Largest Spring-Fed Swimming Pool, Balmorhea State Park

Tyler
Shorty the Squirrel Grave

Valentine
Prada Marfa

Waco
Texas Ranger Hall of Fame and Museum

Waksom
Giant Books Library Façade, Waskom Public Library

Waxahachie
Munster Mansion

Weatherford
J.R. Ewing Statue, Doss Heritage and Culture Center
Peter Pan Statue, Weatherford Public Library

Wharton
Teepee Motel and RV Park

Wichita Falls
Professional Wrestling Hall of Fame

Wimberly
Western Town

Wink
Roy Orbison Museum
The Woodlands
Woodlands Lake Monster

Bibliography

The majority of sites listed in this book have been visited personally by the author. Information regarding them was gathered visually or from historical markers. In some cases, the information was obtained from photos. Other common sources were brochures, the municipal offices of the city where the attraction was located, chambers of commerce and websites of the attractions themselves. In most of those cases, the source is named within the guide listing. When more in-depth information was needed, research sources are listed as follows.

ALABAMA

Alabama Heritage. alabamaheritage.com.
United States Civil Rights Trail. civilrightstrail.com.

ARKANSAS

Abandoned Arkansas. "Peppersauce Ghost Town." abandonedar.com/peppersauce-ghost-town.
City of Rogers. "Mount Ne Today." rogersar.gov/270/Monte-Ne-Today.
Daisy Airgun Museum. www.daisymuseum.com.
Detour Art. www.detourart.com.

Diamond John's. www.diamondjohns.com/teepees.php.

Esse Purse Museum. essepursemuseum.com.

Historic Dyess Colony, Johnny Cash Boyhood Home. dyesscash.astate.edu/
about.

Lum and Abner Jot 'Em Down Store Museum Facebook page.

Mammoth Orange Stand Facebook page.

National Park Service. nps.gov.

Natural Bridge. www.arkansas.com/hiking-backpacking/natural-bridge.

Roadside America. "30-Foot-Tall Dancing Hog." www.roadsideamerica.
com/story/62490.

Terra Studios. terrastudios.com/art-park.

Turpentine Creek Wildlife Refuge. www.turpentinecreek.org.

Walmart Digital Museum. www.walmartmuseum.com.

FLORIDA

Aggles, Theodora. "Dunedin Artist Couple Lives in Mosaic-Covered
Cottage." April 11, 2012. www.tampabay.com.

Atlas Obscura. "Whimzeyland." www.atlasobscura.com/places/
whimzeyland.

Authentic Florida. www.authenticflorida.com.

Aventura Mall. aventuramall.com.

Bottle House of Carrabelle. carrabellebottlehouse.com/index.html.

Boyett's Citrus Attraction. www.boyettsgrove.com/about-us.

Braden Castle Park. bradencastlepark.com.

Brownie the Town Dog of Daytona Beach. www.browniethetowndog.org.

Carrabelle Chamber of Commerce. "World's Smallest Police Station."
carrabelle.org/things-to-do/worlds-smallest-police-station.

Drive-In Church. www.driveinchurch.net/contact_us.

Explore Southern History. "The Possum Monument." www.
exploresouthernhistory.com/possummonument.html.

Find A Grave. findagrave.com.

Florida Fringe Tourism. "Giant Head of Beethoven." www.
floridafringetourism.com/listings/giant-head-beethoven.

Garcia, Patricia. "Can a Parking Garage Be a Work of Art? In Miami, It
Can!" *Vogue*, April 26, 2018. www.vogue.com/article/museum-garage-
miami-design-district.

Hong Kong Willie. hongkongwillie.blogspot.com.

Islamorada Times. islamoradatimes.com.

Jeanine Taylor Folk Art. "Mr. Imagination's Memory Wall." www.jtfolkart. com/product-page/mr-imagination-s-memory-wall.

Jules' Undersea Lodge. jul.com/contact-us.

Mermaid Gift Shop Facebook page.

National Register of Historic Places Program. "Monument of States." www.nps.gov/nr/feature/places/15000862.htm

Orange World. www.orangeworld192.com/pages/about-us.

Roadside America. "Fort Lauderdale, Florida: Hotel Shaped Like a Cruise Ship." www.roadsideamerica.com/tip/46516.

———. "Lake Wales, Florida: Ruins of St. Anne's Shrine." www. roadsideamerica.com/tip/53147.

———. "Madeira Beach, Florida: World's Largest Chicken Wing." www. roadsideamerica.com/tip/28848.

Shell Factory. shellfactory.com.

Spata, Christopher. "Welcome to St. Petersburg's Tiny Town. Population: One Cool Artist Dude." February 2, 2019. www.tampabay.com article.

Georgia

Atlas Obscura. atlasobscura.com

Explore Georgia. exploregeorgia.org.

Historic Oakland Foundation. oaklandcemetery.com.

Lohr, Kathy. "Georgia Town Makes Claim for Fruitcake Capital of the World." National Public Radio, December 12, 2012. npr.org.

Roadside America. roadsideamerica.com

Roadtrippers. roadtrippers.com.

Stuckey's. stuckeys.com.

Waffle House Museum. wafflehouse.com

Kentucky

Apple Valley Hillbilly Garden and Toyland, applevalleyhillbillygardenandtoyland.com.

Atlas Obscura. "Heigold House." atlasobscura.com/places/heigold-house.

Find A Grave. "Henry Woolridge." www.findagrave.com/ memorial/6624469/henry-wooldridge.

Fox 56. foxlexington.com.
Greenville, Kentucky. tourgreenville.com.
Jailer's Inn. jailersinn.com.
Jailhouse Pizza. jailhousepizza.com.
Kentucky's Stonehenge. kystonehenge.com.
Kentucky Tourism. hazardkentucky.com.
Kentucky Vietnam Veterans Memorial. kyvietnammemorial.net.
Lost River Cave. lostrivercave.org.
Noah's Ark Encounter. arkencounter.com.
Oldham, Kentucky. "Oldham KY Trains on Main in La Grange."
    touroldham.com/trains.
Patton Museum. www.generalpatton.org.
Roadside America. "Jerry's Junk." www.roadsideamerica.com/
    story/20850.
————. "Louisville, Kentucky: Finn's Flock." www.roadsideamerica.com/
    tip/56796.
Vent Haven Ventriloquist Museum. www.venthaven.org
Waverly Hills Sanitorium. therealwaverlyhills.com.
Wildwood Inn. httpwildwoodinnky.com.

LOUISIANA

Abita Mystery House. abitamysteryhouse.com.
Adams' Cypress Driftwood Swamp Facebook page.
BMike Studio. http://bmike.com/project/studio-be.
Go NOLA. gonola.com.
Lawrence, Christina. "St. Augustine Catholic Church." New Orleans
    Historical. neworleanshistorical.org/items/show/551.
NOLA. nola.com.
Roadside America. "Darrow, Louisiana: Graves of Married Dogs."
    roadsideamerica.com/tip/61340.
Shreveport-Bossier: Louisiana's Other Side. shreveport-bossier.org.
Town of Logansport. www.townoflogansport.com.
Waymarking. www.waymarking.com.

MISSISSIPPI

Birthplace of Kermit the Frog. birthplaceofthefrog.org.

Block, Melissa. "William Faulkner's Home Illustrates His Impact on the South." All Things Considered, February 13, 2017. npr.org.

Find A Grave. findagrave.com.

Friends of the Mississippi River Basin Model. friendsofmrbm.org.

The Frog Farm Facebook page.

HottyToddy. "Homegrown Hogs Take the Bacon in Mississippi." November 8, 2013. hottytoddy.com.

Mississippi Department of Archives and History. mdah.ms.gov.

Mississippi Encyclopedia. mississippiencyclopedia.org.

Mississippi Folklife Folk Art Directory. arts.ms.gov/folklife.

Mississippi Petrified Forest. www.mspetrifiedforest.com/history.

National Park Service. nps.gov.

Perez, Mary. "The Hermit of Deer Island Was Keeping a Secret. A Researcher Just Revealed What It Was." Sun Herald, October 19, 2017. sunherald.com.

Roadtrippers. "The Frog Farm." maps.roadtrippers.com/us/fayette-ms/entertainment/the-frog-farm.

———. "Lunar Lander Exhibit." maps.roadtrippers.com/us/pearlington-ms/attractions/lunar-lander-exhibit.

Rowan Oak. www.rowanoak.com.

Simmons-Wright Company. thesimmons-wrightcompany.com

Tom Otterness Studio. "Playgarden Park." www.tomostudio.com/artworks/playgarden-park.

Visit Yazoo. visityazoo.org.

Waveland's Ground Zero Hurricane Museum. wavelandgroundzero.com.

Willard, Michelle. "The Bucket Is Back." Murfreesboro Post, October 23, 2011. murfreesboropost.com.

NORTH CAROLINA

Abandoned Explorers. abandonedexplorers.com.

The Art of Gene Dillard. www.genedillardart.com/mosaics.

Atlas Obscura. "Shangri-La Stone Village." www.atlasobscura.com/places/shangri-la-stone-village-2.

bibliography

Clyde Jones' Critter Crossing. https://www.chathamartscouncil.org/artist/clyde-jones-2.

Dairi-O. dairio.com.

Find A Grave. findagrave.com.

Grahamland Fiberglass Figures. grahamlandfiberglass.com.

Guinness World Records. guinnessworldrecords.com,

Hidden History with Heather Leah. candidslice.com.

Innovative Pest Management Facebook page.

Lena Toritch, Master Sculptor | Compassionate Heart. lenatoritch.com.

NCPedia. ncpedia.org.

North Carolina Ghosts. northcarolinaghosts.com.

North Carolina Gourd Society. ncgourdsociety.org.

Roadside America. "Bladenboro, North Carolina: Largest (Real) Tire in the World." www.roadsideamerica.com/tip/28389.

———. "Charlotte, North Carolina: Quill Pen and the Writer's Desk." www.roadsideamerica.com/tip/43451.

———. "Fuquay Varina, North Carolina: Ben Harris Sculptures." www.roadsideamerica.com/tip/56253.

———. "Morehead City, North Carolina: King Neptune." www.roadsideamerica.com/tip/29124.

Shaffer, Josh. "How Durham's Brontosaurus Got Lost in the Woods— And Why We Should Bring It Back." *News & Observer*, March 1, 2018. newsobserver.com.

Strange Carolinas. strangecarolinas.com.

South Carolina

Atlas Obscura. atlasobscura.com.

Dunning, Jennifer. "Peg Leg Bates, One-Legged Dancer, Dies at 91." *New York Times*, December 8. 1998. nytimes.com.

Kazoo Factory and Museum. thekazoofactory.com.

Kingdom of Oyotunji African Village. oyotunji.org.

The Pearl Fryar Topiary Garden. pearlfryar.com.

Raven, Hason. "Unique Barnwell Sundial Stands the Test of Time." May 31, 2018. wrdw.com.

Roadside America. roadsideamerica.com.

TENNESSEE

Atlas Obscura. atlasobscura.com.

Atomic Heritage Foundation. "Oak Ridge, TN." www.atomicheritage.org/location/oak-ridge-tn.

Backyard Terrors Dinosaur Park. backyardterrors.com.

Bliss, Jessica. "How a Five-Year-Old Helped Bring Nashville's Mystical Mosaic Dragon Back to Life." *The Tennessean*, May 18, 2018. tennessean.com.

Cooter's Place. cootersplace.com.

Lost Sea Adventure. thelostsea.com.

Made in Tennessee. tnvacation.com.

Metro Government of Nashville & Davidson County. nashville.gov.

Salt and Pepper Shaker Museum. thesaltandpeppershakermuseum.com.

Sun Studio. sunstudio.com.

Tennessee Renaissance Festival. tnrenfest.com.

TEXAS

Ace of Clubs Facebook page.

Atlas Obscura. atlasobscura.com.

Castroville Area Chamber of Commerce. www.castroville.com.

8th Wonder Brewery Facebook page.

Find A Grave. findagrave.com.

Grapevine Texas. grapevinetexasusa.com

Guillen, Darla. "Galveston's Storied 'Kettle House' History Revealed." *Houston Chronicle*, February 7, 2018. chron.com.

It's a Southern Thing. southernthing.com.

KHOU.com Staff. "Buc-ee's in Katy Breaks Record for World's Longest Car Wash." November 15, 2017. khou.com.

Koloian, Kevin. "Lake Woodlands." *Community Impact*, February 16, 2012. communityimpact.com.

McLeod, Gerald E. "Day Trips: The World's Smallest Catholic Church Is Right Here in Warrenton, Texas." *Austin Chronicle*, May 14, 2004. austinchronicle.com.

Official Tourism Website of Galveston Island, Texas. galveston.com.

The Orange Show. orangeshow.org.

Professional Wrestling Hall of Fame. pwhf.org.

Roadside America. roadsideamerica.com.
7A Ranch, Wimberley, Texas. 7Aranch.co.
Sparky Park. austinparks.org/sparky-park.
Texas Forest Trail Region. texasforesttrail.com.
Texas Hill Country. texashillcountry.com.
Texas Parks and Wildlife. tpwd.texas.gov.
Texas Ranger Hall of Fame and Museum. texasranger.org.
Waymarking. waymarking.com.

Index

About the Author

Kelly Kazek is an author, journalist, blogger and award-winning humor columnist. She has written two books of humorous essays and ten books on regional history. She lives in Huntsville, Alabama, and travels the South's back roads, seeking out quirky history for her blog at KellyKazek.com and It's a Southern Thing (SouthernThing.com).

Visit us at
www.historypress.com